T0301674

Two Faces of Globalization

For
Mish-Mish and Mira,
May God bless you with all the best in life!

Two Faces of Globalization

Munificent and Malevolent

Dilip K. Das

Edward Elgar
Cheltenham, UK • Northampton, MA, USA

Published by
Edward Elgar Publishing Limited
The Lypiatts
15 Lansdown Road
Cheltenham
Glos GL50 2JA
UK

Edward Elgar Publishing, Inc.
William Pratt House
9 Dewey Court
Northampton
Massachusetts 01060
USA

A catalogue record for this book
is available from the British Library

Library of Congress Control Number: 2009930351

Mixed Sources
Product group from well-managed
forests and other controlled sources
www.fsc.org Cert no. SA-COC-1565
© 1996 Forest Stewardship Council
FSC

ISBN 978 1 84844 525 3

Printed and bound by MPG Books Group, UK

Prepare for troubles before they arrive.
Put things in order before they exist.
The giant pine tree
grows from a tiny sprout.
The journey of a thousand miles
starts from beneath your feet.

(Wisdom of *Tao Te Ching*)

Contents

About the author

Professor Dilip K. Das has been associated with several prestigious business schools around the globe, including the European Institute of Business Administration (INSEAD), Fontainebleau, France; the ESSEC, Paris; the Graduate School of Business, University of Sydney; the Australian National University, Canberra and Webster University, Geneva. He also was Professor and Area Chairman at the Indian Institute of Management, Lucknow, India, and EXIM Bank Distinguished Chair Professor in the International Management Institute, New Delhi. The areas of his expertise include international finance and banking, international trade and WTO-related issues, international business and strategy and Asian economy, including Chinese and Japanese economies. His most recent interest is globalization and the global business environment.

Professor Das has worked as a consultant for several international organizations, such as USAID, the World Bank, and the World Commission on Development and Environment in Geneva. He has organized 13 large international conferences during the last ten years. He is presently a Toronto-based consultant to international organizations.

He has an immense appetite for researching. He has written extensively and published widely. He is an author or editor of 27 books. The last two books he authored were entitled *The Doha Round of Multilateral Trade Negotiations: Arduous Issues and Strategic Responses,* published by Palgrave Macmillan Ltd, Houndmills, UK, in 2005 and *The Chinese Economic Renaissance: Apocalypse or Cornucopia,* published by Palgrave Macmillan Ltd, Houndmills, Hampshire, UK, in 2008. The latter has been translated into Mandarin for the Chinese market. He has contributed over 80 articles to professional journals of international repute and 79 of his papers have appeared in prestigious research and working paper series. Twenty-two of them have also been posted on the well-regarded websites of business schools and universities.

He was educated at St John's College, Agra, India, where he took his BA and MA (Economics) degrees. He went on to study at the Institut Universitaire de Hautes Etudes Internationales, the University of Geneva, Switzerland, where he did his M.Phil. and Ph.D. in international economics. He is fluent in French.

Preface

Economic globalization, like environmental degradation, has been one of
the most defining issues of the twenty-first century, a veritable mega-trend
of our time. It is a structural theme that is shaping our time. Its impact –
direct and indirect – is universal. Few substantive policy areas come close
to it in terms of significance. One idiosyncratic feature of the twenty-first
century so far is that globalization has picked up pace and has been widening in scope on an unprecedented scale, which has made the study of
contemporary economic globalization progressively more pertinent, applicable and essential than ever in the past. Paul Krugman (2008a) regards it
as "the second great age of globalization", comparable to John Maynard
Keynes' much-quoted description of globalization[1] on the eve of World
War I.[2] In terms of depth, spread and range, the contemporary phase
of globalization has unquestionably surpassed the previous one. Fast-
accelerating trade and capital flows during the contemporary phase of globalization ushered in rapid economic growth in many countries. A group
of developing and transition economies as well as the advanced industrial
economies have succeeded in enhancing employment, reducing poverty
levels and increasing their real income. However, there is no gainsaying
the fact that these positive and constructive outcomes of global economic
integration have remained far from universal. Welfare gains from globalization have been unevenly and disproportionately divided, causing a great
deal of disaffection, even hostility, among many considerate observers.

The essential objective of this book is to dispassionately examine
the contemporary phase of economic globalization; other important
dimensions of this process have been left out. Beyond this self-imposed
limitation, it attempts to provide a comprehensive, timely and germane
discourse on the contemporary phase of globalization. Economic globalization has proved to be both boon and bane for individual economies and
societies as well as the global economy. Casual empiricism rapidly reveals
that, like the ancient Roman god Janus,[3] globalization has two faces, one
benign and the other malign. The contemporary phase of globalization
cannot be impartially, meticulously and methodically studied without
focusing on both of its facets. My purpose is to do precisely that in this
book. Therefore, I have not undersold the position of the detractors of
globalization.

Owing to the fact that contemporary globalism has had both welfare-enhancing propitious consequences as well as detrimental and negative ones, it has become an acutely contentious subject. Both scholarly and public policy-making communities have been pondering and debating over the two contrary facets of globalization. Viewpoints and opinions vary widely. There have been interminable erudite deliberations, even disputes, over the "good and bad" dimensions of globalization. Numerous scholars of irreproachable standing have participated in this debate. Consequently, the existing theoretical literature on globalization is substantive, enough to fill a small library. In focusing on both good and bad concurrently and contrasting them in an objective manner, this book fills a gap in the literature.

These debates were, and continue to be, starkly polarized. Fervent opinions supporting and opposing globalism have coexisted. Therefore, to be able to comprehensively and gainfully examine the contemporary wave of globalization, a focus on both facets is crucial. Analyzing one side of it, while ignoring the other, will logically provide a partial, incomplete and unbalanced perspective. It will necessarily be a biased and worthless viewpoint, having little value for academic readerships or policy mandarins. An unprejudiced and level-headed scholarly analysis cannot afford to ignore either of the two dimensions of globalization. In this book, I make an attempt to take an equable and level-headed view of the two facets of the ongoing globalization, which are constructive and advantageous on the one side and damaging and harmful on the other.

This book delves into escalating economic globalization by way of trans-border trade and financial flows. Economic forces have been the principal driver of contemporary global integration, albeit politics played an important role in shaping it. In the process of presenting a complete picture of the contemporary phase of globalization, throughout this book we try to examine which facet of globalization is dominating. A wealth of evidence exists that demonstrates that globalization leads to vast economic benefits on the one hand and debilitating costs on the other. Although globalization offers opportunities for higher rates of sustainable growth, these benefits must be weighed against its adverse effects. Some highly useful and valuable questions would be whether globalization is more welfare-enhancing or more hurtful, whether its positive impact overwhelms its negative ramifications, and whether its tangible benefits outweigh the costs.

To be sure, globalization has enormous potential for engendering welfare gains. Recent experiences of different subsets of economies, namely, in the advanced industrial economies and emerging economies of the dynamic South testify to this fact. However, there are many in the profession who are convinced that for many economies and societies, globalism has failed to live up to its potential. In addition, unevenness in its economic outcomes has been widely analyzed by academic researchers and ruminated over by the policy mandarins. Even in the high-income industrial countries it has been argued that buoyed by globalization, corporate income has surged, while average households have gained little. In the US, over the last ten years, the proportion of households making less than \$35000 a year in constant dollars increased, while those making more than \$75000 shrank. Furthermore, that globalization has contributed to increasing income inequality has been increasingly observed and analyzed. However, globalization and the inevitability of income inequality cannot be taken for granted. Also, there is a dubious if rampant belief that governments are growing weaker, while transnational corporations, the agents of globalization, are becoming stronger. While some economies and households have benefited, others have not. The East Asian economies, most remarkably China, have emerged as the triumphant winners of globalization. Conversely, the Latin American economies and the Russian Federation have exemplified its failures. These are some of the contradictory features of the present phase of globalization.

Over the years, a vigorous anti-globalization lobby was born. Although it has presently mellowed, it blamed globalization for a lot of economic and non-economic problems and irately demanded that it be stopped in its tracks. This lobby was strongly averse to the policies of the institutions of global economic governance and the transnational corporations. The former were accused of ignorance and maladroitness, while the latter were considered exploitative and excessively profit-driven. The popular views on globalization were gloomy and downbeat and a seemingly unbridgeable chasm was created between the available economic evidence and popular opinion. The principal reason for this difference in the two perspectives is that increased trans-border flows of goods and factors of production (including labor) can have adverse results when there are domestic market failures or regulatory weaknesses. Both of these need to be dealt with directly by public policy makers, with the help of appropriate domestic policy measures. They can indeed reduce the costs of globalization. If appropriate policy measures are not adopted and implemented without vacillation, the danger of a globalization backlash looms, which could stall, defer or reverse some forms of global economic integration. The ultimate effect would be the undermining or loss of the economic progress that has so far been achieved with the help of ongoing global integration.

The process of globalization does need the helping hand of policy. It should be guided to ensure that it is, first, more inclusive than it has so far been. Second, policy makers should consciously try and strike a balance between risks and benefits. The guidance of the process should be such that benefits are maximized and costs remain controlled. For global economic integration to perform at its best, appropriate national and regional institutions are needed as much as efficacious supranational institutions ensuring global cooperation.

The above exposition justifies my attempt to provide a dispassionate analysis of the favorable and unfavorable impacts of globalization on economies. Globalization per se is neither good nor bad. While in the long run it can enhance systemic efficiency and decisively have a positive impact, it can create problems in the short run. Each economy will have to find its own *sui generis* resolutions for those short-run problems. All things considered, globalization has benefited the global economy. While it has had a negative impact on some economies and certain segments of the population, on balance it has not hurt the poor sections. Empirical research has revealed that global per capita income has markedly risen and on an average the incidence of poverty in the world has declined over the last three decades. Furthermore, the contemporary phase of globalization is more likely to assist in achieving the first Millennium Development Goal (MDG) of halving global poverty by 2015. If so, the anti-globalization lobby needs to be thoughtful and restrain itself. An underlying implicit query that runs throughout this book is whether globalization can help improve living standards and alleviate poverty in the global economy.

Thoughtful people steer clear of extreme viewpoints on globalization. Remaining on the middle ground, they see in it something that is largely positive and can be harnessed in such a manner that it works for the benefit of the majority of economies and societies. Those who hold the middle ground tend to believe that while unbridled globalization can have pernicious micro- and macroeconomic impacts, when handled in a considerate manner, it can open doors of opportunities for many. A one-sided view of globalization will certainly lead to uncalled-for consequences. Considerate analysts and public policy makers need to dispassionately view the various nuanced facets of globalization and identify ways in which the global integration process can yield favorable and constructive results for national and global economies. While remaining realistic about its potential, they need to be cognizant of the potential risks involved.

Perpetuating the folklore about globalization is not the objective of this book. It takes an objective and dispassionate view and delves into the constructive and favorable side as well as the adverse and unfavorable side of the process of globalization. The deficiencies and imperfections have not been overlooked. An outstanding feature of this book is that after a brief historical perspective, it essentially focuses on the contemporary phase of globalization. Second, unlike most globalization-related books, it is written in a comprehensive and authoritative manner. It covers large thematic areas of the global economy and globalization through the channels of multilateral trade and financial flows. It does not leave out newly emerging trends, like accelerating intra-south trade and investment, which has become a new dimension of the global economy, as well as the emerging economies of the dynamic South.

Another outstanding feature of this book is that in taking a contemporary view of the global economy and the phenomenon of globalization, it offers the newest knowledge related to relevant themes on globalization as well as the latest concepts. In a succinct manner, this book deals with the principal normative and positive strands with which one needs to be properly familiar in this subject area. As is essential for a book of this kind, parts of the chapters have been written in a "just-the-facts-jack" style. The picture of both static and dynamic aspects of important economic themes related to globalization has been painted with a broad brush. The selection and rejection of the thematic strands to be covered in this book have been done exceedingly carefully.

In a succinct manner, this tightly written volume covers a great deal of ground and imparts a great deal of knowledge on ongoing globalization-related themes to students, researchers and policy makers alike. It is a worthwhile exercise because a knowledge gap has existed among various stakeholders. In addition, it is neither overly technical nor highly model-oriented. The writing style is squarely based on solid analytical logic and arguments are supported by empirical evidence. Excessive emphasis on formal economic modeling, technicalities, equations and econometrics discourages many potential readers. These characteristics narrow the market to a small expert readership. This book strikes a balance between academic discipline and accessibility for a wide range of readers. In so doing, it stops short of mathematical formulations and econometric modeling. Its descriptive analysis style makes it easy for the target readership to access. Many students, decision makers in business and policy makers, who have good analytical minds and sound knowledge of economic principles, feel lost in mathematical formulations. This writing style makes the book accessible to a large number of readers.

The book is written in a reference-book style, but it can also be used as a textbook. As noted above, students and other readers can find the latest knowledge and concepts on several important themes on ongoing globalization in this book, in a manner in which they can appreciate and absorb them as well as use them as input in their decision making. Students, particularly those from business schools, who may hold global economy-related jobs after completing their studies, will find this knowledge extremely relevant, usable and helpful.

The number of academic institutions offering courses related to global economy is already significant and growing. Several new research centers and institutes have been born over the period of a decade. The target readership of the book is master's level students in economics, international political economy, international relations as well as MBA students. Ambitious senior-level undergraduates as well as policy mandarins and researchers can also benefit from the book. Having a background of initial micro, macro, international trade and monetary economics should be sufficient to comprehend this book because it provides definitions and explanations of the terminology and advanced concepts used in the text as endnotes. Decision makers and public policy makers will find this book an informative and valuable aid.

The book's structure comprises five chapters, as follows: Chapter 1 is a conceptual chapter, which lays the historical and conceptual foundation of the contemporary phase of globalization. The focus of Chapter 2 is the examination of the evidence regarding the welfare-enhancing facet of globalization and examining whether it is a munificent force. Conversely, Chapter 3 takes a serious view of the pernicious and marginalizing side of globalization. It attempts to analyze objectively whether the detractors of globalization are right or wrong. In Chapter 4, the anti-globalization movement, its rise and fall, has been analyzed. The basic premise of the anti-globalization viewpoint has been scrutinized seriously. In an unbiased manner, the chapter investigates the logical basis of the rejection of contemporary globalization. Chapter 5 examines one important positive facet of the contemporary phase of globalization, namely, the emergence of the dynamic South. This subset of developing economies has succeeded in benefiting immensely from the contemporary wave of globalization. As this group of developing economies grew rapidly and began to move to the center of the global economic stage, it initiated changes in the global economic geography. Rapid growth in these dynamic economies of the South began swaying the balance of economic power in the global economy. Consequently, the locus of global economic activity has discernibly changed.

My aspiration is to provide students, business leaders and policy mandarins around the world with a fact base to better comprehend one of the most important transformations shaping the contours of the global economy. I also aspire to bring out that the contemporary phase of globalization is a major systemic economic phenomenon. While disruptive in the short term to some economies, it is on balance a benevolent and positive force of historic dimensions.

NOTES

1. "The inhabitant of London could order by telephone, sipping his morning tea in bed, the various products of the whole earth, in such quantity as he might see fit, and reasonably expect their early delivery upon his doorstep; he could at the same moment and by the same means adventure his wealth in the natural resources and new enterprises of any quarter of the world, and share, without exertion or even trouble, in their prospective fruits and advantages; or he could decide to couple the security of his fortunes with the good faith of the townspeople of any substantial municipality in any continent that fancy or information might recommend. . . . The internationalisation [of the ordinary course of social and economic life] was nearly complete in practice" (Keynes, 1919).
2. Krugman (2008a), p. 14.
3. Janus is the Roman god of beginnings and endings and hence was represented with a double-faced head, each looking in opposite directions. He was worshipped at the beginning of harvest time, planting, marriage, birth and other types of beginnings, especially the beginnings of important events in a person's life. Janus also represents the transition between primitive life and civilization, between the countryside and the city, peace and war, and the growing-up of young people. The month of January was named after him.

Acknowledgements

I take this opportunity to thank my son, Siddharth, for providing prompt and efficient research assistance, and three anonymous referees for providing detailed comments on the manuscript. They were as helpful as they were constructive. I am grateful to Alan Sturmer, Senior Acquisitions Editor, Edward Elgar Publishing, Northampton, MA, for handling the publication and production process of this book in an exceedingly efficient manner. I have been in the business of researching, writing and publishing for over three decades now. I found his level of efficiency an absolutely rare commodity in the publishing industry. I owe profound thanks to Bob Pickens for the care and attention they poured into editing this book. The book's extremely sharp-eyed copy editor Virginia Williams is another person who deserves my grateful thanks. Hélène Côté provided first-rate assistance in research; her humor was as supportive as her library research endeavors. To nurture excellence in any area of human endeavor, credit should be given where it is deserved. One neither needs a sword nor a gun to kill excellence in any society. Ignore and it will wither away.

Indubitably, the largest debt I owe is to my wife Vasanti, for managing the life around me and leaving me to do the researching and writing. Dawn-to-dusk days of non-stop working would not have been feasible without her indefatigable support. She also meticulously read the first drafts and ruthlessly hunted down faulty syntax and mixed metaphors.

1. Conceptual globalism and globalization: an initiation

> This new technology-driven globalization is the new reality to which we are trying to adapt. There truly is no escape from it.
>
> Gerald Helleiner, 2000

> What you cannot avoid, must be welcomed.
>
> A Chinese proverb

1. PRELUDE TO GLOBALISM AND GLOBALIZATION

Although the use of these two terms began in the latter half of the 20th century, they have a longer lineage. The contemporary concept of economic globalism can be traced back to the liberal thinking of classical economists like Adam Smith and Herbert Spencer. Terms like globalize were first used in Reiser and Davies (1944). The *Webster International Dictionary* included them in 1961, while they appeared in the *Oxford English Dictionary* in 1986. The term globalization was coined in 1962.[1] Most major languages were quick to develop an equivalent taxonomy. In business and economics, marketing legend Theodore Levitt of Harvard Business School used it first in 1983 in an article entitled "The Globalization of Markets".[2] His article is regarded as an enduring classic and its insightful language is still relevant today.

Although the contemporary era of economic globalism is barely three decades old, neither is the essential concept of globalism novel nor is globalization a new phenomenon. In its conceptual, corporeal and functional forms globalism is more than two thousand years of age. Was the spread of Buddhism in the fifth century BC from northern India to China, Japan and other East Asian countries not cultural and informational globalism, which we now put under the rubric of social or socio-cultural globalism? Globalism is a defining issue of the contemporary era and has come to acquire considerable emotive meaning and force. It has tended to spark the most highly charged debates, has been the subject of countless articles and books and the cause of major public demonstrations, occasionally violent, in Europe and North America. The last three decades were a period of unprecedented integration of the global economy. Little wonder that the concept of globalism and the phenomenon of globalization acquired a good deal of currency as well as the involvement of various stakeholders. It became and will continue to be the dominant force shaping the world economy. Its relevance and significance extends well beyond academic economists, to business and public policy makers and the public at large. The concepts and nomenclature of globalism and globalization came to be used by different social sciences in the early 1980s, but since the early 1990s they have permeated popular consciousness. Journalists and politicians of varying allegiances have used them recurrently. Therefore, they lack a clean, crisp and consensus definition (Section 3.2). These concepts have also become central to the thinking and analysis of economists and to the actions of business leaders.

The three terms, globalism, globalization and globality simply characterize the gradually evolving interaction and integration of economies and societies around the world. As the three terms are embraced by different social sciences, they have been variously defined. Consequently there are myriad competing definitions. While widely used, these expressions take on imprecise meanings and are often poorly understood and conceptualized (Section 3.2). Comprehension of the issues is compromised by an unclear grasp of the core concepts. These terms are regarded as confusing and confused in the academic literature and a debate continues on what is their precise meaning and definition. Used in an all-encompassing manner, they are frequently turned into a portmanteau. They have become clichéd, trite and stereotypical expressions, which have lost their ingenuity by long overuse – and frequent misuse. There has been a strong tendency to put any new idea, or change of a fundamental nature, under the all-encircling terminology of globalization.

As the concepts of globalism and globalization cover a wide subject area, they are shared by several social sciences. They are deployed across disciplines and across theoretical approaches. Their academic and intellectual significance has been on the rise, particularly since 2000. Business schools, universities and other academic institutions run popular courses and degree programs in the subject. Some have recently come to prominence and are well-attended. Scholarly journals, books, research papers, academic literature, websites on these and related themes have grown rapidly. Since the turn of the century, numerous dedicated research and study centers and professional associations have sprung up on this theme around the world. Mittelman (2002, p. 1) regarded this concept as "an ascendant paradigm in international studies", a novel paradigm of social enquiry.

A good deal of the literature surrounding globalization is multidisciplinary. The multidisciplinary and multifaceted nature of this subject matter is obvious from its compelling economic, financial, business, social, political, technological, informational, environmental, cultural, educational, international relations and security-related dimensions (Section 4). Emphasis on economic and financial dimensions of globalism was always high, while other dimensions were subordinated to it. Of late, the significance of environmental and military dimensions has markedly escalated. While these multiple dimensions are interrelated and often mutually reinforcing, they are exclusive and diverse in their origins. The multidisciplinary nature of globalization has made it an intellectually challenging issue. This is one of the reasons why there is intense academic interest in this area of intellectual curiosity. Numerous bright minds of the day have been drawn to this issue. In tandem, interest in lay circles is no less intense. Books like *The Lexus and the Olive Tree,* which *inter alia* tell the story of the contemporary global economy in reader-friendly prose and put across the conventional wisdom on globalization, hit the bestseller lists.[3] Nearly every issue of *Business Week* discusses one globalization-related issue or another. Business and policy-making conclaves have interminable debates over it, as do parliaments and labor meetings. Extreme disagreement of views coexists on globalism. If one group fervently believes in its capability of enhancing prosperity and economic welfare, the other firmly regards it as a pernicious force that impoverishes the poor of the world and enriches the rich and is the principal villain in causing environmental degradation, among other injurious influences.

The objective of this introductory chapter is to succinctly provide an induction for knowledgeable readers in the concepts of economic globalism and globalization in their contemporary form, their historical antecedents and how economic globalism essentially operates. Although the essential focus is on economic globalism, other kinds have not been totally passed over. There is no pretence that economic globalism is the only, or even the dominant, kind. As the definition of globalism and globalization has been a contentious issue which has generated analytical deliberations and an enduring animated debate, this chapter also dwells on definition-related issues, particularly focusing on economic globalization.

2. A HISTORICAL PERSPECTIVE OF THE LONGUE DURÉE

The concepts and phenomena of globality, globalism and globalization have their antecedents. In their ancient forms they can be traced back to ancient civilizations and empires like Maurya (322–185 BCE), the Roman and Parthian Empires and the Han Dynasty (206 BCE to AD 220). These were the first eras of cross-cultural, economic and social encounters in the pre-modern period. The Roman Empire, which stretched between Great Britain, the Middle East and Northern Africa, is a striking manifestation of early globalization. Markets for goods, capital and labor were integrated during this period (Temin, 2006). However, some (like Wade, 2006) believe that globalization, in one form or another, has been present since the dawn of modern humans, some 50 000 years ago.

Two millennia ago, the Romans unified their widespread empire by building an extensive transport network, common language, legal system and currency. A commonality of institutions successfully promoted trade and economic development (Hitchner, 2003). Maddison (2007) provides a detailed account of the Roman Empire and its economy.[4] Another equally striking example of energetic and thriving globalism in the pre-modern era is the Chinese Silk Road that promoted and strengthened commercial networks between China, the Parthian Empire and parts of southern Europe. The silk route, which began during the Han dynasty, expanded into a full-scale international trade route between China, India, Persia and the Arabian Peninsula (Chow, 2006).

The Arab conquests of the seventh and early eighth centuries united the Mediterranean world of Rome and its ancient empire with Mesopotamia and Iran. The Arabs united the Byzantine possessions of Egypt, Syria, Palestine and North Africa. This was the Islamic golden age and another example of ancient globalism, when traders successfully established a rudimentary form of global economy. Trade in goods and migration of people took place freely. The exchange of both ideas and techniques was also common. Two-way flows of ideas and knowledge took place between East and West "in one vast integrated space united by Islam and Arabic language" (Findlay and O'Rourke, 2007, p. 48). The Islamic golden age matured and became fairly complex during the Mongol Empire of Genghis Khan and Kublai Khan. This epoch witnessed the globalization of crops, commerce, knowledge and technology. The Mongol Empire, one of the largest continuous empires in history, was responsible for a strong wave of globalization.[5] Marco Polo (1254–1324), the most famous traveler of the silk road, was a veritable trading entrepreneur of his period. He found new products and developed markets for them. He became a confidant of Kublai Khan. He provided detailed accounts of the economy of the Mongol Empire, which by his account was prosperous.

The Ming Dynasty (1368–1644 AD) of China, the last dynasty ruled by ethnic Hans, played an important role in economic globalization. Not only did neighboring countries have trade and tribute-paying relations with China during this period, but also distant European countries like Portugal, Spain and Holland had active commercial ties. Abu-Lughod

(1989) provided comprehensive accounts of the voyages of the Ming Dynasty admiral Zheng He (or Cheng Ho) until the early decades of the fifteenth century. The Ming Dynasty navy had over 3800 ships, many of them several times larger than their Portuguese counterparts.[6] China not only led the world during this era in ship-building but was also ahead of Europe in clock-making, hydraulics and iron-smelting.[7]

The famous voyages of discovery by Christopher Columbus, Vasco da Gama and other explorers expanded trade and economic ties over large distances. These voyages were made possible by advances in European ship-building technology and the science of navigation. Noteworthy improvements in the quality of compass, rudder and sail design also contributed to advances in nautical technology. The sea lanes opened up by these voyages assisted in promoting thriving intercontinental commerce. Before the 16th and 17th centuries, the Portuguese and Spanish Empires had expanded to the Americas and to many other parts of the globe, promoting and expanding economic and political globalization. As these voyages had high costs and risk, trade was logically limited to goods of high value relative to their weight and bulk. Some of the important items of trade included sugar, tobacco, spices, tea, silk, porcelain and gems and precious metals. While trade and migration had their positive income effect, inequality was rampant. Estimates show that during the pre-industrial period, income inequality was lower in the East Asian economies than in Europe and the Middle Eastern countries (Milanovic et al., 2007).

The birth of large state-sanctioned trading companies was the next noteworthy development; they began to have increasing control over trade. In the seventeenth century the Dutch East India Company, the first transnational corporation (TNC), was established. It was also the first business firm to share risk to enable joint ownership by issuing shares. Subsequently, the British East India Company and the Hudson Bay Company were created. All of them enjoyed monopolistic powers, aggressively protected their high markups and profits and were instrumental in playing a meaningful role in both economic and political globalization. Believing in a mercantilist philosophy, they regarded international trade as a zero-sum game. As markets were a rich and rewarding source of profits, during this period, European nation-states competed for market dominance. This intense competition frequently crossed the economic arena and turned into military conflict (Bernanke, 2006).

As large parts of the world did not participate in the above-noted periods of pre-modern globalization, some analysts do not think that this could be termed *bona-fide* globalization. However, the non-participation of several countries is also a characteristic of the current period of

globalization. Other arguments for not regarding the past as periods of
globalization are: first, in comparison to the present, the means of transport and communication during these periods were far from swift. They
did not allow firms and markets to be organized and function efficiently
at the global level. Second, the present global financial markets are characterized by a far larger volume of operations in terms of gross flows and
variety of instruments being traded. However, these are inaccurate and
non-tenable arguments for rejecting the globalism of the pre-modern
periods. If they are accepted, then all history, economic or otherwise, is
worthy of rejection.

2.1 Modern Phase: Vintage 19th and 20th Centuries

The period before the Napoleonic Wars (1815) went down in history as an
anti-globalism mercantilist period (Williamson, 2002). The first modern
period began after the end of the Napoleonic Wars and continued up to
World War I. International trade and financial flows as well as the cross-
border migration of labor expanded significantly during this phase of
globalism. The growth rate of world trade was more rapid than that of
world output. It grew at an average rate of 3.5 percent a year, compared
to 2.7 percent in the case of world output. The steady reduction of tariffs
and transport costs, particularly during the latter half of this period,
advanced global economic integration. Due to the advent of railroads and
steamships, transport costs declined sharply and communications costs
fell as telegraph technology and services expanded. The trans-Atlantic
telegraph cable, laid in 1866, was extolled for "annihilating both space
and time in the transmission of intelligence" (Standage, 1998, p. 90).
Ambitious public works projects, like the opening of the Suez Canal in
1869, truncated travel time between Asia and Europe, which promoted
both travel and commerce. These technological advancements were consistently pro-globalization. During this era, the forces of capitalism were
fully unleashed.

Policy measures that buttressed globalization during the first modern
period included the abolition of the Corn Laws in Britain in 1846. As
Britain unilaterally moved to free trade, it set in motion a trade liberalization trend in Europe. The Cobden Chevalier Treaty of 1860 between
Britain and France reinforced this trend. The most-favored-nation (MFN)
clause was the most significant element of this treaty. Accordingly, the two
contracting parties agreed to extend any reduction of tariff agreed between
them to their other trading partners as well. This set the ball rolling and
many European economies signed such treaties. A growing appreciation
of the classical principle of comparative advantage made policy makers

abandon the mercantilist approach of the past. In 1913, the share of exports in world output peaked. World trade did not reach this level again until 1970 (Bairoch and Kozul-Wright, 1996; Irwin, 1996). Expanding trade had increased the variety of goods available, in the process enriching the quality of life. The trade monopolies of the past were supplanted by intensely competing firms. Consequently, global prices converged on a wide range of traded commodities, including spices, wheat, cotton, pig iron and jute (Findlay and O'Rourke, 2002). The pre-World War I period also enjoyed almost entirely free movement of capital and remarkably free movement of labor. Between 1871 and 1915, approximately 36 million people left Europe in search of a life of new opportunities. An unexpected spin-off of this migration was a sharp rise in productivity in those industries that had been facing labor surplus. This was the period when globalization reached its crescendo. The latter half of the 19th century, until World War I, was a period of intense economic integration.

Globalization has ebbed and flowed during different periods. The favorable trading environment changed with the outbreak of World War I. The liberal global economic order collapsed and quantitative restrictions (QRs) and tariffs became rampant among the belligerents. This was the start of de-globalization. The Great Depression stifled the liberalization that began after the war under the gold exchange standard (1925–31) and tariffs began to rise again. The US enacted its ill-conceived Smoot-Hawley Act, raising tariffs to 23 percent, triggering immediate retaliation from its trading partners. QRs also returned. Both world output and trade plummeted rapidly, with world trade declining more sharply than output.

After the end of World War II, the international community joined hands and the Bretton Woods system was conceived by some of the brainiest economists of that period, who included John Maynard Keynes. The General Agreement on Tariffs and Trade (GATT) began operation in 1948; the multilateral trade regime evolved almost ceaselessly. Among the international fora, the GATT system was exclusive in that it brought its entire membership together to negotiate a common set of rules to govern international trade, and in the process promote free trade. These negotiations are conducted during "rounds" of multilateral trade negotiations (MTNs). Eight rounds of MTNs were held under the sponsorship of the GATT, which succeeded in liberalizing multilateral trade by lowering tariff barriers. It is noteworthy that multilateral trade liberalization did not take place at a uniform pace, but in fits and starts. The following seven rounds of MTNs, under the sponsorship of the GATT, were overwhelmingly dominated by industrial economies: the Geneva Tariff Conference (1947), Annecy Tariff Conference (1949), Torquay Tariff Conference (1951), Geneva Tariff Conference (1956), the Dillon Round

(1960–61), the Kennedy Round (1964–7), and the Tokyo Round (1973–9). In the eighth, the Uruguay Round (1986–94), the developing economies participated energetically. The GATT was amended and supplemented progressively with the passage of time. In 1994, the edifice of the World Trade Organization (WTO) was created on the foundation of the GATT, a relatively small organization in terms of coverage of trade rules and membership. The WTO evolved qualitatively from the GATT and is a much larger organization. These rounds of MTNs succeeded in bringing about a dramatic stepwise reduction in trade barriers of different kinds. Multilateral trade exploded after the early 1960s. In constant 2000 dollars, it expanded from $1 trillion per annum in 1970 to $10 trillion in 2004 (World Bank, 2007). It has picked up momentum since the mid-1990s and increased from $5.17 trillion to $11.98 trillion between 1995 and 2006, that is, it more than doubled.

During the post-Uruguay Round period, between 1995 and 2007, multilateral trade in goods and services expanded at almost double the growth rate of the developing economies. Historically, the rate of trade expansion and moves to diversify exports have been uneven. The WTO is engaged in reducing tariff and non-tariff barriers (NTBs) and other kinds of protection; its wider reach extends to areas not covered by the GATT in the past. The first round of MTNs under the aegis of the WTO, the Doha Round, was launched in 2001 (Das, 2007d). Although the Doha Round was officially "suspended" in mid-2006, the concerted endeavors of the GATT/WTO framework fundamentally transformed the global trade institutional structure (Das, 2008d). The WTO, in alliance with the Bretton Woods twins, supported the ongoing phase of trade liberalization and globalization in a significant manner. Together these three supranational institutions formed a strong institutional framework underpinning and advancing globalization.

Like trade flows, capital flows were buoyant in the first modern period between the early 19th century and World War I. Large volumes of investible capital gushed from the industrialized countries of Western Europe to the rapidly developing economies in Australia, Canada, Latin America and some developing countries that were colonies of the European economies. Bairoch and Kozul-Wright (1996) quantified the capital outflows; at their peak they were 9 percent of GNP for Britain. For France, Germany and the Netherlands, this proportion was not much lower than that for Britain. During the first modern period, private global capital movements did not suffer restrictions. Many of these financial flows took the form of bond financing. They were essentially utilized, first, for the purpose of infrastructure construction, particularly railroads and ports, and second, as foreign direct investment (FDI) in the infant industrial sector in the capital-importing countries. Britain was the largest capital-exporter, Canada the largest importer, while the US was a relatively smaller importer. The free flow of capital before 1914 was aided by the fact that much of the world followed the gold standard, that is, national currencies maintained convertibility into gold. According to the principles of international macroeconomics, this meant that countries could not use monetary policy instruments to stabilize domestic economies.

The outbreak of World War I caused global capital movements to come to a near standstill. They did not pick up again until 1970. The liberal pre-war policy stance that propped up free capital mobility was abandoned. The gold standard was suspended by the belligerents and capital controls and exchange controls were put in place. As the Great Depression began, capital controls became increasingly stringent and extensive in their application. The reason was that each economy wanted to use monetary policy and fiscal measures to shield itself from deflation. This international monetary and currency regime proved to be ideal for de-globalization.

The contemporary phase of economic globalization is similar to, yet different from, past episodes (Bernanke, 2006). One lesson of history is that not all forms of global integration can be regarded as beneficial and supportive of economic and social progress. Globalism took a violent, unwholesome and harrowing direction in the past when the instruments of spreading it were the sword, the gun, the gunboat and the slave ships. This vicious aberration must not be allowed to supplant the voluntary spread of globalism even for a short period. Regrettably, numerous periods of history have recorded such deviations from the healthy voluntary variety.

The creators of the Bretton Woods regime drew lessons from the excessive volatility of the inter-war period and destabilizing speculation. The architects of the new international monetary system had committed to maintaining capital controls and opted for a currency regime of a fixed but adjustable peg. This left macroeconomic managers free to use monetary policy to stabilize domestic economies and pursue the domestic objective of full employment. The reconstruction of the major European economies was completed by the mid-1950s, their current account convertibility was achieved by 1956 and they formally accepted the obligations of Article VIII of the International Monetary Fund (IMF) by 1961. Due to policies inconsistent with the maintenance of their exchange rate parities, some European currencies came under speculative attack. The Bretton Woods system came under strain. The US gold reserves began depleting and the Bretton Woods system grew increasingly fragile. In 1965, the US Treasury imposed restrictions on capital outflows. Currency speculation began to get out of control and attempts to quell it failed. The Bretton Woods system collapsed in mid-1971 and the global economy moved onto a floating exchange rate regime for the major currencies in 1973. Japan, Germany, the UK and the US dismantled their capital controls by 1979 and the rest of the European economies did so by the end of the 1980s. Capital mobility was not incompatible with independent monetary policy; therefore it picked up momentum. Some developing economies also liberalized their capital accounts. Capital market integration began and geographically extended beyond those economies that participated in financial globalization during the first modern period, which had ended in 1914.

The 20th century was a period of remarkable transformation in the structure of production, growth in per capita output and developments in domestic and international financial systems. The pace of economic growth was ratcheted up by many notches. Technological advancements during this century drove an enormous increase in the production of goods and services, generating a great deal of material wealth. The 20th century "tamed capitalism" and boosted its productivity by providing the institutional underpinnings of market-based economies (Rodrik, 2007a, p. 195). Declining transport and communications costs boosted international trade and investment. Also, the make-up of the international monetary system changed significantly and repeatedly during this period. Notwithstanding two devastating wars and the so-called Great Depression, economic growth in the 20th century did benefit from brief periods of partial and limited globalization, which spread the division of labor to wider territories after World War II. In addition, the improvements in financial intermediation and market practices alluded to above promoted mutually beneficial exchanges between the net-saver and high-investing economies and economic agents, which in turn enabled them to use capital productively.

The economic impact of this limited period of globalization was clearly discernible in the average global per capita income, which increased five-fold. Conventional long-term GDP estimates show that the value of goods and services produced during the 20th century exceeded the "cumulative total of output over the preceding recorded human history" (IMF, 2002, p. 151). DeLong (1998) computed that between 1900 and 2000, global GDP at constant prices increased 19-fold. This increase was far from evenly distributed; the latter half of the 20th century was far superior to the former. Maddison (2001, p. 125) went as far as to say that the global economy "performed better in the last half century than at any time in the past. World GDP increased six-fold from 1950 to 1998, with an average growth rate of 3.9 percent a year, compared to 1.6 percent from 1820 to 1950, and 0.3 percent from 1500 to 1820." Real per capita income in the global economy rose by 2.1 percent a year during the latter half of the 20th century compared to 0.9 percent from 1820 to 1950, and 0.05 percent over the 1500–1820 period.

In effect, global economic growth in the latter half of the 20th century was so much better and qualitatively different from any earlier periods in history that a "new perspective of the world economy was needed to comprehend it" (Lucas, 2000, p. 159). This rapid growth led average global per capita income to more than triple in the second half of the last century (Kohler, 2002).[8] Maddison (2003) firmly corroborated this fact.[9] For North America, Western Europe and Japan this period was one of unmatched prosperity. Subsequently the East Asian economies followed this group. In particular, real income growth in the advanced industrial economies of North America, Western Europe and Japan during this period was unprecedented compared with all other economies during all the previous periods. In the post-1950 period, the resurgence of Japan and the other East Asian economies demonstrated that a significant degree of convergence with the mature industrial economies was feasible. The post-1978 China also credibly demonstrated the same possibility (Das, 2007a).

This remarkable economic performance was no coincidence. The forces of globalization, in the subset of economies named in the preceding paragraph, were supported by the institutional innovation that had taken place in them, which enhanced both the legitimacy and the efficiency of markets. Globalization not only powered the ascent of the Chinese economy but subsequently also that of India. The two populous giants are presently being regarded as the new locomotives of global growth (Das, 2006). Brisk growth in these two economies and their progressive global integration was bolstered by the "material advancement unleashed by market forces" (Rodrik, 2007a, p. 195). However, the flip side of the coin is that many countries did not benefit from globalization during the 20th century. Global income growth was also unevenly dispersed. The income gap between developing and industrial countries and the haves and have-nots within countries deteriorated.[10] While the richest quarter of the world population saw its income grow six-fold during the 20th century, for the poorest quarter this increase was barely three-fold. Thus, despite its commendable economic achievements, the 20th century was also a period of markedly worsening income inequality in the global economy (IMF, 2001). Income discrepancies were larger at the end of the 20th century than they were at the beginning. Between 1900 and 2000, the Gini coefficient[11] rose from 0.40 to 0.48 (IMF, 2002). Therefore the supranational institutions that played a supportive role and promoted globalism began to appear increasingly uncomfortable in this role.

2.2   Contemporary Phase: Vintage Twenty-first Century

The second, or contemporary, era of market-driven globalization is deemed to have begun around 1980. Paul Krugman (2008a) called it "the second great age of globalization", comparable to the much quoted John Maynard Keynes' familiar description of globalization on the eve of World War I. This time point is significant because for the first time in the contemporary period governments in the mature industrial economies, and increasingly in the emerging economies of the developing world, began to foster liberal economic policy regimes that were broadly supportive of globalization. Slashing trade barriers and liberalizing capital flows reflected this mindset of the policy makers. This is not to imply that liberalization was adopted across the board and by all countries; pockets of protectionism persisted.

The policy ambiance that began to develop from the early 1980s was that of lowering artificial and policy-driven barriers to international transactions, which nurtured a generally permissive policy background for global economic integration. The pace of global economic integration accelerated during the decade of the 1990s, as many governments reduced policy-induced barriers that impeded international trade and investment flows. These two decades witnessed an unprecedented revival of global economic integration. Consequently, the volume and value of global trade and financial transactions rose dramatically. The revival was underpinned by technological advancements and given an impetus by international economic policies, born of multilateral cooperation. This process of global integration affected (and is affecting) the evolution of national, regional and global economies. Few economies, developing or industrial, have remained untouched by the influences of contemporary globalization. It has also had a profound microeconomic impact as well as bearing on how the residents of different nation-states interact with each other.

A general policy shift towards greater reliance on market forces is one of the idiosyncrasies of contemporary globalization. While private enterprise was embraced, statist policies were rejected. Gradually, the post-1980 period saw a momentous transformation of the global economy. Its characteristic features were rapid growth in multilateral trade and global financial flows, including FDI. The long-term average growth rate of FDI is approximately twice that of multilateral trade, which in turn grew almost twice the rate of global GDP growth. Furthermore, during the current phase of globalization, multilateral trade and financial services are far more developed and deeply integrated globally than ever in the past. Transport costs have continued to decline further with advances in containerization and far greater utilization of air freight in international trade.

According to Frankel (2000), average ocean freight and port charges, in 1990 dollars, declined from $90 to $29 between 1920 and 1990. A much larger proportion of cargo is now transported by air than in the past. Between 1930 and 1990, air transport revenue per passenger mile declined from $0.68 to $0.11. The modern transport revolution not only saves time but also dramatically reduces transport costs as a percentage of the value of goods shipped, in the process strengthening the performance and profits of trading firms. With rapid growth in FDI, operations of transnational corporations (TNCs) have expanded briskly. TNCs are widely regarded as agents of economic globalization. The behavior and production organization of companies of all sizes have changed dramatically in response to globalization; production of many goods and some services is increasingly organized globally. In addition, completely new methods of trade, like outsourcing and production networks, have come into being. With the passage of time, they are growing increasingly mature, complex and popular.

Advances in information and communications technology (ICT), the newest sinew of globalization, are responsible for a sea change in the global economy. ICT is a general purpose technology, or meta-technology, having a pervasive impact on economy. This industrial sector was dynamic, that is, rapidly changing, and depended relatively heavily on a highly educated workforce. Brisk progress in ICT influenced the economic and social parameters to an unmatched degree by increasing our ability to communicate and access information. Access to the Internet has grown rapidly and transport and communications costs have continued to drop. In constant (1998) dollars, the cost of a three-minute New York–London telephone call in 1931 was $293; in 1950 it came down to $50 and in 2001 it fell to $1 (Krueger, 2006). By 2007, it was down to a paltry $0.23 (OECD, 2007b).

Advances in ICT have favorably influenced both the speed and scale of globalization during the contemporary phase. Advances in computing power as well as the emergence and widespread utilization of the Internet enabled sharp cost cuts in processing and transmitting information. They also facilitated international transactions in goods and services. Furthermore, ICT-enabled services were instrumental in the creation of regional production networks which exploited vertical specialization as well as the geographical fragmentation of production processes to an unprecedented degree. The mature industrial economies have taken to large-scale outsourcing of production of goods and services. As set out in Section 5, due to the creation of a globalized labor force, many production processes and services can be performed remotely. While vestiges of the model of the international production chain existed in the early 20th century, this process is far more advanced and pervasive now than ever before. Dramatic improvements in value-chain, or supply-chain, management have not only altered manufacturing processes but also reduced costs of production. Production processes have been broken down among globally distributed suppliers; techniques like just-in-time (JIT) enable efficient production (Section 5). The advent of a group of emerging-market economies (EMEs)[12] on the global economic stage, with China gearing up to take a conspicuous place, has affected the global economy in an unmatched manner (Section 2.3). The ultimate outcome is the close integration of a large number of, albeit not all, economies. While exclusive and distinctive in their own right, these remarkable attributes are being driven by the same fundamental forces, and are having similar effects, as they did in the preceding era of globalization. Technological advancement and advances in the mode of transport and communication are still major enabling factors.

One characteristic of contemporary globalization is increased intra-firm cross-border collaborations in the form of joint ventures, non-equity agreements and minority participations, enabling firms to engage in producing products or services that are beyond their individual technical and financial resources and capabilities. Such collaborations have steadily increased since the early 1980s. Large and resourceful firms in mature industrial economies that are technology leaders frequently take the initiative in putting together such collaborations. An increasing number of small- and medium-sized firms have also begun taking such initiatives and devising ways to form cross-border inter-firm collaborative ventures. The commonest sectors for such collaborations include electronics, aerospace, telecommunications, computers and automobiles. R&D-intensive industrial sectors are regarded as particularly appropriate for cross-border collaborations. Therefore, these sectors have become relatively more globalized. The greatest concentration of collaborative activities is presently found between firms in the OECD economies, East Asia and China, Latin America and Eastern Europe. In these parts of the global economy, inter-firm collaborative ventures are made both intra-regionally and inter-regionally. Indeed, firm, industry and country differences play a role in these kinds of global industrial collaborations.

In terms of scale, the contemporary era of globalization is unmatched. Never in history has global integration involved so many people, both in absolute numbers and as a percentage of the global population. For instance, in the latter half of the 19th century when the economically advanced economies of Europe were integrating with North America, Australia and Latin American economies, the total population of the lesser developed nations was half the size of the advanced economies. In contrast, China and India together represent 2.5 times the current population of the mature industrial economies. Similarly, the scale of goods, services and capital traded at present is unprecedented. Contemporary globalization is also marked by a significant broadening of the range of products and services that have become tradable. Trade in services has become the fastest growing component of multilateral trade. This is the consequence of having a far more open global economy than ever before. Trade has consistently grown faster than global GDP. Merchandise exports are 20 percent of global GDP during the current phase of globalization, compared to 9 percent a century ago during the earlier phase of globalization (Alexander and Warwick, 2007). Advances in ICT have not only reduced the cost of communication but also made it possible to actively trade a range of services, such as accounting, which were regarded as non-tradable until the recent past, such as financial, legal, medical services, engineering and R&D. Although trade theory never took into consideration the precipitous decline in the communication costs of voice, text and data, this has considerable implications for trade. Lower costs facilitate communications between buyers and sellers, brokers and middlemen. They particularly affect trade in various kinds of services. In 1994, the WTO created a GATT-like institution, called the General Agreement on Trade in Services (GATS). Its mandate was to facilitate and monitor trade in services, which heralded a new era in the globalization of trade in services (Das, 2007d). The volume of multilateral trade in services in 2007 was $3.3 trillion (WTO, 2008). Restrictions of cross-border financial flows were markedly reduced by governments during the contemporary period and the so-called soft infrastructure, which includes legal and accounting frameworks, has steadily improved.

An amber signal will not be out of place here. The contemporary era of globalization, like the previous ones, is not global. It has not benefited all economies. There exists a country group that has failed to benefit from globalization. The majority of the members of this group are located in sub-Saharan Africa. Not only did poverty not decline in these countries, but in many cases it also increased. The causes include these countries' inability to liberalize their domestic economic structures and integrate with the global economy. Additionally, these countries have suffered from deeper problems of political strife, social tensions, ethnic conflicts and most of all poor governance.

2.3 Progressive Integration of the Emerging-market Economies

In its scale and pace, the contemporary era of globalization is without equal and surpasses all previous eras by a large margin. The volume of

merchandise trade, which was 20 percent of global GDP in 2006, is one
of the proofs of this fact. The corresponding proportion was barely 8
percent in 1913 and 15 percent in 1990. Global financial flows expanded
more rapidly than multilateral trade during the contemporary phase of
globalization. Financial markets are far more mature and investors use
a large array of instruments, equities and derivatives (Bernanke, 2006).
These examples and statistics do not state the full magnitude of current
globalization.

At the end of World War II, several economies in Asia (China, India,
Indonesia, the Republic of Korea (hereinafter Korea), Malaysia, Taiwan
and Thailand), Latin America (Argentina, Brazil, Chile and Mexico)
and Turkey in the Middle East had some experience of running their
own low-technology manufacturing industries in areas like silk, cotton
textiles, foodstuff and light consumer goods. This exposure to indigenous
manufacturing activity provided them with some industrial expertise and
experience and they prepared to move into mid-technology manufacturing. If economic development is "a process of moving from a set of assets
based on primary products, exploited by unskilled labor, to a set of assets
based on knowledge, exploited by skilled labor", these countries were
ready to move from the first set of assets to the second (Amsden, 2001;
p. 7). Around the early 1980s, many of them began adopting proactive
macroeconomic policies to liberalize their economies, structurally reform
them and integrate with the global economy. They gradually emerged as
the EMEs (Section 2.2), although Amsden (2001) prefered the term "late-
industrializing economies", which did not catch on and was rejected as a
cliché. Integration of these EMEs with the global economy implies that
the greater part of the world population is potentially integrating with
and participating in the global economy. The progressive and proactive
integration of the larger EMEs, like the four Asian newly industrializing
economies (ANIEs), namely, Korea, Hong Kong SAR, Singapore and
Taiwan, Brazil, China, India, the Russian Federation and South Africa,
has been of especial significance in this respect. There are no historical
parallels to this watershed development. It cannot be ignored that until
a short time ago China and the Russian Federation were autarkic economies, while India was an inward-oriented economy, almost isolated from
the rest of the global economy.

A traditional distinction was made by development economists and
geographers. According to this taxonomy, the industrial economies were
identified as the core and the developing economies as the periphery.
With the progressively growing importance of the EMEs in the global
economy, this distinction has become irrelevant. The old pattern of the
core countries exporting manufactures, while the periphery economies

exported minerals, raw materials and commodities, no longer holds. An increasing proportion of manufacturing capacity has moved from the mature economies to the EMEs. Their integration with the global economy and contribution to global growth have been rising in the 2000s. According to the *World Economic Outlook 2007*, China, India and Russia alone accounted for one-half of global economic growth in 2006. Led by China and India, EMEs expanded strongly in 2007 also. According to the projections of the IMF, the EMEs would continue to serve as the main engine of global economic growth in 2008 (IMF, 2007b).

Another aspect of the breakdown of the core-periphery paradigm is the reversal of capital flows. In the past, the core countries, in particular Britain, ran large current account surpluses and were large capital export-ers to the periphery economies. In a reversal of this paradigm, presently the US, the largest global economy, has been running massive current account deficits and is also the largest debtor economy in the world. To a substantial extent, its deficits are financed by EMEs that have enjoyed long periods of current account surplus.

3. FUNCTIONALLY DEFINING GLOBALISM

Although it will not be unreasonable to assume that most knowledge-able readers have some familiarity with the concept, beginning with a functional definition would not be unreasonable. A definition is not a mere lexicographical device. It has an intellectual objective, that is, to aid understanding of the issue at hand and provide an insight into it. Broadly defined, globalism implies networks of connections spanning multi-continental distances, drawing them close together economically, socially, culturally and informationally. Globalization in turn is generally conceived as the processes promoting and intensifying multi-continental interconnectedness, and thereby increasing the degree of globalism. The phenomenon of globalization assumes progressively increasing globalism, which in turn stands for an intensification of the network of connections or multiplicity of relationships among economies and countries.

In its quintessential form globalization grinds down national bounda-ries and integrates societies and economies. Although the three terms, globality, globalism and globalization, are often narrowly defined in economic terms, they are broad in their meaning and implications.[13] Driven by innovation and technological progress and with the objective of advancing material well-being, economic globalization has occurred over a long period of history. From an economic point of view, globalization represents a process of increasing international division of labor on the one hand and growing integration of national economies through trade in goods and services, cross-border corporate investment and capital flows on the other. In the contemporary phase of globalization, technological innovations, particularly in digital technology, combined with the rapid worldwide extension of communications and falling transportation costs, have noticeably increased the possibilities for global production and exchange. That said, mere technological advancement cannot usher in the phenomenon of global economic integration. Economic globalization is a policy-induced process. It cannot take place without the adoption of a liberalized policy stance at national level. Trade and financial sector reforms and liberalization, followed by market-based institutional reforms, are the *sine qua non* of global integration. Innovations in ICT and the popularity of the Internet have enabled the modern business community to access information and resources across the world and coordinate production activities in real time.

3.1 Multitude of Definitions

Several other narrow and broad types of definitional concepts have also evolved around globality, globalism and globalization. Given the depth of interest among academic researchers from different social science backgrounds, public policy mandarins and business leaders in globalism and globalization, it is not surprising that there are several categories of definitions. Each set of scholars came up with his or her own definitions from his or her own perspective. The first to emerge were facile, flawed and cul-de-sac definitions. In this category of definitions globalization was presented as internationalization, liberalization, universalization and Westernization. Conceptual globalism on these lines did not provide analytical value-added and was not insightful on any measure (Scholte, 2002). Apart from being sharp, clear cut and revealing, a definition needs to raise insightful understanding of the issues at hand and provide empowering knowledge. Such an understanding would support our endeavors to transform our lives in a constructive, innovative, positive and creative direction. Bhagwati (2004) provided a definition based on the economic dimension of globalization, which included integration of the global economy by way of trade, FDI, movements of portfolio capital and bank capital of varying maturity, technological diffusion and cross-border migration.

Potentially trans-planetary, and more specifically supra-territorial, linkages between people and countries are also regarded and conceptually accepted as globalism. Through the action of economic, socio-cultural, political and technological forces, the process of globalization can potentially unite the world into a single society. It is within the realm of possibilities. Although elements emphasized in different definitions differ, they are also related to one another as they often overlap. The notions of globality and spatiality resonate strikingly well together; they point to the essential arena of human and social activity. Some scholars see globalization as a reconfiguration of social space. To them, globality identifies the planet as a solitary site for various human and social exploits. Globality implies that while people and societies may live together in local, provincial and national realms, they also subsist in trans-border spaces where the world is a single unit or space (Scholte, 2005). Based on the types of networks, flows and "perceptual connections that occur in spatially extensive networks", Keohane and Nye (2001, p. 14) identified four principal dimensions of globalism. These spatially extensive networks distinctly and discreetly fall in the following areas: (i) economic, including financial, (ii) military or strategic, (iii) environmental and (iv) socio-cultural. This typological distinction is indeed incomplete because several other dimensions of globalism can be easily conceived and have been noted above (Section 1). Economic geography has changed at all spatial levels, that is both within nations and globally. For instance, the strengthening urbanization trend is an illustration of sub-regional spatial transformation.

Spatiality, mentioned in the preceding paragraph, is crucial to the modern concept of globalism. There are definitions that transcend the economic, financial and technological know-how variables and extend to other spheres of human activity and cover spatially extensive networks of interconnections. Being spatially extensive is a necessary condition for contemporary globalization, albeit universality is not. Interaction among the spatially connected networks can take place as usual through the flow of goods and services, finance, information, ideas and people. The networks can be environmentally linked. They can also be extended to include national, regional and international security issues. Distance, a continuous variable, matters most in the spatial context. In addition, in order to spatially qualify as global, the network of relationships should be multi-country and multi-continental. Mere national and regional linkages and interdependencies cannot be considered a part of the globalization process.

3.2 Imprecision in the Definition of Globalization

Some economists and serious analysts spurn the use of the term globalization and regard it as vague and imprecise. After innovation, globality, globalism and globalization are arguably the most ambiguous expressions. Helleiner (2000, p. 1) regarded it as "slippery", "ambiguous", "subject to misunderstanding" and recommended "that it should be banned from further use". In its vague form, the concept of economic globalization refers to the growing dimension of economic interdependence among neighboring countries, which in turn has been brought about by the increasing volume and variety of cross-border transactions in goods and services as well as cross-border factor flows. Those who lament the vagueness of the term globalization prefer global integration on the ground of it being more precise.[14] This process implies the connectivity and interdependence of the world's markets and businesses. As alluded to above (Section 2.1), global economic and financial integration occurs when countries lower barriers to trade and financial flows and open their economies up to trade and investment with the rest of the world.

Supra-territorial links between countries and people was another common implication of globalism. During the 1970s and 1980s, the phenomenon of growing inter-economy interdependence was referred to as "economic and financial interdependence", "global interdependence" or simply "interdependence" by academic researchers.[15] A closely related concept and term during this period was "internationalization", which can not be equated with globalization because it merely implies growth in interaction and interdependence between populations in different countries. This is an ancient process and has been going on since time immemorial. In comparison to globalism or globalization, "interdependence" and "internationalization" were partial and limited concepts. Interdependence stands for single linkage between two economies or countries. The postwar Japan–US economic and strategic bond was interdependence, not globalism. The Closer Economic Relationship (CER) Agreement between Australia and New Zealand is another example of economic and trade cooperation and, therefore, interdependence, not globalism. It does not imply a solitary linkage or a one-point bond like the CER. To be sure, such interdependencies are a part of, and contribute to, contemporary globalism.

3.3 Economic Globalism

Economic globalism is a constructive and creative dimension of globalism and visualizes global economy as an integrated marketplace. In its most fundamental form, it implies that cross-border flows of goods and services, factors of production, in particular financial assets, as well as diffusion of technology take place in a frictionless manner. Making political boundaries less significant, this process creates a single market in inputs and outputs and unifies global commodity and factor markets. It crafts complex economic relations of mutual support and interdependence between global economies. A network of micro- and macroeconomic linkages evolves and enlarges, and in the process national economies integrate into a global economy. This is how economists perceive and comprehend globalism. From this perspective, globalization is a process of increasing division of labor on the one hand and progressive integration of national economies on the other. It critically affects the evolution of national economies and offers opportunities for growth and development. Some use globalization to refer to the endeavors of the supranational institutions to create global markets in goods and services and global economic governance; the principal institutions of the global economic governance are the two Bretton Woods twins and the WTO.

Ann Krueger (2000) defined economic globalization in the simplest possible manner as "a phenomenon by which economic agents in any given part of the world are much more affected by events elsewhere in the world than before". Another down-to-earth definition of economic globalism or globalization can be integration and harmonization of economies and countries. This imagery of global markets developing and integrating into a seamless web was conceived by two well-known globalization authorities, namely, Greider (1997) and Friedman (1999), whose views on globalization are absolutely divergent. No doubt, this vision of global economic integration is far from the present reality. While it has made a good deal of headway over the preceding three decades and economic life in many countries is linked to the global economy in numerous ways, integration of the global economy is still partial and limited. This is the conclusion of a wide range of empirical studies, too numerous to be cited here.[16] Even without tariffs and non-tariff barriers, there are numerous barriers that create obstacles to achieving the objectives of frictionless cross-border flows of goods and services. For instance, markets for financial assets famously suffer from "home bias" and diffusion of technology has many intellectual property rights-related (IPR) bottlenecks. This vision of a globalized economy is expected to materialize only in a perfectly globalized world.

The phenomenon of economic globalism has arguably developed into one of the most important economic policy challenges of the 21st century. It has attracted the attention of academic researchers, business leaders and public policy makers, who assume that globalization will continue to shape the global economy in the short and even the medium term. It has become a ubiquitous force that is affecting, if not shaping, the contours of major global economic and financial trends. Important economic and political events of the past three decades, like China's economic liberalization and ascent to the status of an imminent economic superpower, the collapse of the former Soviet Union and the advances in technology, are some of the important events that have helped advance globalization. The onward march of the ICT revolution made an enormous impact and catalyzed the contemporary globalization process. ICT, like electricity and steam, is a general purpose technology (GPT) with huge potential to underpin total factor productivity (TFP) growth. TFP is the measure of improvement in technology used as well as improvements in quantity of labor and technology. The GPT intensified both the penetration and reach of globalization as well as quickening its pace. It was also instrumental in accelerating productivity growth in those economies that integrated globally. ICT is widely regarded as one of the focal components of what became known as the so-called "new economy", which in turn helped advance globalization. Advances in ICT also gave rise to a new generation of information products and technologies and are responsible for the birth of the "information economy". This is a knowledge-based economy where innovative ideas and technology constantly improve and change manufactured products and services.

That said, the contemporary phase of globalization is still in its initial phase, if not its infancy. What future forms globalization will adopt and how it will shape the global economy is open to speculation. A lesson of history, which can not be overlooked, is that globalization tends to be fragile. It can slow down, come to a standstill or even go into reverse. Its advance was stopped in the recent past by two catastrophic world wars and a deep and crippling economic recession. The 1913–45 period witnessed its reversal or de-globalization. However, barring a similar inopportune turn of events, globalization is likely to progress in the foreseeable future. However, whether this progress will be smooth and unabated or tentative and halting is a moot point. Notwithstanding impressive and unprecedented progress over the past three decades, policy ambiance surrounding globalization at the end of the first decade of the 21st century was not without negative strands, antipathy and antagonism.

Economic globalism has synergized economic forces, provided them with a new territorial dimension and accelerated the expansion of market capitalism. In the 19th century, following the Industrial Revolution, the same economic synergy was experienced by the global economy, albeit on a smaller scale compared with the contemporary period. Aided by modern technology, particularly ICT, today it is enabling individuals and business corporations to influence actions and events around the world faster and deeper than ever before. Contemporary globalism is restructuring global capitalism and making concepts like North-South, core-periphery or the First and Third Worlds irrelevant, if not outdated.

In this book, we shall be dealing essentially with economic and financial globalism. Intra-industry trade and accelerating exports of manufactures and services from the mature industrial economies and a set of high-performing developing economies have helped the progress of economic globalization during its contemporary phase. The transfer of information and technology is also a subset of this category of globalism. Furthermore, creating global production networks by slicing the value chain, or vertical specialization, is the latest development and an idiosyncratic feature of this category of globalism (Section 5). Additionally, TNCs and large financial institutions in the mature industrial economies have played a proactive role in devising and creating global networks in economic and financial areas. These economic agents and activities have promoted and appreciably advanced contemporary globalism.

3.4 Primacy of Laissez-faire Concept and Neoliberalism

The meaning of the term neoliberal has been under dispute. It is more often used by the opponents of neoliberalism than by its supporters. I use it to imply that globalization necessitates the adoption of free-market policies. A common theme that runs through the contemporary phase of economic globalism is that of the integration of markets and economies in keeping with the *laissez-faire* theoretical concept in which the state leaves economic activity to private sector business enterprises and individual households alone and limits its role to supervising the fulfillment of contractual obligations and building the required economic infrastructure.

According to neoliberal theory, the state's role is to underpin globalism by dismantling the protective barriers to trade and financial flows which it created in the past. Neoliberal theory requires the shrinking of government bureaucracy, the maintenance of a balanced budget, lowering or eliminating trade barriers, facilitation of exports, privatization, deregulation of capital markets and the domestic economy, and opening banking and telecommunication sectors to private ownership and competition. The next logical step for the state is to create a policy environment that stimulates global integration, as policy neutrality cannot possibly promote global integration. Technological innovation, declining transport costs and ICT advances, while necessary, are not enough for successful integration into a globalizing world economy. An economic policy paradigm that emphasizes the positive features of a liberal policy regime is the *sine qua non* of successful integration into a globalizing world economy. Economic liberalization of both trade and financial sectors is the basic premise of the modern precept of globalization.

In accordance with neoclassical economic principles, globalism calls for the creation of free and open markets, where "production, exchange and consumption of resources should unfold through forces of demand and supply, as they emerge from the uninhibited interactions of the multitude of firms and households in the private sector" (Scholte, 2005). From the *laissez-faire* viewpoint, a broad definition of politico-economic globalization can be a cluster of economic, technological and political innovations that drastically reduce the barriers to economic, financial, political and technological exchanges between economies, in the process creating liberal economic regimes and internationalizing the domestic policy network. However, it was observed during the current phase of globalization that such peeling away of traditional barriers to exchange created policy challenges at the national level. It was not easy to resolve them and they frequently led to social friction.

Supranational institutions and multilateral financial institutions narrowly emphasize, as they should, economic integration brought about by trade and factor mobility. Global economic governance is a public good. The Bretton Woods twins, the WTO and the Organization for Economic Cooperation and Development (OECD) secretariat provide, as well as dominate, global economic governance. They are the promoters of neoliberalism and contemporary globalization. Other supranational institutions like the International Labor Organization (ILO) and the various United Nations bodies[17] are eclipsed by them. The regional bodies that came into being during the postwar period as well as in the recent past have a predominantly economic focus. The only exception in this regard is the Council of Europe, which has a social and cultural focus. Accordingly, the definitions put forth by these supranational institutions have a strong economic and financial flavor. The official World Bank definition of globalization limited itself to "freedom and ability of individuals and firms to initiate voluntary economic transactions with residents of other countries".[18] For the World Bank, this growth in cross-border economic activities is limited to international trade, foreign direct investment and capital market flows.[19] Empirically, this would translate into integration of world economies with greater mobility of factors of production and enhanced trade in goods and services. The former variable includes both direct and portfolio investment. The definition adopted by the International Monetary Fund (IMF) is not much different. It stated, "Economic 'globalization' is a historical process, the result of human innovation and technological progress. It refers to the increasing integration of economies around the world, particularly through trade and financial flows" (IMF, 2001). The OECD defined economic globalization as "a process in which the structures of economic markets, technologies, and communication patterns become progressively more international over time".[20]

4. MULTIDIMENSIONALITY OF GLOBALISM

The distinction between the economic and non-economic dimensions of globalism or globalization has attracted a great deal of popular and scholarly attention. While they are equally significant, the non-economic forms of globalization are older than the economic dimensions. Before delving into the different dimensions of globalism, it must be stated that their demarcation often tends to be somewhat arbitrary. Also, different dimensions of globalism do not co-vary, ascend or descend in unison and are in general independent of each other. They neither have temporal links nor commence during the same period.

Environmental globalization is widely considered the oldest facet of globalization. For thousands, if not millions, of years environmental and climatic changes were the decisive determinants of the ebb and flow of human populations. There were some favorable consequences of environmental globalism. The New World[21] crops enriched cuisine and nutritional standards in the Old World. Principal among them were maize, potato and tomato. Biological globalization turned out to be equally significant in the remote past and has had a considerable impact on various facets of global life. History records the spread of fatal and non-fatal epidemics from country to country and continent to continent. One of the earliest records is that of the spread of smallpox from Egypt to China, Europe, and the Americas and eventually to Australia between 1350 BC and 1789 AD (Barquet and Domingo, 1997). The spread of plague from Asia to Europe in the 14th century and of pathogens from Europe to the New World in the 15th and 16th centuries are all well documented in the medical annals. Several of these diseases and epidemics had lethal consequences in the recipient parts of the globe.

The conquering armies of Alexander the Great, three centuries before Christ, were a prominent example of military or strategic globalism. His empire stretched across three continents, from Macedonia to Egypt and up to the Indus River basin in modern India, where he won a Pyrrhic victory over the local King Porus and was forced to abandon his expedition and retreat. This was probably the first, but by no means the last, example of military or strategic globalism. It continued during the following two millennia, until Pax Britannica in the 19th century and Pax Americana in the mid-20th century. Alexander's victories were not limited to military supremacy. He was responsible for introducing cultural and informational globalism. He was instrumental in spreading Western thought, philosophy and scientific knowledge to the East. His victories resulted in the spread of Hellenism to the parts of the globe he had conquered. Thus, he became one of the first global purveyors of ideas and information. The ebb and flow of ideas and information is the most pervasive, if not the most meaningful, form of globalism. Over the past two millennia, four great religions of the world, namely, Buddhism, Judaism, Christianity and Islam, have managed to diffuse well over several countries and continents. Hinduism, an older religion, was geographically restricted to India and parts of Southeast Asia[22] in the past but its adherents can be found in Europe and North America in the present era.

The concept of national and international security underwent a radical change during the post-World War II era. The potential scale and speed of new military conflicts grew rapidly and assumed enormous proportions. Long-distance networks of interdependence in the areas of national and international security led to the development of another dimension of globalization, namely, strategic globalization. Treaties or promises regarding the use of military force between alliances and threat between adversaries created global strategic networks. The Cold War era spawned globe-straddling military and strategic alliances of power as well as parallel alliances among neutrals and non-aligned countries. Few countries were able to eschew being a part of one kind of strategic alliance or another.

Environmental globalism entails long-distance movements of materials, biological substances and other generic materials that threaten human health through the environment or oceans. Two of the most problematic examples of environmental globalism are ozone layer depletion and rising levels of carbon dioxide and carbon monoxide in the earth's atmosphere causing global warming, which adversely and directly affects the entire global population, flora and fauna. During 2005, the level of carbon dioxide in the earth's atmosphere was measured at its highest ever level. Besides, the spread of the HIV virus from central Africa to the entire globe in a short span of three decades also falls under environmental globalism. By 2000, China and India were suffering a high incidence of HIV and a potentially high mortality rate. Many of these adverse environmental changes were caused by reckless human activity. This is not to deny that some also occur naturally, without any human intervention.

Mobility of knowledge, scientific know-how and economic and financial concepts and techniques comprise socio-economic globalism, as does the spread of other branches of knowledge. The spread of scientific ideas and technology transfer are also an important part of economic globalism. Long-distance movement of ideas, images, and information comprises socio-cultural globalism. Diffusion of religion also falls under this category of globalism. Since the era of Pax Britannica, one socio-culture came to lead the others. The socio-cultures that follow the leader try to replicate its institutions and social practices and mores. This phenomenon is described by the sociological expression "isomorphism". Socio-cultural globalism reacts with other kinds of globalism. Generally, there is a relationship between socio-cultural globalism on the one hand and economic and military globalism on the other. A rule of thumb in this regard is that the former follows the latter two.

Although ideas are a veritable force in themselves, in the past they followed economic and military force. Together they transformed societies. In addition, socio-cultural globalism also affected, and continues to affect, individuals, their personal identities, their attitude towards culture, politics, work and leisure. It determined, and continues to determine, their definition of individual and social achievements. With the advancement of ICT and the advent of the Internet, the cost of the global flow of communications has plummeted precipitously. ICT has compressed space and time and helped to create a global civil society. The flow of ideas and cultural globalism and globalization has become increasingly independent of other forms of globalism and globalization. There are other types of globalism, some of which would necessarily be subsets of the principal types of globalism mentioned above. For instance, political globalism is a subset of socio-cultural globalism.

Educational globalism represents the global spread of modern knowledge. It is aptly represented by the popularity of the MBA degree, which originated in the United States (US) over half a century ago. The near global spread of business schools epitomizes the globalization of educational trends. The most important dimension of educational globalism is the diffusion of technology, which, as stated above, also has enormous economic ramifications and, therefore, is also a part of economic globalism. Legal globalism is represented by a similar spread of legal practices and institutions. Other relatively more visible dimensions of globalism are those in the areas of entertainment, fashion and language. The last-named are comparatively overt in terms of their influence over individuals and societies.

Being multifaceted, globalization has resulted in a myriad non-economic benefits. For instance, the development of the Internet and the World Wide Web has revolutionized the flow of economic, financial, political, educational and cultural information. Global awareness of serious long-standing environmental issues has led to enlightened public policies; two of the recent dramatic policies are the timely reaction of policy makers to ozone layer depletion and the destruction of national forests. The world of academics and researchers has been transformed for ever. As in the previous era of globalization, rapid and easy communication and transportation around the world has further underpinned globalization. In addition, the development and wide use of life-extending medical technologies and drugs have contributed to health and physical welfare in many parts of the globe.

5. ESSENCE OF ECONOMIC GLOBALIZATION?

Like economic growth, economic globalization is a complex meta-process. As regards what is economic and financial globalization, what precisely

it does and how it functions, history testifies to the fact that during
various periods human ingenuity, innovation, endeavors and technological progress have coalesced to form the phenomenon of economic globalization (Section 3.3). It has caused the progressive integration of national
economies, which in earlier periods was regional, while in the contemporary period is wider and global. Even in earlier periods, cross-border
trade in goods and services and financial flows were the principal drivers
of economic and financial globalization (Section 2). In the contemporary
period, cross-border foreign direct investment (FDI) flows, including
corporate investment and capital flows from TNCs, as well as bank and
stock-market investments are also a part of the same process that but-
tresses globalization. Private capital flows from the advanced industrial
economies to the developing economies surged to an all-time high of $1
trillion in 2007 (World Bank, 2008b). This was the fifth consecutive year
of strong global financial flows. It should be noted that the bulk of these
flows conventionally went to the high performers in the developing world,
the EMEs. Financial globalization affects the evolution of national and
regional economies and affords them opportunities to accelerate economic
growth, which is not to say that it does not entail challenges.

Like the latter half of the 19th century, the contemporary period of globalization has also been technology driven. The ICT revolution has favorably affected productivity and improved cost structures in every aspect of
economic life in firms, households and governments. Even in the unlikely
situation of no technological innovations taking place in other scientific
areas, the accumulation of ICT technology would be enough to keep productivity rising for several years to come. Recent advances in ICT have
made an enormous contribution to globalism in general. A particular contribution of ICT to contemporary globalism is the integration of the global
labor force. Technological innovations are creating a single global market
for labor in jobs that can be undertaken remotely. Any product or service
that can be digitized can now be globally shipped at almost zero cost. The
labor force in some countries, which were inward-oriented or near-autar-
kic economies in the past, has now become part of a globally active labor
force. In the process, the effective global labor force has increased fourfold
over the past two decades (IMF, 2007c). As set out in Chapter 1 (Section
5), the collapse of the Soviet bloc brought some 760 million workers to
the global labor market, while the opening of the Chinese and Indian
economies added a further 760 million and 440 million, respectively, to
the global labor pool (Venables, 2006). Some suspect that all service sector
jobs will eventually move from industrial economies to low-wage EMEs
where labor forces are globally active. Therefore, this kind of globalization
of the labor force has generated tension in the labor markets in mature

industrial economies (Section 5.3). However, they ignore the rising salaries in Bangalore and Prague. Supplies of low-wage offshore talent in many EMEs were running low in 2007 (MGI, 2007).

Transfer of knowledge, particularly technological and managerial know-how, across international borders is a vital part of the economics of globalization. Shared production networks, or networked production (Section 2.2), both of manufacturers and services providers, first developed regionally and then became global. Heightened trans-border FDI flows facilitated the creation of these networks. They are another distinctive feature of the contemporary phase of globalization. Production networks were made possible by slicing up the value chain, which made it feasible to exploit the comparative advantage of different economies at lower levels of production by locating different parts of the production process in different countries. Production networks manage and distribute their products globally. They can work as a unit in real time on a global scale. A manufacturer can now have sub-assemblies and components of her product manufactured in different economies, while producing the final product in yet another cost-effective locale. Many parts of the production process, which required face-to-face interaction in the past, and were essentially local activities, have been de-localized and are now conducted across great distances. The geographical dispersion of production processes, with assembly operations migrating to lower-wage economies, has resulted in an increase in vertical intra-industry trade in many EMEs, particularly those in East Asia. The creation of geographically diversified and sophisticated production networks was fostered by FDI. This strategy led to a steady increase in the share of EMEs' trade in multilateral trade. The importance of exports in their economies and exports-to-GDP ratio in these EMEs has risen to unprecedented levels. During the contemporary phase of globalization, millions of factories spread over different EMEs have joined the global supply chains. Dramatic improvements in supply chain management have taken place, transforming manufacturing processes out of recognition. This enumeration of the driving forces of globalization is far from exhaustive because international trade in goods and services relative to world output could not have expanded so rapidly without the adoption of liberalizing domestic macroeconomic policies and the growth of an enabling network at the supranational, or the WTO, level (Section 5.2).

5.1 How the Globalization Process Operates

In essence, there is little arcane about how the economic globalization process works. It implies progressively quicker international transactions among an increasing number of economies, aided by technological advances. Quintessentially, what globalization does is that it extends the operation of free market forces beyond national borders. In the remote past, these forces operated within a village market, then within an urban industrial sector or individual financial center. By promoting the division of labor, specialization and competition over a wider area, free markets allow scale economies to work in a much larger area and raise productive efficiency. As the forces of the free market encourage specialization, the process of globalization allows individuals, firms and economies to concentrate their endeavors in their areas of comparative advantage, on what they do best, that is, to produce at lowest opportunity cost. The final result is enhanced economic productivity, increased productive efficiency and superior utilization of scarce resources.

Successful outcomes of globalism strengthen our belief in the market as an economic institution. Globalization proves that the market economy and the operation of market forces are superior to any available alternatives. Therefore, globalism entails the adoption of market-oriented policies in both the domestic and international spheres. Liberalization of the policy framework is one of the preconditions of globalization. That said, there is no gainsaying the fact that in most cases globalization can and does involve short-run economic and social costs, which for some firms or economies can be high. Individual firms or economies need to seek problem-specific solutions to these problematic issues.

Thus viewed, globalization offers an opportunity for firms to exploit larger markets spread all over the globe. It strengthens the process of international division of labor. National economies grow and integrate with the global economy. Integrated markets expand economic freedom and spur competition among firms, leading first to higher microeconomic productivity and second to macroeconomic productivity. Another consequence of market expansion is that it provides firms with greater access to capital, technology and cheaper imported resources, which in turn has a favorable impact on productivity. The final outcome is that economies that liberalize domestically and establish links with the global marketplace discernibly benefit by improving their TFP and enhancing economic welfare domestically. The EMEs of East and Southeast Asia, as well as China, exemplify such welfare gains – including TFP improvements – which have resulted from domestic liberalization and globalization. Outward orientation and global integration has rendered dynamic the East Asian economies and China. As a result, this region has been economically transformed in a short span of two generations.

Contrary to the popular views, there is copious evidence that demonstrates the welfare-enhancing impact of globalization. However, negative opinions are prevalent in some quarters. They largely emanate from the fact that rapid cross-border flows of goods, services and factors of production can result in adverse economic effects on the domestic economy when domestic market failures and regulatory weaknesses exist. Both of these need to be dealt with directly by public policy makers, with the help of appropriate domestic policy measures. Managed appropriately, they will indeed reduce the costs of globalization. If the appropriate domestic policy measures are not adopted and implemented without vacillation, the danger of a globalization backlash looms, which could stall, defer or reverse some forms of global economic integration. The ultimate effect would be the undermining or loss of economic progress that has so far been achieved with the help of ongoing global integration.

The process of globalization needs to be guided and requires the helping hand of domestic policy. Judicious and well-targeted domestic policy measures can successfully moderate the negative consequences of global economic integration. Policy makers should consciously try to strike a balance between the risks and benefits of globalization. Additionally, the guidance of the globalization process should be such that benefits are maximized and costs remain controlled. For one thing, economic globalization should be guided to ensure that it is more inclusive than it has so far been. For global economic integration to perform at its best, appropriate national and regional institutions are needed as much as efficacious supranational institutions ensuring global cooperation.

Incontestably, globalization can be a pro-developmental force, but for globalization to achieve domestic policy objectives, like poverty alleviation, domestic political decisions, policy support and action are essential. Without them, the pro-development impact of globalization process cannot be taken as a given. The productive and innovative forces of ongoing globalization need to be harnessed. The method of doing so is to adopt development policies and strategies that aim at addressing both the challenges and opportunities offered by ongoing globalization. These strategies are *sui generis* and need to be tailored to the specific needs of each country. There can be few generalizations in this regard. However, some generalizations can be made regarding the creation of a conducive development environment in an economy that is seeking to benefit from ongoing global integration. Having good governance at all levels, transparency and rule of law, a sound economic strategy, and most of all the adoption of market-oriented economic policies would indeed go a long way to achieving this objective. These should be supported by an adequate domestic institutional infrastructure. Thus, for globalization to yield the desired propitious economic results, both the role of the government and the role of the market need to collaboratively intertwine. Briefly put, this is how globalization can work towards providing welfare-enhancing results.

5.2   Neoliberal Policies Promoting Contemporary Globalism

Over the last three decades, free market and neoliberal economic philosophy has taken hold in economic policy and governing circles in a large number of countries. It has supplanted interventionism. This is a major shift in the conventional wisdom and a return to the 19th-century thinking of liberalism and deregulation, along the lines of what Adam Smith had advocated in terms of the elimination of government intervention in economic life, encouragement to free up private enterprise, no barriers to commerce and promoting competition. In its essential form, this economic philosophy promotes the uninterrupted operation of market forces and the laws of demand and supply governing producers and consumers. Institutions that interrupt market forces tend to create systemic and market inefficiencies; therefore, they should keep a low profile in the markets. Privatization, liberalization and deregulation were the principal pillars of the current neoliberal economic strategy that has supported the current wave of globalization. The popularity of maxims like the so-called Washington Consensus,[23] which since 1990 became something of an economic ideology, have had a significant impact on national economic strategies. It held that good economic performance required liberalized trade, macroeconomic stability and getting prices right. The supranational institutions considered it a nirvana for developing economies and that it accelerated globalization, albeit not at a uniform pace. This strategy was posited by John Williamson and named after the Washington-based supranational financial institutions. While the Washington Consensus has had its halcyon period and was regarded as an indispensable element in the repertoire of policy mandarins, it has presently lost its sheen and has been criticized by some noted economists (Serra and Stiglitz, 2008). In accordance with this strategy, many policy mandarins set out to adopt a neoliberal economic strategy to create and underpin world-scale liberal markets, resulting in the onward march of globalization.

With the adoption of neoliberalism, the contemporary phase of globalization promoted government bureaucracies, increasingly staffed by apolitical technocracies. In particular, the running of central banks and formulation of monetary policies became distanced from elected public officials. Independent subject-matter experts or technically trained professionals began to have a greater role in running economic, financial, monetary and commercial affairs in national government systems. However, elected public officials kept the reins of fiscal policy. In many a macro-economy, a consciousness of designing national economic policy in such a manner that the economy is able to improve its TFP as well as its competitiveness in the global marketplace dawned for the first time. The role of technology in underpinning contemporary globalization has been alluded to above.

5.3 Unforeseen Side Effects

Much to the chagrin of these policy makers, they discovered that globalization did not benefit everybody. While it benefited some, it passed others by. The neoliberal policies adopted during the process of globalization had serious downsides: economically and socially injurious effects that were not anticipated. Globalization has impinged on global prices of goods, services and those of factors of production. Several large industrial sectors in the mature industrial economies, particularly at the lower-technology end, began to suffer from serious unemployment. In many cases, these job losses were permanent, which in turn caused social disruption. Globalization was squarely and entirely blamed for these job losses.

Cross-border movement of trade in goods and services was much swifter in the contemporary phase of globalization than in the earlier phases. However, what the operation of free market forces and opening up to the global marketplace do not and cannot ensure is that the benefits of the division of labor, specialization, efficient operations and higher TFP are uniformly shared by the population. Consequently, increasing economic inequality and a worsening Gini coefficient in many EMEs became strong denigrating points against the contemporary globalization.[24] One of the causes of this is that in some economies global integration has caused job losses. The globalizing economies must devise and provide domestic policy support to achieve income equality and address unemployment.

The growing income inequality argument has also been made at the economy level, that is, globalization is said to have spurred income inequality among countries. Many of the poorest economies, like the countries falling under the rubric of the least developed countries (LDCs),[25] were adversely affected by the onward march of globalization. From time to time, the international community has extended a helping hand to them. Further help can be extended in the form of policy advice as well as transfer of tangible resources.

While growing integration of financial markets has progressed at a brisk pace and resulted in several welfare-enhancing effects, there was an unforeseen downside.[26] Financial globalization is seen as a disturbing source of financial market volatility by some, who regard it as a serious byproduct of globalization. Since the "tequila" crisis in Mexico in 1994, several EMEs have suffered a financial crisis. The Asian financial crisis of 1997–8 savaged not only several dynamic Asian economies but also the regional economy. The spread of the US sub-prime mortgage crisis globally in early 2008 was the latest example. Growing financial globalization does predispose the global economy to crises. The reason is that it makes regulatory authorities relax or repeal financial restrictions and regulations that had made this kind of crisis impossible three decades ago. The accumulation of significant short-term external debt during that period was difficult, if not impossible.

A characteristic of the contemporary phase of globalization is that the cross-border movement of the labor force has been far from swift.[27] This is a weak link in contemporary globalization. Large-scale movements of labor were instrumental in the integration of the global economy during the first modern period of globalization during the 19th and early 20th centuries, but not in the contemporary phase.

These downbeat developments gave rise to skepticism and disaffection regarding neoliberal economic strategy and spread of globalization. Apart from the media and political leaders, some noted economists drew attention to both the conceptual and implementation-related flaws that contemporary globalization suffers from (Stiglitz, 2003a).[28] Individual economies need to devise tailor-made solutions to their specific globalization-driven predicaments. Strident calls for de-globalization have become frequent. Reforms and re-globalization in a Keynesian direction have also been proposed.

6. HOW THE CONTEMPORARY PHASE OF GLOBALIZATION DIFFERS

In the contemporary period of globalization, the EMEs have become active economic players, unlike the previous era of globalization which was overwhelmingly dominated by the older industrial economies. Several of the EMEs have grown into not only sizeable producers of goods and services but also leading markets. Going by sales statistics for the first half of 2008, Russia became the largest car market in Europe, outstripping Germany (O'Neill, 2008). US exports in mid-2008 were growing at a rate close to 20 percent. The same phenomenon was discernible in Japan, Germany and the United Kingdom. Rapid market expansion in the EMEs was one of the principal factors responsible for the acceleration in export expansion in the advanced industrial economies.

Since the early 2000s, a sharp increase has been noted in firms from the large EMEs acquiring prestigious established corporations in the mature industrial economies. Acquisition of the renowned US beer manufacturer, Budweiser, by a Belgian-Brazilian conglomerate, of GE Plastics of the US by a Saudi Arabian firm, of Corus Group of Britain by the Tata Group of India and Aluminum Corporation of China taking a large stake in Rio Tinto, are some of the prominent examples of acquisitions in the last two years (2006–8). During the post-August 2007 credit crunch period in the US, sovereign-wealth funds (SWFs), cash-rich state-owned investment funds from the EMEs and Gulf Cooperation Council (GCC)[29] countries, invested massive financial resources in several prominent US financial institutions, like Citigroup. Many of these financial institutions were in dire straits during the sub-prime financial crisis and sorely needed a capital infusion to strengthen their capital bases. The role of the SWFs in global finance increased significantly (Chapter 5, Section 5).

Rapid growth in the EMEs has worked to the benefits of the large and established firms in the advanced industrial countries. During the current phase of globalization, as the EMEs grew in economic importance, some of the large established TNCs from the advanced industrial countries increased their stake in them. For instance, IBM employed 2000 information technology (IT) engineers and technicians in India in 2000, this number shot up to 73 000 in 2008. Between 2008 and 2013, IBM expected to increase its revenues from these economies from 18 percent to 30 percent (*The Economist,* 2008a).

The conventional meaning of economic globalization thus far has been the flow of economic ideas, capital, technology, business knowledge and acumen, and resources from the high-income industrial economies to the emerging-market and developing economies. Since the advent of the contemporary phase of globalization, the latter country groups integrated with the advanced industrial economies and in turn benefited. Meanwhile, business firms and TNCs from the advanced industrial economies expanded into the EMEs and the developing world through their subsidiaries and other means, in the process enabling EMEs to integrate with the global economy and improve their TFP, which had enormous welfare implications.

Unidirectionality has been progressively eroded. Contemporary globalization is multidirectional and polycentric. Against the contemporary shifting backdrop, economic globalization flows both ways, that is, from the EMEs to the high-income industrial economies and back again. It also flows among the various EMEs, and they influence each other's economies. For instance, a little-known Indian company overwhelmingly dominates the small-motorcycle market in several high-growth markets, like Colombia, Egypt and Mexico. A Brazilian company owns the largest Canadian nickel mining company. A Chinese baby-stroller maker not only has a strong grip on the domestic market, with 80 percent market share, but also caters for almost a third of the US market. Thus viewed, the unidirectionality of economic globalization is rapidly becoming an attribute of the past. The past imagery of economic globalization, which was conceived in terms of "coca-colaization" or "Americanization", is not applicable in the contemporary period.

Business firms from the EMEs have increasingly been adopting significant postures and making their presence felt in the world marketplace. In 2008, the so-called *Fortune*-500 list included 62 firms from the large EMEs, up from 31 in 2003 and 23 in 2000. EMEs have their own TNCs, some of which have become a force to reckon with. Embraer, Lenovo and Arcelor Mittal, owned by Brazil, China and India, respectively, are three such examples. Haier, a white-goods firm from China, Cemex, a Mexican cement producer, Infosys, an Indian software giant, have earned respect for their global operations and finely honed competitiveness. Samsung of Korea and Acer of Taiwan are well-recognized brands. Such corporations from the EMEs are changing the world of business. They followed innovative practices not only in their product designs but also in operational techniques and business models. This category of multinational has been assuming leadership positions in their respective markets, posing a serious challenge to established leaders from the advanced industrial economies.

History repeats itself. This challenge by the multinationals from the EME is reminiscent of the vigorous and fast-expanding firms from the US that challenged those from Europe in the early 20th century, and more recently, Japanese firms that challenged those from the US during the post-World War II period. The new market leaders from the EMEs are providing established players with valuable lessons in competing in an era of globality. Many of them have devised creative and ingenious approaches to cost control, local customization, building multinational executive teams, which have enabled them to acquire their global leadership positions. The reasons behind the intensified competitiveness of the EME firms include the fact that they grew up in cost-challenged and hypercompetitive markets in the period before they began to globalize, which honed their business acumen and prepared them for the challenges of contemporary global markets. Also, in a globally integrated economy, they could readily access modern technology, expertise and business practices and adapt them to their objectives. In many of the EMEs, senior executives are trained in top-flight business schools in the West. Their aspirations for success drive them hard.

In the contemporary world of business, every firm competes with every other firm for markets and resources. Sirkin et al. (2008) termed the multidirectional flows of business and financial operations the new "globality", which is fast supplanting the old globalization model. Large business corporations and TNCs have been distancing themselves from the concept of a center. In this regard, some, like Lenovo, the Chinese computer giant, went as far as working without a corporate headquarters. In this newly evolving corporate ethos, no market is regarded as too small or too remote from the perspective of cost advantage, obtaining resources and exploitation of business opportunities. The concept of foreignness has grown outmoded and irrelevant. The incumbent corporate leaders from the advanced industrial economies have been adapting to the transforming global business scenario by adapting the principles of globality, in the process decentralizing decision-making and redeploying assets to build commerce within the emerging regions. By breaking down the old silos, the established corporate leaders of the past can regain, or continue to maintain, their positions. Their new frame of thinking will need to include drawing on the uniqueness of the assets, capabilities and perspectives of the EMEs (Sirkin et al., 2008).

In the past, when the TNCs from the high-income economies expanded their operations, their objective was to cater to the local demand in the economies they were entering. No more. The long-established business model which was centralized, top-down and process-driven, with trends and influences running from West to East, is a receding breed. During the current phase of globalization, the basic intent of the TNCs is to expand and integrate their enterprises and operations globally. They now endeavor to create a single corporate entity in which work is sourced wherever it is performed most efficiently, in a cost-effective manner. Their new focus is to build a global corporation that is seamlessly integrated across time zones and cultures (*The Economist,* 2008b, p. 20).

7. SUMMARY AND CONCLUSIONS

While terms like globality, globalism and globalization came to be used in economics and other social sciences in the latter half of the 20th century, the concepts have a long pedigree. Although the contemporary era of economic globalism is barely three decades old, the essential concept of globalism is not novel nor is globalization a new phenomenon. As the three terms are embraced by different social sciences, they have been variously defined. Consequently there are myriad competing definitions. While widely used, these expressions take on imprecise meanings and are often poorly understood and conceptualized. As the concepts of globality, globalism and globalization cover a wide subject area, they are shared by several social sciences. They are deployed across disciplines and across theoretical approaches. Since the turn of the century, their academic and intellectual significance has been on the rise. Economic globalism is only one strong and constructive dimension of globalism. Much of the literature surrounding this concept is multidisciplinary.

Briefly, this chapter provides a historical perspective on two millennia of economic globalism, touching upon various salient periods and time points. Several recently revealed facets of history have been mentioned. Globalism tends to be multidimensional; therefore the distinction between economic and non-economic dimensions of globalism or globalization has attracted a great deal of popular and scholarly attention. The definition of globalism has been the focus of animated debate among scholars. Therefore, after providing and discussing a functional definition of globalism, other broad definitional concepts have been considered. The phenomenon of economic globalism has arguably developed into one of the most important economic policy challenges of the 21st century, attracting academic researchers, business leaders and public policy makers, who assume that globalization will continue to shape the global economy in the short – and even the medium – term.

NOTES

1. It was first seen in an article in the *Spectator* magazine.
2. This article appeared in the *Harvard Business Review,* in which he had boldly stated, "The world's needs and desires have been irrevocably homogenized. This makes the multinational corporation obsolete and the global corporation absolute" Levitt (1983, p. 92). Levitt argued that due to advances in communication technology, the pattern of consumer demand was progressively homogenizing all over the world. Therefore, large international companies should cease to be "multinationals", customizing their products to match local market tastes everywhere, but should become global by standardizing production, distribution and marketing of their products. This uniformity of products, according to Levitt, would be the source of production efficiency and result in higher profit than having different products in each market. Scale economies would be a rich source of competitive advantage.
3. The author is the well-known Thomas L. Friedman (1999).
4. See chapter 1 in Maddison (2007).
5. After Kublai Khan's conquest of southern China in 1279, the Mongol Empire extended from the coasts of southern Siberia, Manchuria, Korea and China down to Amman in the East, and to Hungary and Belarus in the West. It covered India, Indochina, the Persian Gulf and Turkey.
6. In 1492, Christopher Columbus sailed in three ships to discover the sea route to India. The largest ship, Santa Maria, was a 60 footer. Admiral Zheng He commanded over 300 ships on each of his voyages. His flagship was 400 feet long.
7. See Frank (1998), Bairoch (1999), Findlay and O'Rourke (2007), Das (2008d) and Hamashita et al. (2008).
8. Horst Kohler, Managing Director, International Monetary Fund, "Strengthening the Framework for the Global Economy", a speech given on the occasion of the Award Ceremony of the Konrad Adenauer Foundation, Berlin, November 15, 2002.

Available on the Internet at http://www.imf.org/external/np/speeches/2002/111502. htm.
9. See Table 8-B, Maddison (2003).
10. The term industrial country has become a misnomer, because some of the emerging-market economies, like China, have become extensively industrialized. The contribution of the industrial sector to their GDP is larger than that in the wealthy countries of the developed world, whose economies are overwhelmingly dominated by the services sector. The EMEs countries have become large exporters of manufactured products as well.
11. The Gini coefficient is a standard measure of income inequality. It ranges between 0 and 1, with 0 being perfect equality and 1 complete inequality.
12. The term emerging-market economy (EME) was coined in 1981 by Antoine W. van Agtmael of the International Finance Corporation, the private sector arm of the World Bank. The developing countries in this category vary from small to large, even very large. They are regarded as emerging because they have adopted market-friendly economic reform programs, resulting in sounder macroeconomic policy structures. China is the largest and most important EME, along with several smaller economies like Tunisia. The common strand between these economies is that they have embarked on reform programs and consequently recorded rapid GDP growth. They have liberalized their markets and are in the process of emerging onto the global economic stage. A sustained rapid rate of GDP growth is the first indispensable characteristic of an EME. Many of them are in the process of making the transition from a command economy framework to an open market economy, building accountability into their system. The Russian Federation and the East European economies that were part of the Soviet bloc in the past fall into this category. Second, other than adoption of an economic reform program, an EME builds a transparent and efficient domestic capital market. Third, it reforms its exchange rate regime because a stable currency creates confidence in the economy and investors in the global capital markets regard it as fit for investment. Fourth, a crucial feature of an EME is its ability to integrate with global capital markets and attract a significant amount of foreign investment, both portfolio and direct. Growing investment – foreign and domestic – implies a rising confidence level in the domestic economy. Global capital flows into an EME add volume to its stock market and long-term investment into its infrastructure. For the global investing community, the EMEs present an opportunity to diversify their investment portfolios. Investing in the EME has gradually become a standard practice among global investors who wish to diversify, although they have added some risk to their portfolios.
13. See for a detailed exposition on this issue Clark (2001), Das (2004a and 2004b), Norris (2001) and Keohane and Nye (2001).
14. This is not without flaw. Although the term "global" implies worldwide, in the strict sense of the term contemporary globalization is not worldwide. Many low-income countries have not been integrating with the global economy.
15. Some of the noteworthy writings are Keohane and Nye (1977) and Rosenau (1980).
16. See for instance Helliwell (1998) and Frankel (2000).
17. In particular, the Economic and Social Council of the United Nations (ECOSOC) and United Nations Educational, Scientific and Cultural Organization (UNESCO).
18. Cited by Milanovic (2002).
19. See "What is Globalization" on the World Bank website at http://www1.worldbank.org/economicpolicy/globalization/ag01.html.
20. See OECD (1997), chapter 1. A corollary of this definition is that competition becomes increasingly global market-based rather than national market-based.
21. The expression New World is an old expression. Originally, it stood for Australia, Argentina, Brazil, Canada, and the United States.
22. The renowned ancient temples of Angkor Wat in Cambodia are dedicated to the Hindu god, Lord Vishnu, the preserver of the universe.
23. John Williamson reasonably argued that the set of policy reforms that would serve

the developing economies, particularly those of Latin America, should encompass the following ten propositions: an emphasis on fiscal discipline, a redirection of public expenditure priorities toward fields offering both high economic returns and the potential to improve income distribution, such as primary health care, primary education and infrastructure, tax reform (to lower marginal rates and broaden the tax base), interest rate liberalization, a competitive exchange rate, trade liberalization, liberalization of FDI inflows, privatization, deregulation (in the sense of abolishing barriers to entry and exit) and secure property rights. Its essential emphasis was on deregulated markets.

24. See Milanovic (2006) for an explanation of how globalization affects income inequality in the developing economies.

25. In its latest triennial review of the list of Least Developed Countries (LDCs) in July 2006, the Economic and Social Council of the United Nations used the following three criteria for the identification of LDCs, as proposed by the Committee for Development Policy (CDP): (1) a low-income criterion, based on a three-year average estimate of the gross national income (GNI) per capita (under $745 for inclusion, above $900 for graduation); (2) a human resource weakness criterion, involving a composite Human Assets Index (HAI) based on indicators of: (a) nutrition; (b) health; (c) education; and (d) adult literacy; and (3) an economic vulnerability criterion, involving a composite Economic Vulnerability Index (EVI) based on indicators of: (a) the instability of agricultural production; (b) the instability of exports of goods and services; (c) the economic importance of non-traditional activities (share of manufacturing and modern services in GDP); (d) merchandise export concentration; and (e) the handicap of economic smallness (as measured through the population in logarithm); and the percentage of population displaced by natural disasters. A total of 49 countries fall under the category of LDCs.

26. One logical outcome of this kind of integration of the global economy should be convergence of interest rates, which has not come about.

27. In spite of technological advances and resulting improvements in modes of transport of labor in the contemporary period of globalization, cross-border movements of labor force are far less than those during the Pax Britannica. The world grew far less liberal in the area of labor migration than it was during the previous era of globalization. For cultural and political reasons, movements of labor have tended to become restricted. Some industrialized economies have also experienced a potent backlash against inward flows of immigrants, which has been sharply worsened by illegal immigration. An identical observation can be made regarding the advancement in financial globalization.

28. The earnest tone and thorough analysis of this scholarly book instantly made it one of the most widely read books on globalization during the recent period.

29. The Gulf Cooperation Council (GCC) was established in 1981. Its members are Bahrain, Kuwait, Oman, Qatar, Saudi Arabia and the United Arab Emirates (UAE).

2. Winners of globalization

Globalization is here to stay, one cannot back away from that fact, but today's new order can be tapped for the advancement of the entire world economy through peaceful economic efforts.

Lawrence Klein, 2005; Nobel Laureate, 1980

Globalization is neither good nor bad in itself; in the long-run it is a step towards efficiency; in the short-run, however, it involves all kinds of painful social and cultural adjustments. Every country has to meet the challenge of globalization in its own individual way.

Robert Mundell, 2000; Nobel Laureate, 1999

1. GLOBALIZATION: A WELFARE-ENHANCING MUNIFICENT FORCE?

The preceding three decades were a period of unprecedented integration of the global economy through trade and financial channels. Economic globalization is regarded as "the most powerful force to have shaped the post-war world" (Frankel, 2006). It became an indisputably vigorous driver of epoch-making structural changes in national, regional and global economies. Some consider it the most powerful transformative force in the global economy. It has been influencing the evolution of several national economies in a consequential manner. It enabled a group of developing economies to achieve what is known as 'income convergence'. China's globalization and vertiginous growth – and moving to the center of the global economic stage – is one such example (Das, 2008b). Without denying the challenges and policy constraints that it imposes, it is fair to say that economic globalization is a source of dynamic change and has myriad positive, innovative and dynamic traits. Although this is reflected in the increasing volume and value of international trade in goods and services relative to world output and expansion in short- and long-term capital flows, there is much more to it than that. A large body of literature has established that liberalizing an economy for trade raises both aggregate income and growth rates.[1] Trade and financial integration can play a catalytic role for a range of economic benefits. That said, one cannot ignore the fact that not everyone has benefited from globalization, nor have those economies that have benefited done so evenly.

A notable quantitative and qualitative transformation in global living standards has taken place over these decades. By strengthening and advancing *inter alia* specialization, the division of labor and competition as well as promoting the efficient use of factors of production, globalization has become a compelling source of welfare enhancement. Facilitating foreign direct investment and technology transfer were two of the other channels through which globalization impacted economies. Its benefits gush through both static and dynamic channels to the globally integrating economies.

As the global integration of economies progresses and grows more intense, it causes rising efficiency of resource and input utilization in the world economy as countries and regions specialize in line with their comparative advantage and produce goods and services at their lowest opportunity costs. In 2007, the volume of multilateral trade in goods and services added up to $16.9 trillion, which was 33.91 percent of global GDP. This proportion was at a historic high. Multilateral trade in merchandise pierced the threshold of 30 percent of global GDP for the first time ever in 2007 (WTO, 2008). Likewise, private capital flows from the mature industrial economies to the developing ones crossed the $1 trillion threshold for the first time in 2007 (World Bank, 2008b). This was the fifth uninterrupted year of strong global financial flows. As set out in Chapter 1 (Section 5), financial globalization affects the evolution of national and regional economies and offers them opportunities to for accelerated economic growth. This is not to refute the fact that global financial flows also entail challenges.

As in days of yore, declining transport and communication costs are among the factors advancing rapid globalization (Chapter 1, Section 2.2). Global integration unleashes pro-growth forces like liberalization-generated enhancement of the productivity of domestic firms (Arnold et al., 2007). It eliminates price distortions and promotes efficient resource allocation in the domestic economy, leading to increases in total factor productivity (TFP). TFP measures the improvement in technology quality as well as that of labor and capital.

Empirical studies associate the integration of global markets and economies with TFP increases (Winters et al., 2004). Also, empirical evidence shows that capital account liberalization leads to an increase in real wages in the domestic economy (Henry and Sasson, 2008). Casual empiricism reveals that the phenomenon of economic globalization has worked as a transformative force for several economies and groups thereof. It has produced enormous *aggregate* benefits for the global economy and a dramatic rise in the standard of living around the world. In particular, it has profited those who had products and services, skills and resources to market worldwide. A munificent and benign force that has generated so much value-added and tangible wealth must be protected from harm and nurtured, so that its positive aspects can be gainfully harnessed.

An oft-cited illustration of the economic gains and tangible benefits of globalization is the much-vaunted economic achievements of the East Asian economies (Das, 2005b). This was followed by rapid pace growth and the global integration of Southeast Asian economies and recently by China's rise as an emerging economic superpower (Das, 2007a).[2] Fischer (2006, p. 178) regards it as the "most critical" global development of recent economic history. India is the latest economy to be in the process of joining this high performing group (Das, 2006). Global economic and financial integration have on balance yielded rich dividends for this sub-group of Asian economies. Vietnam seems to be another economy that is likely to join this dynamic group in the medium term. Since it liberalized its economy to the outside world and launched market-oriented reforms in 1986, it has achieved strikingly rapid and equitable growth. Vietnam learned many strategy lessons from China's success; the official policy commitment to export-led growth and accelerated global integration is exceedingly high. Over the 1997–2007 period, its average annual growth rate was 7.5 percent in real terms. By 2007, it had emerged as the principal destination for foreign direct investment (FDI) in manufactures in Asia.[3] It has become a favorite of foreign investors and transnational corporations (TNCs), which are regarded as agents of economic globalization. Intel invested $1 billion in a microchip factory near Hanoi. Not too long ago, Vietnam was not able to feed itself; the economy slid into famine in 1980. However, soon it turned into one of world's principal providers of farm produce and a large rice exporter. It also grew into a substantial exporter of textiles, shoes, furniture and other labor-intensive products. With a trade to GDP ratio of 160 percent in 2007, it is one of the most open economies in the world.

1.1 Genesis of the Contemporary Phase of Globalization

The birth of the contemporary phase of globalization took place around 1980, when the political and policy climate changed in favor of neoliberal economic strategies. As explained in Chapter 1 (Section 3.4), the meaning of the term neoliberal has been in dispute. It is used more by the opponents of neoliberalism than by its supporters. I use it to convey the fact that globalization necessitates the adoption of free-market policies. Several important policy measures that promoted and advanced global integration were taken in important countries around this period (Rachman, 2008). These policy measures come under the rubric of neoliberalism. To name the most significant, China launched its macroeconomic reform program at the end of 1978 with the objective of turning from Maoism to markets. In 1979, Margaret Thatcher came to power in Britain and Ronald Reagan in the United States (US) in 1980. Neoliberal economic policies were implemented and deregulation and tax cuts were promoted in both economies, giving a substantial boost to pro-market ideology. In the mid-1980s, the European Union (EU) made a commitment to create a single market. With the collapse of the Berlin Wall in 1989 and disintegration of the Soviet Union, a large number of East European economies and the countries newly created after the break-up of the Soviet Union began the onerous task of turning their centrally planned economies into market economies, so that they could eventually integrate globally.

During the decade of the 1980s, protectionist strategies in the Latin American economies fell out of favor. Also, under the pressure of a major macroeconomic crisis, India decided to give up its socialist economic structure and launched a major macroeconomic restructuring. Inspired by the success of the East Asian economies with an outer-oriented development strategy during the 1970s and 1980s, a good number of developing economies began their economic turnaround during the 1980s by adopting economic liberalization. Many developing economies incessantly improved various aspects of their external policy. Most-favored-nation (MFN) tariff rates on average declined from 14.1 percent during 1995–99 to 11.7 percent during 2000–04 and further to 9.4 percent in 2007, which is a total decline of 33 percent (WTO, 2008). In addition, a significant proportion of world trade began to be conducted at zero MFN tariffs, or under various preferential tariff arrangements. Consequently, several industrial, developing and especially emerging-market economies (EMEs),[4] began the steady process of integration into the global economy. This mindset among policy makers influenced the other channels of global economic integration.

Over the preceding three decades, multilateral trade flows expanded dramatically, usually faster than the global output growth. This rate of growth has accelerated since the mid-1990s. Between 1995 and 2006, global merchandise trade more than doubled, increasing from $5.17 trillion to $11.98 trillion. Merchandise trade increased further to $13.57 trillion in 2007 (WTO, 2008). During this period, not only did international trade in manufactures and commodities grow as a proportion of GDP in various sub-groups of economies, but such economies also became increasingly open to capital inflows, particularly FDI (IMF, 2008a).[5] Membership of the GATT/WTO system steadily increased and reached 153 in July 2008, when Cape Verde, an archipelago located in the Atlantic Ocean, acceded to the WTO. This rush for membership began in the mid-1980s, before the Uruguay Round of multilateral trade negations was launched in September 1986, and continued thereafter. Membership of the GATT/WTO system makes a significant contribution to an economy of a member country *inter alia* through the twin fundamental GATT/WTO principles, namely, the MFN and the national treatment. The first requires a country not to discriminate among its trading partners, and in return it cannot be discriminated against by its trading partners. The second principle requires that a country must treat imported and domestic goods and services the same, once tariffs have been paid. While empirical evidence exists that demonstrates that the GATT/WTO system's endeavors to reduce trade barriers have expanded trade among member countries, a consensus on this issue is elusive. Subramanian and Wei (2007) concluded that a positive effect of GATT/WTO membership did exist but only for some member countries and in selected sectors. They found that a positive impact of membership resulted in 120 percent of additional multilateral trade. Likewise, Tomz et al. (2007) found a positive overall impact on trade of members if the definition of "participation" is broadened. An empirical study by Martin, Anderson and Pham (2007) came up with the most positive impact. It was focused on Asian economies that were GATT/WTO members. During the 1950–2000 period, these economies traded 380 percent more than they would have done without membership of the GATT/WTO system. *Ceteris paribus*, pairs of GATT/WTO members with one in the Asia Pacific and one outside were found to be likely to trade 30 percent more with each other than if both were non-members. In contrast to these empirical studies, Rose (2004) found no significant positive impact of the GATT/WTO membership on trade.

This rapid multilateral trade expansion has advanced trade-driven globalization. It has provided an impetus not only by lowering tariff and non-tariff barriers but also by increasing FDI through trade and investment negotiations. Many EMEs and developing economies undertook macroeconomic policy measures, such as autonomous unilateral trade reforms, which promoted trade-driven globalization. Declining costs of transport and information communication had the same effect. Trade-driven globalization has changed the economic geography of the world. In addition to the advanced industrial economies, a dynamic group of developing and emerging-market economies has emerged, which has become an increasingly more significant engine of world trade and investment. In addition, intra-developing country trade, also known as South–South trade, in goods, services and commodities, is on the rise. The pace and scope of trade-driven globalization has reached an unparalleled level (UNCTAD, 2008c).

As set out in Chapter 1 (Section 2.2), information and communication technology (ICT) is a meta-technology or a general-purpose technology. It is skill-enhancing and characterized by pervasive effects on the economy as a whole. It affects scientific and technological advancements well beyond the ICT sector per se. It has had a pervasive impact on the global economy during the contemporary phase of globalization. It owes a great deal to the post-1980 advances in ICT, which introduced a new paradigm for the configuration of global economic activities. The externalities generated by the ICT sector went a long way in influencing the global production pattern and economic development. They created new modes of organization of production of goods and services as well as altered manufacturing patterns in industries and consumption patterns in households. The final result was wide-ranging cost reduction and faster and better communication between economic agents, which in turn had an enormous global impact. The most notable was the opportunity for a group of developing economies to diversity production activity and become a part of global value chains. The conceptualization and creation of production networks was not feasible without ICT innovations. In addition, it was because of advances in ICT that a lot of commercial services that were regarded as non-tradable, such as accounting, can now be provided from afar. Countries like India have had remarkably success in developing their ICT sector and providing commercial services. India has emerged as the world's largest exporter of ICT services. In 2006, the Indian ICT industry accounted for 5.4 percent of GDP and 37 percent of total exports (UNCTAD, 2008c). Economies that succeeded in rapidly and steadily diffusing ICT, like Hong Kong SAR, the Republic of Korea (hereinafter Korea), Singapore and Taiwan, now straddle the line between developing and high-income industrial countries. ICT is a dynamic and rapidly growing industrial sector, having enormous growth potential. The positive macroeconomic impact of ICT on GDP growth has been well demonstrated and widely acknowledged. It leads to both capital-deepening and technological progress. As an important productive sector, ICT contributes to both TFP and GDP growth (UNCTAD, 2007b).

Several sub-groups of economies that integrated globally during the contemporary phase of globalization benefited markedly from it. Indubitably, the extent and pace of trade and financial integration differed for different sub-groups of economies and regions, but the common factor was that trade in goods and services and financial flows continued to progressively integrate national economies with the global economy. Since 1990, volume of cross-border financial flows soared nine times (Kose et al., 2008b). In addition, other forms of financial integration also rose. Some of the important channels included cross-listing of stocks, cross-border ownership and control of exchanges as well as banks and securities settlement systems. Stock ownership grew increasingly global. According to the statistics compiled by the Federal Reserve Board, outside the US, 15 percent of the assets in private equity portfolios were in foreign equities in 1997; the corresponding proportion rose to 24 percent in 2007. For the US, the comparable proportion grew from 9 percent of total equity portfolios to 19 percent over the same time span (Kohn, 2008).

Since the turn of the century, the surge in globalization has coincided with surging world market prices of primary commodities, in particular oil. This is a reversal of the past commodity price trend, which had been in decline for a couple of decades vis-à-vis manufactured unit value (Cashin and Scott, 2002). The ongoing commodity price boom is notable in that its coverage is broad and its duration has lasted for much longer than its predecessors. The long-term supply elasticities of many commodities are large; therefore, this boom will eventually reverse as soon as supply responses pick up momentum. However, the probability of an energy price reversal does seem remote, even totally non-existent.

1.2 Global Economic Integration through Upgrading Policies and Institutions

The above-mentioned group of dynamic economies has noticeably benefited from globalization, in particular from the successful exploitation of market-led outer-oriented development strategy and climbing the ladder of development by first producing and exporting labor-intensive manufactures and then by capital- and technology-intensive manufactures. Assisted by their adherence to an outer-oriented economic strategy, they integrated first regionally and then globally, particularly with the mature industrial economies. India climbed the same ladder by exploiting the information and technology enabled services (ITeS) sector. Freeing market forces and enhancing their legitimacy in the economic system rendered these economies more efficient, which in turn led to the material advancement of these societies.

In the process of globalization, several economies improved their domestic macroeconomic policy structures and institutions. This observation applies to both developing economies and EMEs, that is, those that essentially export commodities and those that export manufactured goods and services. They pursued external liberalization by dismantling trade barriers, both tariff and non-tariff. They also took policy measures to liberalize current account transactions and preliminary measures to liberalize the capital account. That is not to say that all restrictions on FDI and other financial flows were dismantled, albeit they were significantly reduced.

These economies put in place economic reform programs and markedly improved their macroeconomic policies. Instances of large fiscal deficits and current account deficits have dropped to a small number. There has been a discernible improvement in the general quality of economic institutions as well as the depth in their financial markets. As globalization has proved to be an important driver of growth in the developing economies, some spillover effect in adopting internal and external policy liberalization among economies cannot be denied.

A large econometric exercise undertaken by the International Monetary Fund (IMF, 2008b) analyzed data for a broad sample of 80 countries over a long period (1970–2005) to examine several aspects of global economic integration. The econometric framework essentially consisted of cross-sectional and panel regressions. It came up with several valuable inferences. In brief, export volumes as a proportion of GDP grew for the sample countries by an average of 30 percent between 1980 and 2005. Improvements in institutional and financial frameworks accounted for as much as 25 percent of this increase. Another quarter of the increase was accounted for by reduced policy distortions. These included loosening exchange restrictions, dismantling tariff barriers and reduction in currency overvaluation. Thus, with progress in globalization, the policy and institutional environment and performance have been undergoing marked upgrading in a large number of economies.

The recent rise of the BRIC economies, which is an acronym for Brazil, the Russian Federation, India and China, is credited to the launching of economic reforms and the adoption of restructuring policies in these economies. They espoused a market-oriented liberal policy framework, which in turn was instrumental in relatively closer integration of this subset of economies with the global economy.[6] The same policy framework is considered to be responsible for the growing salience of 20 or more EMEs on the global economic stage. Sub-groups of developing and emerging-market economies that benefited during the contemporary phase of globalization are divided into several overlapping country groups. For instance, other than the four BRIC economies, the seven largest EMEs (China, India, Brazil, the Russian Federation, Indonesia, Mexico and Turkey) comprise one such group, while the EMEs that are the non-Group-of-Seven (G-7)[7] members of the Group-of-Twenty (G-20),[8] is another such group. It is a group of systemically significant countries that account for close to 90 percent of global economic production. The non-G-7 members of the G-20 have lately begun to play a meaningful role in global economic policy-making and governance. The Soviet Union broke up into 15 independent countries. Some of these economies, along with the East European economies which were satellites of the Soviet Union, have transformed themselves into market economies and democracies. They have made valiant attempts to turn into EMEs and integrate with the global economy. Globalization also succeeded in poverty alleviation of an impressive order and integrating the global economy by production networks, with far-reaching benefits to the global economy.

These developments in the latter half of the 20th century, particularly in the preceding three decades, have not only bolstered globalization but also markedly changed the economic geography of the world economy. The winners from globalization denote that it is a benign and productive force and was instrumental in improving living standards in many countries, albeit not worldwide, and that there is serendipity in it. How does globalization work as a welfare-enhancing, munificent mechanism? Economists' response is uncomplicated and direct: globalization enhances the economic opportunities of a country by allowing it to sell its goods and services in a much larger market, have access to a far bigger capital market to finance its growth and development process and have a larger opportunity to import technology and knowledge, which eventually enhances TFP. Thus viewed, the direct consequence of increased economic opportunities is tangible economic benefits and enhanced well-being for the globalizing economy. According to classical economists like David Ricardo (1817), the basis of these welfare gains is the theory of comparative advantage based on differences in factors of production and technology. Exploitation of comparative advantage allows the production of more goods and services with the same resources because firms produce at lower opportunity costs. Meanwhile, the modern theory of international trade attributes the welfare gains to economies of scale. They also occur due to mobility of factors of production, which makes them far more efficient than when they are static.

In the following section, we take a broad and comprehensive look at how these sub-groups of economies have benefited from globalization during the contemporary period.

2.   SOME FRONTRUNNERS OF GLOBALIZATION

Some economists regard globalization as an unambiguously salutary, constructive, valuable and welfare-enhancing force, with a few negative effects that thought and effort can mitigate straightforwardly. They believe that globalization has a "human face", not that is needs one, and contend that, if anything, the world economy – particularly its poorest regions – needs greater integration not less (Bhagwati, 2004). The simple line of logic taken by them is that globalization promotes economic growth, which alleviates poverty and its concomitant social ills. This group of thinkers provides theoretical and empirical evidence to support their proposition, and there is indubitably plenty of it. They present persuasive facts and substantiation of the economic and social benefits of global integration. For instance, the postwar global economy not only discernibly benefited from it but also, once the short recession of 2001 caused by the bursting of the dotcom bubble ended, the global economy again picked up notable momentum. The 2002–07 period is regarded as one of robust growth of the global economy. This section identifies several country groups and highlights the evidence that they provide regarding globalization as a force for enhancing economic welfare and a premise for well-being. Given the appropriate macroeconomic policy structure and supportive institutions, globalization can indeed be a benign and creative force. The analysis in the following sections points to several country groups that have benefited from the contemporary phase of global integration. Chronologically, some groups of economies benefited earlier than others.

2.1 Ascent and Economic Integration of East Asia

The East Asian economies provide the strongest evidence in favor of the positive effect of globalization on an economy. The East Asian economic miracle was squarely premised on globalization, in the form of export-led or trade-induced growth. Their outer-oriented growth was instrumental in closing the technology gap between them and the mature industrial economies.[9] "These countries managed globalization: it was their ability to take advantage of globalization, without being taken advantage of by globalization, that accounts for much of their success" (Stiglitz, 2006, p. 32). Japan had become the second largest economy in the world by 1968. The four East Asian economies followed Japan and turned into the much admired dragon economies. These dynamic economies were followed by the Southeast Asian economies and more recently by China. This was the so-called "flying-geese" pattern of shifting comparative advantage (Ljungwall and Sjoberg, 2007).

The sustained GDP growth of this sub-group of economies was achieved at the same time as remarkable stability; some of them did not have a single year of negative growth in a span of two decades; for some this period was extended to a quarter century. The outer-oriented economic growth and rapid global integration benefited and improved the economic lot of virtually the whole of East Asia. A noteworthy feature of the globalization of these economies was that the benefits of globalization were widely shared in the economy. The annual average rate of per capita incomes shows that the benefits did not go to only a small segment of these societies. Policy makers focused on maintaining economic stability and ensuring that fresh employment was generated as the new entrants entered the labor force (Stiglitz, 2006). In their rapid growth period, what Asian dragon economies achieved in a decade was achieved in the past by rapidly growing advanced industrial economies in a century. This phenomenon has been copiously analyzed by the economics profession.

Chronologically, the first to launch into rapid growth were the four Asian newly industrialized economies (ANIEs), namely, Korea, Hong Kong, Singapore and Taiwan. They were followed by the four larger members of the Association of Southeast Asian Nations (ASEAN), namely, Indonesia, Malaysia, the Philippines and Thailand. These economies had been making overtures since the latter half of the 1990s to come together as a common market and form a formal regional economic bloc, somewhat on the lines of the European Union (EU), complete with a unified financial system and a euro-like common currency. The concept was blessed by Robert A. Mundell (2002), widely regarded as the originator of the concept of the euro. While these developments will take time, a good deal of market-driven economic integration and regionalization of the East Asian economies successfully took place over the preceding two decades. The East Asian economies have succeeded in slicing the value chain and building efficient production networks covering several regional economies (Das, 2005c). Although China and Japan can play a leading role in bringing about a formal institutionalized East Asian economic union, the two East Asian giants, China and Japan, have had a troubled past. A future Sino-Japanese reconciliation may become a driving force and play a constructive role, identical to the one played by France and Germany in bringing about the EU structure.

What is feasible and being attempted is an institutionalized ASEAN-Plus-Three (APT) regional grouping, comprising the ten members of ASEAN, plus China, Korea and Japan (Das, 2007b). The Asian crisis of 1997–8, which pushed some of the most successful of the developing countries into unprecedented recessions, imparted urgency to this endeavor and official attempts to cooperate were launched in earnest after 1997. In November 2007, the tenth anniversary of APT cooperation was commemorated in Singapore by the 13 member countries. They reaffirmed their commitment to the Chiang Mai Initiative and Asian Bond Market Initiative as well as to the establishment of the APT Regional Foreign Exchange Reserve Pool in the near future so that regional financial stability could be enhanced. A plan for a regional financial facility, proposed at the time of the Asian crisis, did not pan out, but it has not been abandoned. These developments will engender interesting politics between the two East Asian giants, China and Japan. The former is predicted to surpass the latter at some point in the not too distant future. Consequently, China will also expect to take a leadership position in the regional institutions in the future. Since 2005, another larger regional grouping has been in an embryonic state. This was a pan-Asia forum and comprised the ten ASEAN members, plus six other countries (Australia, China, India, Japan, Korea and New Zealand). In November 2007, hard on the heels of the ASEAN conference, the third East Asia Summit (EAS) was organized. The EAS has produced no tangible results so far.

2.2   Ascent and Economic Integration of China and India

Until the early 1980s, both China and India were considered among the most impoverished economies in the world. In most tables of economic and social indicators, they were near the bottom. Rapid growth in the recent past and global integration of China first, and more recently, of India, has had a marked favorable impact on these two economies. They are considered different from other developing, emerging-market or transition economies because not only are they large, populous economies but also they have become the most rapidly growing economies in the world. Their rapid growth spell made them into prime catch-up candidates; therefore, they are frequently referred to as the 'mega-emergers'. In 1980, they accounted for a paltry 2 percent of global output, which almost quadrupled to 7 percent in 2005. It is well within the realm of probabilities that these two economies will achieve a fair amount of convergence with the mature industrial economies in the foreseeable future (Section 2.2). However, notwithstanding their rapid growth, their per capita incomes are still low. According to statistics published by the World Bank in 2008, China's per capita income was $2360 in 2007, while that of India was $950. These per capita incomes are far lower than those of the United States ($46 040), United Kingdom ($42 740), Japan ($37 670) and Germany ($38 860). In 2007, average per capita income of the Eurozone economies was $36 329.[10] This income disparity between China and India on the one hand and the industrial economies on the other points to the possibility of large gains from trade for both China and India. They could earn large benefits from the gap in wage levels, adjusted for productivity. The two economies have recently started exploiting these possible gains from trade.

In 2007, China's GDP was $3280 billion, at market exchange rates, making it the fourth largest economy in the world, and India's GDP was $1170 billion, making it the 12th largest economy in the world.[11] When economies of this size begin to integrate globally, they are bound to have a large impact on global trade and financial flows as well as the pace of globalization. Indications are that their future roles in the global economy are going to be larger. According to the projections made by Maddison (2005), by 2030 Chinese economy will account for a little more than 18 percent of global GDP, measured in purchasing power parity (PPP) terms. At this point, it will have overtaken the US economy. In this projection exercise, India's GDP was about half the GDP of China.

The economic weight of China and its integration into the global economy has been increasing faster than that of India. That China gave the global economy a positive supply-side shock is widely recognized (Das, 2008d). Over the next few decades the growth generated by China and India could make these economies a much larger force in the global economy compared to what they were at the turn of the century. As they integrate more with the global economy, China and India are likely to have an impact on global trade, the structure of production, distribution of income and they may become important engines of global growth. They have begun swaying not only goods and services markets globally but also flows of savings and investments. With rising prosperity in these rapidly emerging economies, millions of consumers will join "the global middle class" (Bussolo et al., 2008, p. 2). They will *pari passu* place heavy demands on the global commons as well as on markets in energy and commodities. The voracious appetite of China and India for energy imports and industrial raw materials has produced a commodity price boom. It has helped many developing countries as well as commodity-rich industrial countries like Australia and Canada.[12] Energy prices hardened to their historically high level by early 2008; strong Chinese and Indian demand was partially responsible for this. Rapid growth in China and India affects the other economies through a variety of channels. International trade is arguably the most direct and important one (Das, 2006).

In the post-1995 period, the two economies performed far more strongly than the others. Over the 1995–2004 period, China accounted for 12.8 percent of growth in global output, while India accounted for 3.2 percent. The impetus for the world economy presently comes from China and India, with the US economy stumbling with its twin deficits and a costly war (Klein, 2005). According to projections made by Winters and Yusuf (2007) for the two economies for the 2005–20 period, China's contribution to global growth will rise to 15.8 percent and India's to 4.1 percent. In 2007, growing at rapid rates of 11.4 percent and 9.2 percent,[13] respectively, China and India proved these projections too modest to be correct. In 2007, China alone contributed close to 25 percent to global growth (IMF, 2008b).[14] The spread of tertiary education and growth in the number of college graduates and trained engineers, as well as growth in savings, investment and physical capital in the two economies, point to a promising economic future. TFP growth in the two economies since 1995 was a respectable 2.5 percent per annum (Winters and Yusuf, 2007).

By 2007, the two economies had grown to a significant size. In PPP terms, China's share of global output was 10.8 percent, while that of India was 4.6 percent. The share of the United States, the largest global economy, was 21.4 percent (IMF, 2008b). Other economies were concerned about how rapid growth in these two economies would impact on them as well as on the global economy. Research on how to dance with these giants, without getting one's toes stepped on, is burgeoning (Das, 2006). They have become important locomotives of global growth and have begun to make their mark on the global economy.

Both these economies are among the largest players in the export of ICT goods and services, with China taking the lead in hardware and India in software. Strong growth in this sector contributed significantly to the expansion of these two economies. In 2004, China surpassed the US in ICT goods and high technology exports. India became the world's largest exporter of ICT services and ICT-enabled services. It is also one of the principal suppliers of business process outsourcing (BPO). Offshore outsourcing by advanced industrial economies played an important role in the rapid GDP growth of these two economies (Section 4.1). Both of them are in the process of shifting their economic structure from labor-intensive to technology-intensive and knowledge-intensive goods and services. It is reasonable to expect that their domestic markets will soon be huge and they in turn will become important markets for other economies, developing and industrial, in their own right. Gradually they will become innovators and producers of new knowledge and technology, which will further contribute to the ongoing global shifts in ICT production, trade and employment (UNCTAD, 2007b).

On many key indicators of growth, China's economic performance is superior to that of India. In brief, China is far more open to trade and FDI, has a better record of macroeconomic stability and has invested much more in education and infrastructure. China's macroeconomic reforms and restructuring are also some two decades ahead of India's. A detailed comparison of the two economies is available in Das (2006).

The APT, noted above, could be reasonably regarded as a sub-regional economic bloc dominated by China and Japan. A reasonably sized regional cooperation bloc called the South Asian Association for Regional Cooperation (SAARC) has emerged in South Asia and India is expected to play a central role in it. It has plans to have a free trade agreement, but for largely political reasons, progress has been slow. Substantial regional integration will only take place after further economic growth leads to increased complementarity in the economic structures of the seven South

Asian member economies (Das, 2007c). The dynamics of this economic bloc, if and when it comes into existence, will necessarily be different from those of the East Asian bloc indicated above.

2.3 Ascent and Economic Integration of the BRICs

Along with China and India, Brazil and the Russian Federation are part of the BRIC grouping. At market exchange rates, according to 2007 statistics, China is the third largest economy in the world, followed by Brazil as the tenth largest, the Russian Federation as the 11th largest and India as the 12th largest.[15] In per capita income terms, the Russian Federation ($7560) and Brazil ($5910) are much better off economies than China ($2360) and India ($950).[16] The first Goldman Sachs (2003) BRIC study focused on the growth generated by these large developing and transition economies and concluded that they could become a much larger future force in the global economy than they were believed to be. By using a formal framework to generate long-term forecasts, they demonstrate that India's economy could be larger than that of Japan by 2032 and China's larger than that of the US by 2041. Assuming reasonably successful development and adherence to sound policies in the BRICs, the combined size of the four economies has been projected to be larger than that of France, Germany, Italy, Japan, the UK and the US together by 2039. If they fulfill their growth potential, in a matter of decades, the BRICs could become critical to the global economy. Together these economies have begun playing a proactive role in multilateral trade governance (du Preez, 2007; Das, 2007d).

The second Goldman Sachs (2005) study was a *mea culpa*. It revealed that all the four BRIC economies turned in stronger growth performance than the projections made in the first study. These economies were playing a critical role in how economic globalization was evolving. The methodology of projections was refined and projections were revised to a shorter time span than those in the first study. A case was made for including them in global policy-making and economic governance. The update also proposed the inclusion of Korea and Mexico in the category of BRICs because their future role in the global economy was expected to be of a comparable order to the BRICs.

It must be pointed out that in the BRIC appellation, each economy not only has a very diverse per capita income level but also quite dissimilar economic and political characteristics. There is a slightly different grouping put together by Nayyar (2008) which includes China, India, Brazil and South Africa (CIBS) but excludes the Russian Federation. He contends that these four are already the new engines of growth. Rapid growth in these large EMEs has begun affecting the balance of economic power in the global economy and changing the locus of global economic activity. In future, these economies could provide technologies for growth and resources for investment. The BRIC or CIBS groups of economies are not the end of the list of large emerging economies. There are other economies that have a near-BRIC status and are jostling to be grouped with them. This group includes Korea, Mexico and Taiwan.

2.4   Ascent and Economic Integration of the Emerging Market Economies

A much-extolled achievement of globalization is rapid economic growth during the last two decades of the last century in 20 or more developing countries, known as the EMEs, that came to be better integrated into the global economy. These EMEs are low-to-middle per capita income countries. They have benefited discernibly and measurably from globalization. Some of the EMEs are large like China, while others are small, like Tunisia. The EMEs comprise those economies that reformed and liberalized their economic structure and markets and consequently reaped the benefit of a sustained high growth rate. An EME is usually more open to the global economy than other developing economies. The major players in this subset of economies are the large seven EMEs (or the E-7), namely, Brazil, China, India, Korea, Mexico, the Russian Federation and South Africa. Economic liberalization, which includes liberalization of both the trade and financial sectors, and global integration in the EMEs improved the welfare of the citizens of these economies through gains from trade. In aggregate terms, the macroeconomic payoff from globalization has been high for the EMEs.

The EMEs seem to be catching up with the industrial economies by *inter alia* consciously promoting the scientific and technological advancement of their economies, particularly the industrial and services sectors, and by maintaining rapid and sustained endogenous growth. It should be cautiously added that adoption of the so-called Washington Consensus (see note 23, chapter 1) also contributed to their economic performance. Liberalized trade, macroeconomic stability and getting prices right were mandatory under it. Under the tutelage of supranational institutions like the Bretton Woods twins, many developing economies regarded the economic strategy of liberalized trade, macroeconomic stability and getting prices right as a high-priority macroeconomic policy tool. Their macroeconomic reform programs on the one hand and efficiency and transparency in the capital markets on the other were responsible for stronger growth performance than in the past. Because of reforms of the external sector and exchange rate regime, these economies were able to attract foreign investment, both direct and portfolio. The decades of the 1980s and 1990s was a period of rapid GDP growth for the EMEs and helped them establish their distinct identity. Following two principal channels, the EMEs also integrated well with the global economy. The first was integration through the real sectors of the economy, that is, through trade expansion and inward flows of FDI. Inflow of foreign capital reflected the fact that the EMEs were successfully building international confidence in their economies. After 2000, FDI flows to the IMEs surged further, owing to abundant global liquidity. The second channel was the financial sector or attracting financial inflows through portfolio investment.

The McKinsey Global Institute (MGI) studied the impact of FDI on 14 industrial sectors in China, India, Brazil and Mexico. Sample industries included both manufacturing and services sectors. Their research concluded that, irrespective of the policy regime, industry or time period, FDI was good for the host economy. Thirteen out of 14 case studies found that FDI improved productivity and output in the sector in which it was made, raising national income. It lowered prices and improved quality and choice for consumers. Foreign investors were also found to pay higher wages than local firms. Efficiency-seeking investment, made by foreign firms seeking lower costs, consistently improved sector productivity, output, employment and standards of living in the host countries. Market-seeking investment, made by foreign firms that sought to expand markets, resulted in a mixed impact on employment. Also, benefits came at the cost of less productive incumbent firms. When Wal-Mart entered the Mexican food market, the average profit margins of local firms were driven down (Farrell, 2004).

The EMEs did not come into their own abruptly and unannounced. They had an understated, if subtle, preparatory phase. In a tentative and inchoate manner, they were under formation during the mid-20th century. They had knowledge and experience of manufacturing industries at this point in time and were producing silk, cotton textiles, foodstuff and light consumer goods (Chapter 1, Section 2.3). This familiarity with and knowledge of medium-technology manufactures prepared them subsequently to move into high-technology sectors. The economies in question were China, India, Indonesia, Korea, Malaysia, Taiwan and Thailand in Asia; Argentina, Brazil and Mexico in Latin America and Turkey in the Middle East. All of them later on acquired the status of EMEs. Some of these economies went further than others in becoming knowledge-based economies. China, India, Korea and Taiwan began to invest heavily in their own proprietary national skills. This helped them not only to develop medium-technology industrial sectors but also to invade high-technology sectors. Leading national firms had become capable of that.

Of the seven largest EMEs (China, India, Brazil, the Russian Federation, Indonesia, Mexico and Turkey) some, like China, India and the Russian Federation, were almost closed economies in the past. They have progressively liberalized and globalized. Their economic performance has gained marked momentum and their GDP is growing rapidly. In keeping with economic growth theory, Hawksworth (2006) used a Cobb-Douglas production function with constant returns to scale and constant factor shares to estimate the size of GDP in these EMEs in 2050. His long-term projections concluded that, measured in current dollars at market exchange rates, by 2050 their combined GDP will be 25 percent larger than the present members of the G-7 industrial economies. In PPP terms, it is estimated that they will be 75 percent larger. Measuring GDP in PPP terms is a better indicator of average living standards, or the volume of output and input. However, measuring it in dollars at market exchange rates is a better measure for estimating the size of the markets for export purposes and for investors operating in hard currencies. At present, the seven largest EMEs are merely 20 percent of the size of the G-7 economies at market exchange rates and 75 percent of the G-7 economies when measured using PPP. A sensitivity analysis suggests that these projections are susceptible to assumptions regarding trends on educational levels, net investment and the pace of catch-up. Rapid growth and GDP expansion in the EMEs would inevitably reduce the relative share of the G-7 economies in the global economy, albeit their per capita incomes will continue to be much larger than those of the EMEs. Rapid growth in the EMEs will create major new market opportunities for the G-7 economies and will boost their income levels in absolute terms. Larger global markets will enable firms in the G-7 economies to specialize more narrowly in their areas of comparative advantage as well as benefiting from low-cost imports from the EMEs.

Apart from the seven largest EMEs, there were several that turned in admirable economic performances and integrated with the global economy. A majority of them successfully used the external sector as a lever for growth and globalization.

3.   LATECOMERS TO GLOBALIZATION

The socialist or non-market economies of the former Soviet Union and Eastern Europe performed the difficult task of transforming their economic structures over the decade of the 1990s. Some of them subsequently succeeded in globally integrating as well. The sub-Saharan African economies turned to global integration even later, but they began showing some evidence of it in the mid-2000s.

3.1 Former Non-Market Economies

As these economies were regressing, the failure of a non-market economic system had become obvious for a long time. The fall of the Berlin Wall in 1989 and the break-up of the former Soviet Union in 1991 and the disintegration of the socialist bloc economies were epoch-making events. With the collapse of this economic system, a group of transition economies was born that was eager to make up for their economic mismanagement under a centrally planned non-market system. Their need to progress towards their growth potential was pressing. They attempted to adopt neoclassical economic principles and modernize their economies, which put them on the long road to globalization. The Russian Federation and some of the East European economies have made some progress in this direction. This sub-group of transition economies has done better than the rest of the transition economies. The centrally planned system not only suffered from egregious allocative inefficiencies but also created dislocation and isolation. During their centrally planned period, these economies had limited their economic relations with the rest of the world and followed an inward-oriented economic strategy. Their objective was to develop cohesive economic ties with each other and focus on domestic economic growth by import substitution.

Before the collapse of the Soviet Union, the Central and Eastern European countries formed an almost closed trading bloc. The Soviet Union was close to an autarky, with 90 percent of its trade with the Council for Mutual Economic Assistance (CMEA) countries. These economic and trade relations did not readily break down even after the dissolution of the Soviet Union. In order to end their isolation and reintegrate with the rest of the global economy, the transition economies liberalized their trade and payments regimes. Their economic transformation was significantly underpinned by their endeavors to reintegrate into the global economy. The pace and extent of liberalization varied from economy to economy but the majority of them removed exchange restrictions on current account transactions within a period of five to seven years.

Many of the transition economies reoriented their trade flows away from their former trade partners during the 1990s. Estonia, the Czech Republic and Hungary were the leaders in shifting their trade away from the CMEA and towards the EU. Gradually more transition economies began to alter their trade structure and replaced it with a balanced and market-determined distribution of trade. The EU economies, being larger and geographically proximate, became close trading partners. Reintegration into the global economy began to influence the transition countries' domestic economies by favorably influencing growth in productivity. These trade links also improved their access to global technology and helped them acquire modern managerial skills. Although multilateral trade picked up pace, reintegration into global financial markets was slow. Development and growth of financial relations are determined by an investor-friendly legal system in the host economy, property rights and contract laws, which take time to develop. Besides, a sound domestic financial system and macroeconomic and financial stability are preconditions for the development of global financial relations. This is a time-consuming process. After these are established, the global investor community develops confidence in the economy and begins to invest.

Progress in the reintegration of the various transition economies with the global economy differed widely. As a generalization, it is correct to state that those transition economies that progressed enough in terms of implementing stabilization and reform policies, tended to make more progress in reintegration with the rest of the global economy. In contrast to this group, many lagged and made little progress in reintegrating with the global economy. Slovenia and the Czech Republic have been rated the best performers in terms of reintegration with the global economy through trade and investment. Hungary and Croatia also made impressive progress. Slovakia, Romania, Poland and Ukraine were among those that have advanced well in this direction. The performance of the Russian Federation has been ranked below these economies (Carter, 2007). This is notwithstanding the fact that Russia had accumulated a critical mass of economic reforms in the first half of the 1990s (Aslund, 2007). As the largest gas and second largest oil exporter, Russia became a major source of energy for the global economy. The former group of non-market economies that succeeded in reintegrating and globalizing has performed better than those that did not succeed, or were slow in doing so.

The disintegration of the socialist economies and the failure of the economic system espoused by them seriously influenced the mindset of public policy makers in the developing world. They belatedly focused the attention of policy mandarins on the wastefulness and futility of a statist policy regime. The value of the role of market forces and a pro-market policy environment was made apparent to anybody willing to see. Watchful and discerning policy makers in many developing economies realized which set of policies to reject. Countries like India, which had obstinately adhered to a statist policy regime for an inordinate length of time despite its poor consequences, made an unprecedented attempt to change tack in 1991. The end of the era of a planned economy and statism encouraged a policy preference for an open, market-oriented policy regime and global integration.

3.2 Evidence of Africa Rising

Thus far, a little acknowledged fast is that belatedly several sub-Saharan African countries have begun benefiting from global economic integration and growing at a relatively faster pace than in the past. There are indications of slow but surefooted progress in this direction. Supported by a favorable global environment, the average real GDP growth rate of the sub-Saharan African countries reached 4.9 percent in 2003, and accelerated to an average of 6.5 percent over the four-year period between 2004 and 2007. According to the projections of the International Monetary Fund (IMF), this growth rate is to continue in 2008. In the recent past, per capita GDP for this region also rose to 4 percent or higher. After improving to 19.5 percent of GDP in 2003, the rate of gross domestic investment increased to 21.2 percent for the four-year period between 2004 and 2007. This has been projected to rise to 22.2 percent for 2008 (IMF, 2008d). Macroeconomic management in sub-Saharan economies has improved.

With rising global economic integration, capital receipts from global capital markets in the sub-Saharan countries have been increasing. Between 2000 and 2007, private capital inflows in the form of FDI, portfolio investment and bank loans quadrupled. This mirrored trends in the EMEs, and also the advanced industrial economies, where global capital flows surged due to an abundance of global liquidity (Section 2.4). However, equity and debt flows to these economies remained relatively small; they were a mere $53 billion in 2007, a diminutive proportion of total global flows of $6.4 trillion (IMF, 2008d). Transparent capital account policies and financial sector reforms are needed to encourage capital inflows as well as to ensure productive use of these resources.

Importantly, private capital flows to sub-Saharan Africa overtook official aid flows for the first time in 2006. A large proportion of private capital was attracted by South Africa and Nigeria, while portfolio flows went essentially to Ghana, Kenya, Tanzania, Uganda and Zambia. In response to the improved risk ratings of the latter group of countries, as well as attractive yields, the trend in portfolio capital flows has been gaining momentum. These capital inflows provide an alternative source of financing development and investment expenditures, particularly for much needed infrastructure. They should contribute to higher growth, which enhances the prospects of meeting the Millennium Development Goals (MDGs).

The raw material-producing economies of sub-Saharan Africa have benefited from the commodity price boom and large purchasers' increasing demand. First China and then India and the Russian Federation, followed by the other EMEs, emerged as buyers of large quantities of raw materials from sub-Saharan Africa. Several countries have begun to develop stock markets. Apart from South Africa, the largest African stock market, 15 other sub-Saharan countries have stock markets that list close to 500 companies, with market capitalization of $100 billion (Goldman Sachs, 2008). Until the third quarter of 2008, these stock markets were thriving. Rising by 30 percent in the first six months of 2008, Ghana outperformed the rest.

4.   GLOBALIZATION AND POVERTY ALLEVIATION

How the present phase of globalization has affected people living in absolute or extreme poverty is another imperative issue. Absolute or extreme poverty entails never having enough money for the necessities of life, malnutrition during childhood, little medical care and therefore low life expectancy, scarcity of potable water and fuel and eking out a miserable livelihood, feeling insecure and helpless. Put euphemistically, this is a life of acute indignity and ruthless mental and physical suffering. "Life for people this poor is brutal" (Stiglitz, 2006, p. 10). Little wonder that poverty has become not only a national but also a global concern.

The impact of globalization on poverty alleviation became an ardently debated and intensely researched subject in economic literature. A categorical response to the question whether globalization is positively correlated with poverty alleviation is that it should logically be so. A basic and plausible argument could be that if growth of the real economy is spurred by globalization, then the poor benefit from higher growth by having better housing, nutritional levels, education and other social services. A study of low-income developing economies by Hoekman et al. (2007) concluded that globalization by way of liberalization and reforms of trade and financial markets has a favorable impact at both the macro and micro level (or household level), which in turn improves the plight of the absolute poor. This empirical study emphasized the value, relevance and wisdom of the adoption of complementary policy measures for these low-income developing economies when they are implementing their liberalization measures and trying to globally integrate. Its logically supporting argument was that globalization does not take place all by itself. It is a policy-induced process.

As production activity expands as a result of the globalization-induced expansion of manufacturing and services sectors, it has a direct and positive effect on employment opportunities for the poor. They leave behind grinding rural poverty and move to urban areas, where they find far more employment opportunities. This relocation also has a structural effect on the economy; for one thing, it increases labor productivity in the economy. Besides, if globalization leads to higher income, a more equal income distribution can be achieved from a higher income than from a lower income. Does this cause-and-effect relationship work in the simple and direct manner indicated? Taking a long-term historical perspective, Bourguignon et al. (2002) found that extreme poverty in the world declined from 84 percent in 1820 to 66 percent in 1910. The definition of absolute poverty was people living at or below $1 a day, measured in 1990 PPP and inflation adjusted.[17] Absolute poverty fell again from 55 percent in 1950 to 24 percent in 1992. Turning to a more current period, 450 million were lifted out of extreme poverty between 1980 and 2005 (World Bank, 2007).[18] A caveat is essential here. Economies like China, India, Korea, Chile, Mauritius and Botswana that successfully achieved poverty alleviation did so by not benefiting from ongoing globalization alone. These economies also imaginatively tailored their economic policies to their own *sui generis* economic realities. By following pragmatic and eclectic macroeconomic policies and adopting complementary policies, they maximized the benefits from ongoing globalization (Rodrik, 2007a).[19]

Those who contend that globalization has exacerbated poverty around the world ignore all the poverty reduction that has occurred in economies where it was chronic and concentrated. Numerous globalizing economies support this observation. In countries where liberalization and globalization of the economy have been followed by stable, or declining, inequality, the poorest in the population have tended to benefit significantly. Vietnam is an excellent example of this (Section 4.5), where the share of the population below the poverty line has fallen markedly, and average consumption levels have improved. Indian efforts to liberalize and globalize present the same scenario, that is, higher rates of economic growth have advanced poverty reduction efforts in the economy (Nayar, 2007). China and Thailand, which are two premier examples of rapid globalization during the contemporary period, also demonstrate strong poverty alleviation trends. A detailed World Bank (2002) study asserted that globalization in general decreases poverty because globally integrated economies tend to grow faster and their growth is usually widely diffused among different population groups.

Bourguignon and Morrisson (2002) estimated that 1.4 billion people in the world subsisted on $1 a day in 1980. China and India were two geographical concentration points of poverty in the world. At least 60 percent of these absolute poor lived in these two economies, particularly in the rural areas. The other areas where a large number of them were trapped in 1980 included sub-Saharan Africa and some large Asian economies, such as Bangladesh, Indonesia, Pakistan and Vietnam. Bourguignon and

Morrisson (2002) also show that the number of poor in the world went on increasing between 1960 and 1980. Their number grew by about 100 million over this period. After globalization in China and India began, the poor people in these two economies discernibly benefited. However, even at the end of the last century, a large proportion of the world's poor continued to live in the rural areas of these two economies. As regards poverty alleviation, China recorded an average GDP growth of 10 percent in real terms during the post-1978 period, and the proportion of the poor fell from 31 percent in 1987 to 4 percent in 2000, a remarkable performance by any standard. Similarly, India has also experienced an acceleration in the real GDP growth rate of to close to 6 percent per year since economic liberalization began in 1991. The average GDP growth rate for three decades before liberalization began was 3.25 percent in India.[20] The proportion of the poor in the Indian population dropped from an average of 50 percent during the 1950–80 period to an average of 25 percent in 2000 (Srinivasan, 2002). This demonstrates that in China and India, global integration and poverty alleviation went hand in hand.

An acclaimed and influential research paper by Sala-i-Martin (2006), who compared four specific poverty lines for the 1970–2000 period for income data for 138 countries, also inferred a sharp poverty reduction in the global economy. His first conclusion was that global poverty rates declined significantly over the period under consideration. In 2000, they were between one-third and one-half of what they were in 1970 for all four poverty lines. This is the fastest reduction in extreme poverty in world history. This deduction is supported by ongoing World Bank research on poverty. Recent World Bank statistics from surveys of the living standards of nationally representative samples of households provide evidence of progress in reducing poverty, particularly after 2000. Over the 1981–99 period, people living below the $1-a-day poverty line (measured in 1990 PPP and inflation adjusted) declined from 40.14 percent to 22.10 percent.[21] This proportion fell further to 18.09 percent in 2004. When the second measure of poverty is considered, that is, when the poverty line is moved to $2 a day, over the 1981–99 period, poverty declined from 66.96 percent to 54.24 percent. It further declined to 47.55 percent in 2004 (Chen and Ravallion, 2007).

There is another distinct possibility, which cannot be disregarded. In reality, the theoretical globalization-poverty-alleviation nexus may not always work in the simple and direct manner suggested above, although instances of it working as indicated by the theory abound. There are rapidly globalizing economies with weak poverty alleviation records. Brazil, Mexico, Peru and Zambia fall into this category. Chen and Ravallion (2004) reported that while the absolute number of poor fell only in Asia, it rose in other parts of the world, particularly in Africa and Latin America. If the poverty line is moved to $2 a day, then the number of poor increased all over the world, significantly so in Africa. The anti-globalization movement takes its inspiration from such computations.

4.1 Analyzing the Globalization-Poverty-Alleviation Nexus

As we saw in the preceding section, theoretically it is plausible and rational for globalization to alleviate poverty, but in a real-life situation it may work in some cases while not in others. The reason is that it is a complex and heterogeneous relationship and it is simplistic to assume that one leads to or causes the other. It may well be a non-linear relationship, having multiple channels and thresholds. Non-linearity is vital in the transmission mechanism of the globalization-poverty-alleviation nexus. Sindzingre (2005, p. 1) argues that "institutions constitute a critical factor in creating these threshold effects in the transmission of impact of globalization on poverty". Using a composite index of globalization and cross-country regressions that relate measures of real and financial integration to poverty, Agenor (2004, p. 23) inferred that globalization may have an inverted U-shaped effect on poverty. That is, "at low levels, globalization appears to hurt the poor, but beyond a certain threshold, it seems to reduce poverty – possibly because it brings with it renewed impetus for reform. Thus, globalization may hurt the poor not because it went too far, but rather because it did not go far enough."

Besides, often globalization succeeds in alleviating poverty only when certain economic preconditions are fulfilled. Another explanation for a weakness in the link could be policy distortions in the globalizing economy. These distortions can weaken the impact of globalization-induced growth on poverty. How exactly the process of globalization affects growth of income and its distribution has been analyzed with the help of different methodologies, but there is little agreement on views and inferences. Globalization can affect poverty through multiple channels. Which ones are functional will necessarily vary with the case under analysis. As if multiplicity of channels of impact was not enough, they can be controversial and contentious per se. Ravallion (2004) noted that the impact of globalization on poverty through growth has created both winners and losers from globalization, which in turn has affected both vertical and horizontal inequalities. As the "multifaceted channels interact dynamically over space and time, the net effects of globalization on the poor can only be judged on the basis of 'context-specific empirical studies'" (Nissanke and Thorbecke, 2007a, p. 25). Only detailed empirical research in a country- and region-specific context can provide acceptable insights.

It appears rational and acceptable that growth, induced by global integration, can diminish the incidence of poverty. Yet, the contemporary phase of globalization is not conducive to the structural transformation in domestic economies which is necessary to engender and sustain pro-poor growth. Without creating such a policy structure, the distributional consequences of globalization could be unfavorable, and globalization-induced growth may not be pro-poor. It is possible, and has been observed, that globalization has often led to adverse distributional results at the national level. While globalization creates opportunities for pro-poor growth, only appropriate domestic policies can ensure it. Poverty alleviation is neither a guaranteed outcome of globalization, nor is it its involuntary result. Nissanke and Thorbecke (2007a, p. 28) put it aptly that globalization-induced growth could only be achieved by those "countries that create patterns of comparative advantage towards high-skill and high-productive activities will gain significantly from globalization. Passive liberalization may lead to marginalization." If this growth leads to inequality, the poor cannot be expected to benefit in a globalizing economy. Under certain circumstances, they can even be hurt by it. This growth could subsequently be converted into being pro-poor by modifying and fine-tuning the pattern of growth. Evidently, globalization-induced pro-poor growth would call for a strategy for pro-poor distribution of the gains from globalization. Furthermore, a low level of economic development renders it difficult to benefit from globalization. Economies need to reach a certain threshold of economic development to extract meaningful benefits from global integration. In order to take off and reach that threshold, they need to first invest in agricultural development and, second, to formulate a fitting structural transformation strategy for their economies.

Analysts used various standard techniques like cross-country regressions to analyze the globalization-poverty-alleviation nexus. This technique dominated the empirical research in this area. Cross-country studies are popular among researchers for good reason; they allow them to draw inferences from more than one specific case. Other techniques used have included partial-equilibrium/cost-of-living analysis, general equilibrium simulations and micro-macro synthesis. However, they face a basic problem of definition and measurement of the two key variables, globalization and poverty. As both are broad and multidimensional concepts, it is difficult to measure them with any degree of precision. Multiple definitions lend themselves to different measures of each one of these concepts. This has made the econometrician's task difficult, and lends her exercise inexact, if not vague. Conducting cross-country studies without precise measurement or indices is a challenging and problematic proposition.

Little wonder that some of the empirical studies came up with inferences that seem counterintuitive. For instance, a regression analysis by Heshmati (2007) for 62 countries found a weak and negative correlation between globalization poverty and income inequality. Taking a macro-micro view, Ravallion (2007) also concluded that the link between globalization and poverty was tenuous and that liberalization did not lead to poverty reduction. However, his data were suggestive of the impact of trade openness on poverty. Under certain circumstances, openness to trade could be effective in alleviating poverty. Estimates of income and inequality elasticities of poverty by Kalwij and Verschoor (2007) varied considerably between regions. They found that the average income elasticity of poverty was –1.06, but it varied between regions. The range was from –0.47 for South Asia to –4.21 for Eastern Europe. Similarly, their Gini elasticity of poverty was 0.21 on average. But it varied regionally from -0.06 in South Asia to 2.94 in Eastern Europe.

4.2 An Insight beyond Controversial Assertions

A macro-meso-micro approach to studying how globalization impacts upon poverty was taken by Jenkins (2007). As global supply chains or value chains are an idiosyncratic feature of the contemporary phase of globalization, studying them to come to a conclusion in this regard was indeed a meaningful and valuable approach (Section 5). These value chains integrate large areas of global economic activity. This insightful analysis addresses the issue of the globalization-poverty-alleviation-nexus through the intensive study of three value chains in four sample countries, namely, Bangladesh, Kenya, South Africa and Vietnam.

The value chains per se have been closely studied in academic literature. In particular, inter-firm relationships, issues of governance and distribution of profits within chains have been suitably analyzed. How a value chain operates will have "major implications for those who are integrated and who are marginalized as producers and hence who will be the winners and losers from globalization" (Jenkins, 2007, p. 164). The outcome of this research was that one cannot categorically say whether globalization eradicates poverty or not because globalization processes are completely context-dependent. They essentially depend on two things, the institutional framework and government policies which interact with the process of globalization. How globalization interacts with the rest of the policy and institutional environment holds the key to the question whether it will help in eradicating poverty. If the institutional framework and government policies are properly crafted, global integration could lead to poverty alleviation. This conclusion is both realistic and plausible. While global integration does engender opportunities for poverty alleviation, it cannot function as the primary policy measure for achieving the objective of poverty alleviation. The majority of the poor are not generally engaged in the production of goods and services for global distribution. Other precise anti-poverty, or complementary, policies are required to reach this target group in order to alleviate poverty.

These anti-poverty or complementary policies will necessarily be economy-specific, responding to a particular distortion or problematic issue. For instance, investment in human capital and improving industrial and agricultural infrastructures are the most frequently needed complementary policies. Providing credit and technological assistance to farmers are another important set. Examples of economy-specific anti-poverty or complementary policies could be as follows: in India, globalization could be far more beneficial to the poor if complementary policies reducing impediments to labor mobility are adopted. In several sub-Saharan African countries, where agriculture is the mainstay of the economies, poor farmers can only benefit from exports if they have access to credit, farm inputs and modern technological know-how. Land reform legislation is another major policy issue. If it is ignored by governments, for farmers in many least developed countries (LDCs) globalization will be nothing more than a buzzword. The same logic applies to financial globalization as well. It could be pro-poor and have a poverty-alleviation impact if it is accompanied by good governance, institutional development and macroeconomic stability (Harrison, 2006). While it could assist in eliminating poverty, as an isolated strategy, globalization cannot achieve this policy objective.

4.3 Contribution of Domestic Policy and Institutional Development

As a large majority of the poor people in the developing economies do not work in industries and services that are integrated into global markets, they cannot be expected to accrue direct benefits from globalization. A large proportion of them work on their farms and in small household enterprises, eking out a meager living. The constraints that this category of people usually face cannot be eliminated by merely globally integrating. Frequently, they are locked into a low-income equilibrium because of lack of access to credit, absence of physical infrastructure, institutional limitations, corrupt and venal officialdom and insecure land tenancy rights. Corrupt politicians, weak rule of law and inefficient bureaucracies compound these problems further. These domestic economic constraints on the one hand and social and political malaise on the other cannot possibly be cured by mere global integration.

Analyses that delve into globalization and poverty increasingly stress the importance of institutional development. If domestic policies and institutions are in place and first, engineer a structural shift in production towards marketable goods and services, and second, assist movement of workers into these newly created jobs, globalization will indeed go a long way toward directly benefiting the poor population groups. A recent consensus has emerged around the significance of domestic institutions, without which the benefits of globalization cannot be properly and advantageously reaped. Among the most important institutions are improved safety nets in high-income industrial countries and improved governance in developing countries. Rodrik (2007b) went further and prepared an extensive list of important institutions to be developed and strengthened. It includes enhanced trade adjustment assistance and more progressive taxation in the industrial economies. Institutional reforms required internationally include implementation of the Doha trade agenda, implementation of the World Bank governance agenda, careful IMF surveillance of exchange rate movements, aid-for-trade and international financial codes and standards.

Several examples vividly illustrate the significance and contribution of domestic policy and institutions to economic growth and eventual social prosperity. In the early 1960s, Korea and the Philippines had comparable per capita incomes. However, it was the development of a robust domestic economic policy and institutional structure that helped Korea achieve a much higher level of economic performance than the Philippines. The 2006 per capita income of Korea was $17 690, while that of the Philippines was $1420. In 1996, Korea became a member of the august OECD club of industrial nations. Likewise, Mauritius and Jamaica had comparable per capita income in the early 1980s. Since this time, their economic performance has diverged. Superior economic policy and institutions and rule of law led to prosperity in Mauritius, whose per capita income in 2006 was $5450, while Jamaica ignored its domestic institutional development and had a poor record on the rule of law. It stagnated with a per capita income of $3480. The value of domestic economic policy structure and institutions cannot be overestimated. Expecting globalization to perform economic miracles without endeavoring to streamline domestic policies and build institutions would be futile.

4.4 Does East Asia Have a Lesson?

A striking case of globalization, where rapid growth has been accompanied by impressive poverty alleviation, is the experience of the East Asian economies. This country group successfully utilized pro-poor policies and institutional organization to eradicate poverty in the process of globally integrating. In keeping with Akamatsu's age-old paradigm of "flying geese", Japan was the first economy to emerge from the ravages of the war and grow into a vigorous industrial economy, followed by the four newly industrialized Asian economies (NIAEs), namely, Korea, Hong Kong, Singapore and Thailand. The ASEAN-4 (Indonesia, Malaysia, the Philippines and Thailand) followed the NIAEs. China and India began climbing the ladder of economic development, with China preparing to be an economic superpower of global proportions. Vietnam is the latest to join this country group of dynamic economies. The incidence of extreme $1-a-day poverty first disappeared in Japan. It was markedly reduced in the NIAEs and the ASEAN-4 economies made significant progress in eradicating extreme poverty. Both China and India have reported progress in extreme poverty eradication over the preceding two decades, with China achieving dramatic results.

The distinct manner in which the East Asian economies grew and rapidly integrated with the global economy contributed to poverty eradi-cation. The most important policy element in their growth was their adoption of an outward-oriented strategy. They started by utilizing their most abundant resource, unskilled labor, to produce labor-intensive manufactured products for exports because they had a comparative advantage in them. In the initial stages, their success in export markets was labor-driven. Production of competitive labor-intensive goods for world markets provided a useful framework for effective poverty alleviation. While these economies benefited from the growth effects of globalization, their unskilled labor or the poor were benefiting from the expansion of employment opportunities.

Having achieved initial success in world markets, these economies went on moving up the technological ladder in a sure-footed manner as their comparative advantage moved up. Interestingly, poverty alleviation in these economies also followed the "flying geese" pattern. It is reasonable to expect East Asian economies to achieve the UN Millennium Project objective of halving the 1990s' proportion of extreme poor by 2015. Some may even meet this target earlier (Das, 2005b; Ozawa, 2006).

4.5   China and Vietnam: Case Studies of Poverty Reduction

China and Vietnam provide two of the paramount examples of how econ-omies can effectively alleviate poverty while globally integrating. Granted that correlation is not causation, globalization contributed significantly to the policy objective of poverty eradication in these two economies. If trade-to-GDP ratio is taken as a measure, China is a more open economy than the US. Trade (exports + imports) accounted for 69.4 percent of GDP in China in 2006; the corresponding proportion was 39.6 percent in 2000.[22] At the time of launching its macroeconomic reform program in 1978, China was substantially poorer than sub-Saharan Africa. Over the last three decades, it has moved more people out of poverty than any other country and succeeded in bringing about the largest and fastest poverty reduction in history. Poverty in China was essentially a rural phenomenon. Measured by international poverty lines, absolute poverty in rural areas declined from 250 million in 1978 to 26.1 million in 2004 (OECD, 2005b). The incidence of rural poverty declined from 31.6 percent in 1978 to 2.5 percent in 2005. In 2006, it declined further to 2.3 percent (Huang et al., 2008). This is regarded as the largest single contribution to global poverty reduction in the global economy. Lipsky (2007) remarked that "China alone accounted for over 75 percent of poverty reduction in the developing world over the last 20 years". While poverty has declined, income inequality in China increased. According to the recent (December 2007) revised calculations of PPP by the World Bank, China's success in poverty alleviation was superior to what old computations showed. The old estimate of $1-per-day (measured in PPP and inflation adjusted) poverty reduction in China was from 64 percent of the population in 1981 to 10 percent in 2004. The new estimate showed a reduction from something like 74 percent to 15 percent over the same time period (World Bank, 2008e). It is well on track to eliminate $1-a-day poverty by 2015 (Dollar, 2007).

At the end of 1986, Vietnam launched the *doi moi* (economic renovation) with the objective of stimulating economic growth. Although Vietnam drew a lot of economic inspiration from China, what it achieved by opening up its economy and globalizing is superior even to the superlative achievements of China. The *doi moi* reforms brought tangible success, making Vietnam one of the fastest-growing developing economies in the world. From 1996 to 2006, Vietnam maintained an annual growth rate of 7 percent, or higher. In 2007, its GDP growth rate was 8.5 percent, making it the third consecutive year of above 8 percent GDP growth. In 2007, its investment rate reached 40.4 percent of GDP, which was essentially driven by the private sector. An exceedingly low-income country, its per capita income in 2007 was $790.[23] Its poverty alleviation efforts are noteworthy. In 1993, 61 percent of its population lived below the $1-a-day (measured in PPP and inflation adjusted) poverty line. In 1999, this proportion fell to 35 percent and in 2007 to below 20 percent. Between 1985 and 2005, its GDP quadrupled from $14.1 billion to $52.4 billion. Like China, trade played the role of principal locomotive in pulling the economy out of low-growth equilibrium. Vietnam acceded to the World Trade Organization (WTO) in 2007, which provided an impetus to its market-oriented reforms.

Initially, FDI remained at a modest level, but it soon gained momentum. Commitments in 2007 doubled from those in 2006, to $20.3 billion (World Bank, 2008a). Vietnam, a country on the move, seems to be a winner from globalization.

5. GLOBALIZATION GAINS FOR THE INDUSTRIAL ECONOMIES

The economic payoff for the mature industrial economies from globalization was enormous. Due to its enthusiastic "embrace of globalization", Britain is "enjoying a period of extraordinary prosperity" (*The Economist, 2007a*, p. 12). On balance, Europe has been a sizeable beneficiary from the ongoing globalization.[24] Greater trade opportunities, lower barriers to investment, rapid technological diffusion and reforms have resulted in greater flows of goods and services, labor, capital and ideas within Europe and between Europe and the rest of the world. Conservative estimates show that "one-fifth of the increase in living standards in the EU-15[25] was the result of integration with the world economy" (CEC, 2005, p. 7).

Europe's integration into the global economy is borne out by the fact that the trade-to-GDP ratio for the EU-15 economies jumped from 39 percent to 75 percent over the 1960–2005 period. Imports from developing economies increased from 2.7 percent of GDP in 1990 to 4.9 percent in 2004 in the EU-15. Outward FDI stock from the EU-15 also recorded a sharp increase from 6 percent of GDP in 1980 to 39.9 percent in 2005 (EGW, 2008). The gains from globalization were not evenly shared by workers, firms and communities. Some benefited more than others. Tangible benefits to the European economies included vigorous trade expansion, strong outflows and inflows in FDI, greater technological diffusion, net portfolio inflows, net inflows of labor, downward pressure on inflation and interest rates, employment generation, higher household income and a modest increase in wages. All these coalesced to engender higher GDP growth rates. Owing to globalization, Europeans are living better today than they did when the Iron Curtain fell in 1991.

Uneven distribution of the gains from globalization brought uncertainty and disruption for many. It had a negative impact on many stakeholders, namely consumers, workers, companies, communities and even governments. Some of them succeeded in locating and devising solutions, while others could not and sought to block the advance of globalization.

Largely due to globalization, Europe continues to be the largest trading entity in the world. Its share of world exports has increased over the last two decades. The net outcome of rapid trade expansion was a boost to real economic growth and to earnings of European firms, which in turn caused growth in employment and workers' incomes. Comparable benefits have accrued from Europe's expanding FDI in the rest of the world. Being both a recipient and supplier of FDI, Europe has succeeded in deepening its economic linkages with the global economy. Between 2000 and 2006, it accounted for 64 percent of global FDI outflows and 50 percent of inflows. Europe has been benefiting from two sources of freer labor mobility: first, intra-EU labor movements, which have been a windfall to both sending and receiving EU countries; second, high- and low-skilled labor coming into the EU from the rest of the world. Although cross-border movement of people has been a contentious issue, the EU economies are net importers of labor, presently importing 9 million annually (Hamilton and Quinlan, 2008).

In the postwar era, Japan pioneered outer-oriented economic policies, which helped it not only to globalize but also to catch up with the mature industrial economies of North America and Western Europe. By 1968, it had become not only prosperous but also the second largest economy in the world. It benefited immensely from globalization and will continue to do so. It cultivated close trade and investment relations with both the neighboring East Asian economies and the mature industrial economies. The competitiveness of Japanese firms in a significant range of high-technology manufactured goods and electronics in the markets of industrial economies during the 1980s led to serious trade friction, leading to strong protectionist tendencies in the large industrial economies. Plaza Accord led to a sharp appreciation of the yen in 1985, which provided an impetus for FDI outflows from large Japanese firms and transnational corporations (TNCs). Their overseas production links expanded. Soon, the size of overseas production grew larger than the value of Japanese exports. The Japanese economy entered an expansionary phase in the latter half of the 1980s, which ended in 1991 and a decade-long stagnation followed. Sluggish domestic demand impelled Japanese firms to seek global markets. Looking for low labor costs, they increasingly moved their manufacturing activity into the Asian economies. By the first half of the 1990s, Japan had developed remarkable manufacturing prowess and led the world in production volumes of autos, semiconductors and a large array of high-technology products. Several global Japanese firms, like Sony and Toyota, grew at an unprecedented pace and became a force to reckon with. The economy bottomed out of stagnation in 2002.

Although Japan is a major global economic power, its influence over the East Asian economies has been even more decisive. Many of their economic lessons were learned from Japanese economic experiments and experiences during its rapid growth era. Adopting an outward orientation and taking the initiative to globally integrate were among the lessons learned by the East Asian economies. As manufacture of a large number of goods was moved first to the East Asian economies and then to China, Japan began to run a considerable trade deficit with these economies. The challenge for Japanese firms is to maintain their comparative advantage in technology- and knowledge-intensive industries.

Over the years, the US became increasingly integrated into the global economy. In terms of trade and FDI flows, it has been a highly globalized economy. US firms produce in and do business with virtually all the small and large economies in the world. US firms and TNCs have been among the largest investors in the world. What is often ignored is that it has also been the largest recipient of FDI. Granger causality tests of FDI inflows have found strong evidence of favorable FDI effects on output and employment in the US. Most notably, the result of Granger causality running from FDI stocks to the GDP was found to be robust (Ajaga and Nunnenkamp, 2008).

Measured in terms of trade-to-GDP ratio, the US was a fairly closed economy until 1970, when this ratio was 10. The economy steadily opened up to trade and its trade-to-GDP ratio doubled to 20.6 in 1980 and further increased to 28 in 2005. US firms, including TNCs, have expanded abroad more and more and have increased their reliance on offshore inputs. The US can do business with the whole world in its own currency. Growth in the global expansion of US financial markets was nothing short of explosive and the US continued to be the largest recipient of inward FDI. According to the rankings of the *Global Competitiveness Report* (WEF, 2008), the US economy topped the global competitiveness index league table. The US championed the cause of liberalization of multi-lateral trade and investment in the post-World War II era. Its abstemious and clear-headed leadership was behind the creation of the General Agreement on Tariffs and Trade (GATT) in 1948, after the International Trade Organization (ITO) was stillborn. Policy makers were convinced of the static and dynamic gains from trade. The US liberalized its markets and provided an example for other countries to follow. Trade expansion with the global economy resulted in substantial benefit to the US. The halcyon period of broad-based economic expansion in the US was the quarter century following the war. At this point, industrial capacity in Japan and Western Europe had been decimated. In contrast, in the US the manufacturing sector was not only left unscathed but was also scaled up for wartime production. The US economy was in a strong position to meet growing domestic and global demand. Several studies that quantified gains found, without exception, that they resulted in substantial past and potential future payoffs. The strength of the dynamic US economy lay in its flexibility and adaptability. Bradford et al. (2006) found that postwar trade liberalization provided between $800 billion and $1.4 trillion worth of gains to the US economy. In terms of gains per household, the globalization payoff was estimated to be between $7000 and $13 000. Additional gains from removing trade barriers ranged from $400 billion to $1.3 trillion. In terms of gains per household, they came to between $4000 and $12 000. These gains are worth almost 10 percent of US GDP. As these benefits permanently raise national income, the gains accrue annually. Aldonas et al. (2007) computed similar gains accruing to the US economy from global engagement. The all-round economic gains from the liberalization of trade, investment and immigration are worth $1 trillion annually to the US economy. This translated into average gains of at least $10 000 per US household per year. Hufbauer (2008) confirmed that computations based on the liberalization of the principal channels of growth opened up by policy liberalization and technological innovation resulted in a $1 trillion annual globalization payoff for the US economy. As for the future, Hufbauer (2008, p. 4) states that "total policy liberalization by the US and all its commercial partners would add another $500 billion annually to the US economy".[26]

5.1 Offshore Outsourcing

During the contemporary phase of globalization, the basic concept of trade posited by David Ricardo (in 1817) has undergone a fundamental transformation.[27] Globalization of labor has led to the creation of a new economic dynamics. Increasing integration of low-wage countries into the global labor force – and therefore global division of labor – has created new ways of organizing production and trade. Advances in ICT, noted in Section 1.1, made offshoring cost-efficient. Investment-led trade in goods and services coalesced to create large offshore outsourcing from firms in the advanced industrial economies[28] to those in the developing economies and the EMEs. Consequently, the makeup of multilateral trade has changed spectacularly.

Offshore outsourcing grew at a rapid pace over the last quarter century. It became a feature of contemporary globalization that was as emotionally charged as it was misunderstood. As it created job migrations in the industrial economies, it became a politically sensitive issue and caused a huge stir in the industrial economies. It was indignantly criticized, strongly resented and accused of creating losers from globalization. It became a raucous political issue at election times, in both the EU and the US. Fear of shipping jobs abroad became a public platform and political parties exploited it. Several thousand websites angrily debated the injurious impact of offshore outsourcing for domestic economies. Conservative politicians, like Senator Charles Schumer of the US, repeatedly warned about offshore outsourcing converting industrial countries into developing ones. It has given a fresh lease of life to emotionally charged debates on neo-protectionism.

As the trend in offshore outsourcing picked up momentum, it reshaped the structure of the global economy. It led to both major macro- and microeconomic benefits. It enabled firms in the industrial economies to achieve significant bottom-line savings and improve profits. Not only did firms benefit from it but also consumers and economies gained. A Ventoro survey of 5000 firms in the EU and the US indicated that firms achieved cost restructuring and quality improvements by offshore outsourcing. They could also access intellectual property and wider skill sources by offshore outsourcing. Intra-firm operations were redesigned by firms which reduced time to market. Offshore outsourcing facilitated taking advantage of time zones and operating around the clock, in the process using productive resources and technology more efficiently.[29] Competently handled, offshore outsourcing considerably enhances TFP and the competitiveness of firms. In the Ventoro survey, firms unequivocally reported that the largest benefit of offshore outsourcing was savings made by way of cost reduction.[30] Given these benefits, if a firm chooses not to offshore innovatively, it is sure to become uncompetitive. The macroeconomic benefits that emerged from offshore outsourcing included control of inflation, improved returns on capital, larger investment and export growth. Competitive prices result in an increase in consumers' real income. Thus, from an economic perspective, it is a win-win situation.

Offshore outsourcing has accelerated the pace of structural change in the global economy. The manufacturing sector took most advantage of this practice; its popularity has succeeded in reshaping global manufacturing activity over the last two decades. In comparison with two decades ago, an auto plant in Detroit has an entirely different production structure today. These plants no longer produce cars from start to finish. A large number of globally scattered firms participate in building them. The services sector followed the manufacturing sector into offshore outsourcing in a big way. The latest development is routine offshore outsourcing of services operations by the manufacturing sector in the industrial economies. In Belgium, the Netherlands, Austria and Denmark, manufacturing firms tended to offshore the largest proportion of their manufacturing and services operations. Conversely, manufacturing firms in France, Germany, the UK and the US offshored to a lesser degree, but the volume of offshore outsourcing in these economies is large because these are large economies (OECD, 2007a).

In the manufacturing sector, offshore outsourcing changed the production structure in the industrial economies from vertically integrated to fragmented, and in the process provided a large cost advantage to firms in the industrial economies. Fragmentation of the production process was not economical in the past. It has been made feasible by the ICT advances and declining freight charges. Manufacturing in the US has not been weakened by offshore outsourcing, but if anything has become stronger. If job losses have occurred in some manufacturing industries due to offshore outsourcing, new jobs have been created in many other manufacturing sectors, higher up the technology ladder. The economy had a comparative advantage in these new higher-technology and higher-value-added sectors. If productive resources, in particular labor, are mobile and move to these new industrial sectors, offshore outsourcing results in greater prosperity for the economy. This kind of industrial dynamism is not only beneficial, but also necessary for long-term growth and affluence. Manufacturing production in the industrial economies has risen over the past decade. It has also become more productive and efficient than before. The proportion of the workforce employed in the manufacturing sector declined because of the ongoing structural changes in the economy, that is, the expansion of the services sector and the shrinking of the manufacturing sector. This was not unique to industrial economies. It has been happening in all economies, developing and industrial, that were growing.

Trade in commercial services inputs was low initially. Services were regarded in the past as a non-tradable activity. An old dictum was that what cannot be packed, cannot be traded. No more. Lately, offshoring intensity has increased in commercial services. Due to the ICT revolution, a large variety of services have become tradable. As set out in Section 1, multilateral trade in services is not only sizeable and extensive but is regarded as the most rapidly growing component of global commerce. In 2007, world commercial services exports rose by 18 percent to $3.3 trillion, compared to a 12 percent growth rate in merchandise trade (WTO, 2008).

In spite of rapid growth in services outsourcing, it is still very low. In the US international outsourcing of services accounted for less than 1 percent of total intermediate service inputs (Amiti and Wei, 2005a). Besides, all the major advanced industrial economies are major net exporters of intermediate service inputs, that is, 'insourcing' of services is far greater than outsourcing (Amiti and Wei, 2005b). Future liberalization of trade in services promises a large payoff. Several developing economies have succeeded in expanding their export of services markedly; as a group, their exports of services increased from $54 billion in 1984 to $400 billion in 2004. High-technology giants like IBM routinely outsource many of their software programming needs to India; this was a carefully calculated business decision with consequent financial implications. Although India has grown into one of the largest providers of offshore ICT-enabled services, East European countries, the Russian Federation, Portugal and Spain have also been active players. In a number of industrial economies, including Canada, Germany and the Netherlands, imports of services have increased substantially.

Many of the East European and Central Asian economies have benefited from opening up to the global economy and merging with the EU; the tertiary sector in these economies grew rapidly. A large contribution to the rise in developing countries' service exports over the last two decades was made by these economies. Industrial countries like Australia, Canada and Ireland are also identified as offshore locations that are responsible for large services exports. Exact statistical measures of individual tradable services are often difficult to determine because they are not methodologically maintained or compiled. However, offshore outsourcing of services has gained considerable momentum and importance since the mid-1990s. Growth in this market has been dynamic; double-digit annual growth rates have been common (DBR, 2004). Offshore outsourcing is here to stay and is projected to expand. This applies *a fortiori* to lower-skill services.

EU and US firms that are winners in offshore outsourcing successfully took advantage "of potentially very large cost savings". The mechanism functioned as follows: by offshore outsourcing and exporting some jobs, firms were able to keep many businesses profitable, which enabled them to preserve other jobs in the domestic economy. Higher TFP and profitability allowed these firms to invest more "in new technologies and business ideas", which in turn created new jobs in the higher-value-added sectors (Hamilton and Quinlan, 2008, p. 96).

The efficiency gains from outsourcing of services are nothing short of revolutionary. Those who stress the specter of displaced workers are remiss in ignoring the efficiency and cost benefits from the outsourcing of services. The kind of jobs that can be moved abroad at low cost digitally will continue to be moved. This does not imply that service sector jobs will disappear from industrial economies. However, one consequence of offshore outsourcing will be that the proportion of the workforce in these service jobs will shrink, which will lead to a structural change in the economy as well as societies. The workers freed from service sector jobs in the industrial economies, as noted above, will move to other gainful employment. Furthermore, offshore outsourcing need not result in large unemployment.

Blinder (2006, p. 116) went so far as to call offshore outsourcing the "third industrial revolution". "The world gained enormously from the first two industrial revolutions, and it is likely to do so from the third – so long as it makes the necessary economic and social adjustments" (Blinder, 2006, p. 117). As long as firms in the industrial economies retain high levels of skills and reposition their businesses for higher levels of productivity on the one hand and the workforce remains flexible and mobile on the other, high-value-added services will remain at home. The petrifying visions of high unemployment being created by offshore outsourcing will be belied.

Protectionists who accuse offshore outsourcing of job migration in the industrial economies take only a narrow view and restrict themselves to an incomplete picture. Its impact can be decomposed into a labor-supply effect, a relative price effect and a productivity effect. Two empirical exercises have demonstrated that it is the productivity effect that dominates the other two. Offshoring lower-technology and lower-skill jobs tends to raise the domestic wages of workers. The same logic applies to offshoring of white-collar jobs; it ends up increasing the salaries of white-collar workers. Advancements in the ICT may eventually "boost the wages of domestic workers" who performed the tasks that cannot be moved offshore (Grossman and Rossi-Hansberg, 2006a, p. 14). Offshore outsourcing eventually results in a factor augmenting technological process. When some tasks or processes can be performed more economically abroad, the offshoring domestic firm that had used domestic labor intensively for these tasks or processes gains. Increased profitability gives such a firm an incentive to expand faster relative to the firms that did everything domestically, using in-firm resources. Faster expansion by the firms that offshore selected operations and products eventually results in increasing demand for domestic labor. In addition, offshore outsourcing enables producers and consumers to capture the traditional benefits, in the Ricardian sense, of trade and specialization, plus the additional gains that are generated when tasks or production processes are located where they can be performed most cost efficiently. Furthermore, offshore outsourcing is "equivalent to technological progress that augments productivity" (Grossman and Rossi-Hansberg, 2006b, p. 94). The effect of offshore outsourcing on wages and employment is the same as technological advancements and productivity improvements. If the adversaries of globalization are not critical of technological advancements and productivity improvements, why should they be averse to offshore outsourcing?

6.   PROLIFERATION OF GLOBALLY NETWORKED PRODUCTION AND ITS BENEFITS

Manufacturing firms in the past were usually vertically integrated and their production was centralized. They typically undertook all of the production operations within their premises. Jay Forrester (1958, p. 37) is credited with foreseeing the advent of a new trend in production and making a prescient statement over half a century ago. In a *Harvard Business Review* article, he prophesied,

> Management is on the verge of a major breakthrough in understanding how industrial company success depends on the interactions between the flows of information, materials, money, manpower and capital equipment. The way these five flow systems interlock to amplify one another and to cause change and fluctuation will form the basis for anticipating the effects of decisions, policies, organizational forms and investment choices.

Forrester conceived and identified what the contemporary business literature refers to as supply chain management (SCM). As skills, capabilities and demand rose, the old mode of production was transformed. Subcontracting operations expanded profusely to supply parts, components and sub-systems competitively. This is known as a build-to-order supply chain (BOSC) strategy and has been successfully implemented in many large business corporations.[31]

The BOSC succeeded in launching a veritable revolution. Gigantic manufacturing firms like Airbus and Boeing increasingly rely on BOSC and risk-sharing partner firms, some of which remain involved from the design stage to production of components, sub-assemblies and entire sections of the aircraft. For the last two decades, China's aviation industry has been producing increasingly sophisticated components and parts for both Airbus and Boeing. Doors, airframes, tailfins, rudders for the A320, A350, 737 and 787 Dreamliner are made by Chinese aviation firms in a highly cost-effective manner. Falling costs of transport and communication (Chapter 1, Section 2.2) encouraged globalization of production. Subcontracting firms that are part of the BOSC are often scattered globally. Globalization of production has acquired significant dimensions and large business firms, particularly TNCs, consider it routine. BOSCs have become the principal instrument of the globalization of the production of goods and services.

Typically, these sub-contractors were not one-batch suppliers but they endeavored to develop long-standing relationships with their customer firms. As trade barriers and transport costs fell over the last quarter century, transport and communications costs fell drastically. Air shipping costs fell dramatically, resulting in a rapid increase in airborne trade (Hummels, 2007). Therefore, manufacturers and service suppliers were increasingly exposed to global competition. With a reduction in the global life-cycle time of products and services, firms were forced to adopt new decentralized modes for their products and services. This impelled manufacturing and services operations to disperse geographically and become increasingly globally networked. A broad pattern of cross-border activities of firms evolved. This entailed global investment, trade and collaboration for the purpose of product development, production and sourcing and finally marketing. The global value chains that evolved soon became the new paradigm of production as well as international trade. Assembly operations migrated to lower-wage economies. Progressively more trans-border transactions began to take place within firms and within integrated networks of production. Firms' abilities to disaggregate production processes and geographically disperse production also grew. Trade in parts, components and sub-assemblies enlarged to form an ever increasing share of international trade. Efficiently operating networked production activities enabled firms to enter new markets, exploit their technological and operational advantages, as well as reduce their costs and risks. The increased mobility of factors of production was essentially driven by the liberalization of markets (Chapter 1, Section 2.2).

In networked production, firms tend to focus on a single activity in the value chain. Typically, they adapt and engage in one or more links in the value chain, that is, from R&D through production to service provision. How to choose operations for in-house production and outsourcing is a complex process, which depends upon the maturity and complexity of the product and the intricacy of its production processes. A thorough understanding of the value chain and the link between activities provides a significant advantage. Managing a geographically spread-out value chain is demanding, particularly in areas where technology is changing rapidly and relationships with suppliers are constantly shifting.

Coordinating across the full value chain provides firms with an opportunity to capture a large value from integrated operations. For instance, in 1995, Hewlett-Packard designed and manufactured PCs in Europe and the US for the two markets. No more. By 2008, designers, assemblers and marketers are scattered geographically across a large number of firms. Another example is Apple Computer, which focuses on product design and coordinates across a large value chain. The 450 parts of its latest iPod video player are outsourced to subcontracting firms in Japan, China and other Asian countries. The chip that controls the player is outsourced from a US company, which in turn licenses the microcircuit from another company in the UK. In emerging industries, where production is linked to science-based knowledge and sophisticated production is linked to R&D, firms can capture significant value from such production activities.

Globally networked production and value chains have resulted in persuasive interdependence of economies, lower production costs, lower prices for consumers and higher profits for firms. Several economies and regions have exploited the opportunity to be parts of globally networked production and value chains and in the process, have benefited from accelerating the economic catch-up and received welfare gains. These benefits have been widespread. In particular, Asian economies, principally China, remarkably succeeded in creating and expanding sophisticated production networks. The BOSC linked the production and trade networks of the Asian economies to China. These networks nurtured and increased China's trade in high technology products. This trend has reorganized production in Asia and made it progressively global. A triangular trading pattern has developed, that is, firms in Asian economies, particularly in advanced ones like Hong Kong, Korea, Singapore and Taiwan, used China as their export base. Instead of exporting finished goods to the advanced industrial economies, they tend to export intermediate products to their affiliates in China, where they are turned into finished products for export to the industrial countries (Gaulier et al., 2007).

The achievement of this group of economies in managing and running the BOSC is nothing short of commendable. Due to the increase in vertical specialization, intra-industry trade rose sharply in East Asia. The share of this region in total world trade reached 34 percent in 2006, up sharply from 21 percent in 1990 (IMF, 2007d). Globalization of the marketplace resulted in supply chains facing more and more challenges in the form of global economic milieu and economic strategy, whose support is critical for the smooth operation of the supply chains and their general management. The complexity of supply chains gradually went on increasing. With increasing complexity, the risk of production disruption also increased. While lean supply chain operations increase the efficiency of production operations and save inventory costs, they also make production susceptible to natural disasters and other non-economic disruptions like pandemics. Efficient supply chain operations have led to complaints of price discrimination.

7. DISCERNIBLE BENEFITS FOR THE GLOBAL ECONOMY

The 20th century was so productive that the value of goods and services produced during that period exceeded the cumulative total of output over the preceding recorded human history (IMF, 2002). Britain, the leading economy of the 19th century, managed an average per capita annual growth rate of 1.5 percent. In comparison, in the post-World War II period, several rapidly growing economies managed to grow between 6 percent to 8 percent annually in per capita terms (Krueger, 2003). Between

1900 and 2000, global GDP at constant prices soared 19-fold (DeLong, 1998). Undoubtedly, this growth was far from evenly distributed. In another context (Chapter 1, Section 2.1), I have noted that economic growth in the latter half of the last century was much faster than in the earlier half, in fact during any earlier centuries. The average annual global economic growth rate was 3.9 percent during the latter half, compared to 1.6 percent for the first half (Maddison, 2001). According to Maddison (2003), this was the half century of the most rapid economic growth since the birth of Christ (see tables 1–3, and 8-b).

Economic growth and global integration expanded contemporaneously during the latter half of the last century. The forces of globalization in many economies were supported by the institutional innovation that took place in them, which enhanced both the legitimacy and the efficiency of markets. Relatively easy access to a buoyant international market greatly facilitated faster growth for a group of rapidly growing economies. The so-called dragon economies of East Asia and the EMEs benefited from the experiences of the mature industrial economies. The manner in which it was possible for these groups of economies to exploit their comparative advantage and division of labor was not possible for the rapidly growing economies of the 19th century. "This process led average global per capita income to more than triple in the second half of the last century" (Kohler, 2002). Over the 1980–2005 period, it doubled (World Bank, 2007). In effect, global economic growth in the latter half of the 20th century was so much better and qualitatively different from any earlier periods in history that a "new perspective of the world economy was needed to comprehend it" (Lucas, 2000, p. 159). For North America, Western Europe and Japan, this period was one of unmatched prosperity. The miracle economies of East Asia and China followed the industrial economies and attempted val- iantly to catch up. According to Krueger (2007, p. 337), the credit for the economic performance of the latter half of the 20th century goes to "the open multilateral system, which has enabled the emergence of a truly inter- national financial system, reciprocal reduction of trade barriers, and the emergence of many previously poor countries into the status of 'emerging markets'. . .".

A caveat is in order: that is, not all economies gained from globalization during the latter half of the 20th century. The winners of globalization benefited from globalization *inter alia* by participating in the competitive global economy. Therefore, the winners are restricted to those economies, or firms, that participate in the ongoing globalization process. Also, protected sectors of the economy – and firms and workers in them – evi- dently cannot possibly gain from globalization. If anything, they stand to lose a great deal from globalization. Countries and regions that did not participate in the ongoing globalization lagged behind. Some of them were unable to do so because they had failed to improve their investment climate, had problems with enacting corporate law and protection of property rights. Myanmar, Nigeria and Pakistan are cases in point.

The pace of globalization picked up during the 1990s and 2000s, leading to technological transformations and structural changes in the global economy. Several economies began turning from industrial to innovative, which made a discernible contribution to the global economic growth rate. Trans-border flows of trade and finance, particularly FDI, maintained strong momentum and the global economy demonstrated strong resilience to high oil prices and increases in interest rates. Until the sub-prime mortgage crisis precipitated financial turmoil in the most sophisticated financial market in the world, the US, and adversely affected the global economy in 2008, the global economic growth rate was exceedingly impressive. Few periods of comparable sustained global growth rates can be found during the post-World War II period.

8.   EXPANDING GLOBAL MIDDLE CLASS

The expansion of the global middle class, as a consequence of the ongoing wave of globalization, is a clearly identifiable structural theme of the contemporary period. O'Neill (2008, p. 16) called it "an explosion of the world middle class". This will influence the global distribution of income and spending power. If it is defined as households with incomes falling between $6000 and $30 000, or €3800 and €19 000, in terms of purchasing power parity (PPP), some 70 million people have been globally entering this income group annually. This expansion of the global middle class is set to continue over the next two decades and is "likely to be critical to how the world is changing" (Wilson and Dragusanu, 2008, p. 3). This novel trend is reminiscent of the formation of the middle classes in the high-income industrial economies during the latter half of the 19th century.

Wilson and Dragusanu (2008) analyzed data for 75 countries, representing 97 percent of world GDP, to estimate the emerging trends in income and purchasing power. They identified a clear trend towards rising income and spending by the middle classes. Although China and India were the most significant part of this trend, these dynamics stretched well beyond them. In terms of economies, this would result in a shift in spending power towards the middle-income countries and away from the present high-income industrial economies. As large population countries become the middle-income countries, they may begin to dominate global spending for the first time. By 2050, apart from Brazil, China and India, at least six more countries will have a large middle class. This will include Egypt, Indonesia, Iran, Mexico, Vietnam and the Philippines. By then, this group of nine may well account for around 60 percent of world GDP.

In terms of people, purchasing power is likely to shift to the middle-income group in an unprecedented manner. While this shift has been discernibly happening since the mid-1990s, its pace will pick up markedly in the next decade. By 2020, it is likely to peak. Close to 2 billion people have been estimated to join the global middle class by 2030. As the expansion of the global middle class gathers momentum and becomes more pronounced, global income distribution is sure to narrow.

9. SILENT REVOLUTION: A NEW BREED OF MULTINATIONAL COMPANIES

A new breed of EME-based multinational corporation (MNCs) is emerging that produces low-cost, appealing world-class products or services and modern facilities and systems. The presence and force of these TNCs are on the rise. The forces of globalization are the impetus for this new and fundamental trend. In a more open and globally integrating world economy, the EMEs have been busy establishing their own giant firms. This is sure to lead to a new shape for global business. Lenovo of China and Arcelor Mittal, owned by an Indian family, epitomize this trend. Managed by teams of multinational executives, these MNCs are regarded as being at "the leading edge of new phase in the evolution of the multinational corporations" (*The Economist,* 2008b, p. 20).

As MNCs from the EMEs invest in both developing and industrial economies, investment increasingly flows from South to South as well as from South to North. The business world woke up to the presence of this new breed of MNCs in 2004, when the Lenovo Group of China bought IBM's PC business and when in 2006, Mittal, an international steel group owned by an Indian expatriate family in London, bid for Arcelor, the biggest steelmaker in Europe and succeeded against severe French opposition. Also, when Jaguar and Land Rover were on the block in 2007, the two largest bidders were Tata Motors and Mahindra & Mahindra, two Indian MNCs. The former became the new owner of two prominent auto brands, of which Jaguar is globally regarded as high status. Firms from Brazil and Mexico have also been going global in an impressive manner in industries ranging from cement to consumer electronics to aircraft manufacture. These MNCs bring not only finances but also managerial and entrepreneurial talent. Airbus and Boeing "may have learnt a thing or two from the global supply chain of Brazil's Embraer" (*The Economist*, 2008b, p. 63).

MNCs from EMEs are successfully selling their products and services in global markets. As this movement unfolds, the incumbent global leaders will face strong competition from these EME-based firms and MNCs. The two will not only compete for markets but also for talent, resources and innovation. This silent revolution is transforming the global industrial landscape. While this poses a threat to the incumbent global leaders, it also offers opportunities for partnering and cooperation. A good number of EME-based globally ambitious firms are on the move and have been making their presence felt. Some of the most prominent include Haier and Lenovo Group of China, Infosys and Wipro of India, BYD Company of China, Cemex of Mexico and Embraer of Brazil. Boston Consulting Group (BCG) identified 100 MNCs from 14 EMEs in 2007, from a pool of 3000, that have acquired global status. They are at the leading edge of their businesses. Of these, 18 have assumed a global leadership position and are successfully competing with industrial-country firms in their own lucrative markets (BCG, 2006 and 2007). These MNCs are at varying stages of globalization and have different strategies of globalization (See Chapter 1, Section 3.4).

The latest BCG 100 are based in 14 EMEs, namely, Argentina, Brazil, Chile, China, Egypt, Hungary, India, Indonesia, Malaysia, Mexico, Poland, Russia, Thailand and Turkey. Asia is home to 66 MNCs and Latin America to 22. The maximum number of MNCs (41) comes from China, followed by India (20) and Brazil (13). Other than expanding sales and profit maximization, the motives for globalization for the BCG 100 include continued growth, long-term viability, increasing the scale of production, acquiring intangible assets, such as brands, and experimenting with new business models. They typically enjoy a set of compelling competitive advantages that they leverage in various ways to pursue global growth. They have been expanding their global market share, making major acquisitions and emerging as important customers.

10.   SUMMARY AND CONCLUSIONS

The phenomenon of globalization is neither good nor bad in itself. Its impact can be both salutary, constructive and welfare-enhancing on the one hand and injurious, destabilizing and dislocating on the other. In this chapter, I delve into the positive impact of contemporary globalization and examine the evidence for its beneficial effect on several country groups as well as on the global economy. This chapter provides wide-ranging evidence of its being a definitive transformative force for several economies and groups thereof.

No claim has been made for the universally positive impact of globalization. Global economic and financial integration on balance has yielded rich dividends for many economies. Evidence is available to demonstrate that globalization on balance is a welfare-enhancing force. By successfully exploiting a market-led outer-oriented development strategy and climbing the ladder of development by first producing and exporting labor-intensive manufactures and then switching to exports of capital- and technology-intensive manufactures, several country groups have integrated with the global economy and have commendable results to show for it. In a succinct manner, this chapter provides an account of how various groups of economies have benefited from globalization.

The rapid economic growth of the global economy during the latter half of the 20th century is attributed to ongoing globalization. This period is justifiably regarded as the paramount half century of global economic growth ever seen. Contemporary globalization also provides evidence of impressive advances in poverty alleviation and development of vertically integrated production networks. The supply chains thus created have produced a global manufacturing revolution of their own.

NOTES

1. See Berg and Krueger (2003) and Hallaert (2006) for literature surveys, Topalova (2004) for a case study on India and Amiti and Koning (2005) for one on Indonesia.
2. Until 1980 China was grouped with the poorest countries in the world. It recorded double-digit long-term real GDP growth over the 1980–2000 period, doubling its per capita income every decade. For the six-year period between 2002 and 2008, its real GDP growth was higher than 10 percent per annum. This long-term growth performance has no historical parallel.
3. In 2007, Vietnam attracted investment pledges worth over $20 billion, which was a surge of 70 percent compared to that pledged in 2006. Since the beginning of 2007, almost 1500 new projects were licensed. Most of them focused on construction, electronics production, telecommunications and other high-technology areas. Vietnam's low labor costs and young, industrious and literate workforce have made the country a popular manufacturing hub in Asia.
4. The term emerging-market economy (EME) was coined in 1981 by Antoine W. van Agtmael of the International Finance Corporation, the private sector arm of the World Bank. The developing countries in this category vary from small to large, even very large. They are regarded as emerging because they have adopted market-friendly economic reform programs, resulting in sounder macroeconomic policy structures. China is the largest and most important EME, along with several smaller economies like Tunisia. The common strand between these two economies is that both of them embarked on reform programs and consequently recorded rapid GDP growth. Both of them have liberalized their markets and are in the process of emerging onto the global economic stage. Sustained rapid pace GDP growth is the first indispensable

characteristic of an EME. Many of them are in the process of making a transition from a command economy framework to an open market economy, building accountability within the system. The Russian Federation and the East European economies that were part of the Soviet bloc in the past fall into this category. Second, other than adoption of an economic reform program, an EME builds a transparent and efficient domestic capital market. Third, it reforms its exchange rate regime because a stable currency creates confidence in the economy and investors in the global capital markets regard it as fit for investment. Fourth, a crucial feature of an EME is its ability to integrate with the global capital markets and attract a significant amount of foreign investment, both portfolio and direct. Growing investment – foreign and domestic – implies a rising confidence level in the domestic economy. Global capital flows into an EME add volume to its stock market and long-term investment in its infrastructure. For the global investing community the EMEs present an opportunity to diversify their investment portfolios. Investing in EMEs has gradually become a standard practice among global investors who wish to diversify, although they have added some risk to their portfolios.

5. See IMF (2008b), chapter 5, for a detailed analysis of the latest trends in global integration.
6. See Goldman Sachs (2005) and Goldman Sachs (2003).
7. The Group-of-Seven (G-7) comprises the seven largest mature industrial economies, namely, the United States (US), Japan, Germany, France, United Kingdom (UK), Italy and Canada. In 1976, Canada was the last to join the G-7.
8. The inaugural meeting of the Group-of-20 (G-20) took place in Berlin on 15–16 December 1999. It was jointly hosted by the German finance minister Hans Eichel and chaired by the Canadian finance minister Paul Martin. The G-20 had been set up on the recommendation of the G-7 finance ministers (in their report to the economic summit in Cologne on strengthening the international financial architecture) and was confirmed by them and the central bank governors in their joint communiqué in September 1999. The members of the G-20 are the finance ministries and central banks of 19 countries: Argentina, Australia, Brazil, Canada, China, France, Germany, India, Indonesia, Italy, Japan, Korea, Mexico, Russia, Saudi Arabia, South Africa, Turkey, the United Kingdom and the United States. The 20th member is the European Union, represented by the Council presidency and the European Central Bank. To ensure that the G-20's activities are closely aligned with those of the Bretton-Woods institutions, the managing director of the IMF and the president of the World Bank, plus the chairpersons of the International Monetary and Financial Committee and Development Committee of the IMF and World Bank, also participate in the talks as ex-officio members.
9. For detailed treatment, see Krueger (1995) and Stiglitz (1997).
10. World Bank (2008a).
11. Ibid.
12. The term industrial country has become a misnomer, because some of the emerging-market economies, like China, have become extensively industrialized. The contribution of the industrial sector to their GDP is larger than that in the wealthy countries of the developed world, whose economies are overwhelmingly dominated by the services sector. The EMEs have become large exporters of manufactured products as well.
13. IMF (2008b), table 1.1.
14. See IMF (2008b), chapter 1.
15. The source of these statistical data is the *World Development Indicator Database: Quick Reference Tables* (World Bank, 2008c).
16. Ibid.
17. This international poverty line was recently updated to $1.25 a day in 2005 PPP (Ravallion et al., 2008).
18. See World Bank (2007), chapter 2.
19. See Rodrik (2007a), chapter 7.
20. The People's Republic of China adopted the Deng doctrine or the "Gai Ge Kai Feng" program in December 1978. Translated, it means "change the system, open the door".

In contrast, India started its first major economic liberalization program in July 1991. India had earlier tried unsuccessfully to launch liberalization programs in 1984 and also 1988, which had resulted in some furtive, if superficial, liberalization measures being taken.

21. It was clarified in n. 18 above that this international poverty line was recently updated to $1.25 a day in 2005 PPP (Ravallion et al., 2008).
22. The source of these statistical data is World Bank (2007).
23. *Quick Reference Tables,* published by the World Bank in July 2008.
24. Europe here implies the 27 members of the European Union (EU), as well as Switzerland and Norway. The EU-15 stands for the older EU member states, including the United Kingdom (UK), Ireland, Belgium, Luxembourg, the Netherlands, Austria, Spain, Italy, Greece, France, Germany, Portugal, Sweden, Finland and Denmark.
25. The EU-15 comprised the following 15 countries: Austria, Belgium, Denmark, Finland, France, Germany, Greece, Ireland, Italy, Luxembourg, Netherlands, Portugal, Spain, Sweden and the United Kingdom. This was the number of member countries in the European Union prior to the accession of ten countries on 1 May 2004.
26. These computations and results are not free from controversy. Several empirical studies challenged them and others came up with considerably different results. For instance, see Rodrik (2007b), Bivens (2007b), Schwab (2007) and Anderson et al. (2006).
27. The classical theory of comparative advantage is attributed to David Ricardo who explained it clearly in his 1817 book *On the Principles of Political Economy and Taxation* in an example involving England and Portugal. In the erstwhile Portugal, it was possible to produce both wine and cloth with less work than it takes in England.
28. I prefer to use the term offshore outsourcing instead of "offshoring" or "outsourcing". The former implies the tasks or processes that were previously being undertaken domestically or in-house by a firm have moved to another country and are being done at arm's-length prices. The latter means that the tasks performed in-house previously are being performed by another firm at arm's length, not necessarily in another country. A clearer meaning emerges from offshore outsourcing. This means a firm in another country is performing tasks and processes that were being executed domestically by the outsourcing firm in the past. This could entail both having part of a manufacturing process done by a firm in another country, and employing them to provide certain services digitally from their home base.
29. Ventoro is an organization founded by business executives from the Offshore Outsourcing world, in Portland, Oragon. The study entitled *Offshore 2005 Research* is available on their website. It can be accessed at http://www.ventoro.com/Offshore2005ResearchFindings.pdf.
30. Ibid.
31. Gunasekaran and Ngai (2005) provide a literature review of BOSC.

3. Globalization, that versatile villain

It is no longer safe to assert that trade's impact on income distribution in
wealthy countries is fairly minor. There is a good case that it is big, and getting
bigger. I'm not endorsing protectionism, but free-traders need better answers to
the anxieties of globalization's losers.

> Paul Krugman, 2007a

Since 2001 the pay of the typical worker in the United States has been stuck,
with real wages growing less than half as fast as productivity. By contrast, the
executive types gathering for the World Economic Forum in Davos enjoyed a
Beckhamesque bonanza.

> *The Economist*, 2007b

1. GLOBALIZATION: A PERNICIOUS, MARGINALIZING AND MALEVOLENT FORCE?

The contemporary phase of globalization has produced enormous aggregate benefits for the global economy as well as for several individual
national economies. Convergence of income is one of its benign outcomes.
Because of the great potential for economic growth and development, most
economists have tended to be fervent supporters of globalism and globalization (Chapter 2).[1] However, globalization is Janus-faced. One glance in
the rear-view mirror is enough to persuade us that if globalization created
opportunities for accelerating growth and development over the preceding
three decades, it also became the root cause of serious economic and social
challenges in many economies, both developing and industrial.[2] Milanovic
(2003) presented a detailed account of the malignant aspects of historic
globalization, which makes it look like a nauseatingly exploitative phenomenon. Winners and losers from globalization exist at both macro- and
microeconomic levels. In the equation of tangible gains and losses from globalization, the gains to the gainers may well be larger than the losses to the
losers, yet the win-win premise of globalization has been increasingly dis-
puted. There are many in different social disciplines who were passionately
in favor of globalization, but have subsequently turned into naysayers. This
includes some prominent names in the economics profession. Globalization
has *inter alia* been discredited for creating unemployment, increasing
income inequality and for immisirizing the poor in the global economy.

Economic globalization that takes place by way of trans-border flows of goods and factors of production (including labor) can indeed be a source of adverse economic impacts, particularly when domestic market failures or regulatory weaknesses exist. These need to be treated directly with the help of appropriate domestic policy measures. Without the required domestic policy cures, the costs of globalization may well be high and the dangers of a globalization backlash may assume ominous proportions. The negative potential of the process of globalization can be ignored only at exorbitant economic and social costs.

Some economists not only regard contemporary globalization as essentially a source of serious problems, but they also point out that the costs of ongoing globalization can be serious for some industrial and developing economies, particularly for certain population and employment groups. Vivid evidence is available to show that the benefits of globalization have been asymmetric, in that they have gone disproportionately to the owners of capital at the expense of the providers of labor. This trend has set off an acutely skewed income distribution in many countries. Consequently, the progress of globalization does not look as inevitable and inexorable as it did only a few years ago. Some scholars (see Abdelal and Segal, 2007, p. 104) have begun asking whether the current phase of globalization has "started to come to a close".

Myriad economic and social problems are indiscriminately blamed on globalization. Many, logically or illogically, consider it a negative, harmful, destructive, marginalizing and malevolent influence upon economies and societies. Not all the denigration is ill-founded. It cannot be dismissed as the parochial pique of the uninformed. The economics profession concurs that globalization entails inescapable and inevitable economy-specific short-term costs. There may also be long-term costs of adjustment and reallocation of resources, in both developing and industrial developing economies. These are *sui generis* challenges and each economy has to devise its own short- and medium-term strategies to cope with them. Those who are disillusioned with the consequences of globalization should try to temper and modify this process, in lieu of reinforcing it.

In the popular media, globalization is often regarded as villainous for *inter alia* severely worsening the plight of the poor in the world. Such criticism tends to be sweeping. To be sure, the impact of globalizing on the poor has often been questioned by academic and policy researchers as well. Although it is difficult to attribute any poverty or income inequality trend exclusively or mainly to globalization without rigorous analyses, the assertion that the recent progress of globalization has had some adverse effects on poverty and income inequality cannot be rejected out of hand.

Over the years, some noted scholars have changed their position on the impact of globalization. This is clearly illustrated by two papers by Paul Krugman written in 1995 and 2008, respectively (Section 5.2). The latter article (Krugman, 2008b) starts with an expression of remorse for the viewpoint expressed in the former, which estimated a modest impact of globalization on wages and income inequality in the industrial economies. Other researchers of this period also presented comparable evidence of a moderate impact on wages (Borjas et al., 1997; Cline, 1999). The reason these studies concluded that trade with the emerging-market economies (EMEs)[3] and the developing economies essentially had only a minor impact was that these researchers were using out-of-date statistical data (Bernanke, 2007). With the help of current statistical data, this view was subsequently refined and had to be modified.

Populist views on globalization frequently tend to be mixed, or on the negative side. Public perception in the mature industrial economies is dominated by anxieties regarding job losses and downward pressure on wages. Anecdotal accounts often draw a downbeat and damaging image of globalization, strengthening its disconcerting and harmful aura in the minds of communities in general. A popular TV commentator blames globalization for economically crippling the American middle class; if he is to be believed, it is ready for extinction.[4] Periodically, the global economy finds itself in the clutches of one kind of financial, currency or economic crisis, which epitomizes another limitation of globalization. Both the macro- and microeconomic costs of these crises are severe and often borne disproportionately by the poor in the societies where these crises strike. According to this view, capital movements and the volatility associated with them can potentially lead to disasters. The benefits of globalization do not come without risks, and costs of globalization are exorbitant, while the benefits are puny. Consequently, a strong backlash has been a frequent occurrence in the past.

The facile and simplistic denigration of globalization is easy and is often indulged in by various individuals and institutional entities. Adherents of contemporary globalization point to the conspicuous and much-extolled achievements of globalization, namely, rapid economic growth and rising per capita incomes in the global economy during the latter half of the 20th century (discussed in Chapter 2). Of especial interest is the performance of the East Asian economies and the EMEs over the last three decades as they became better integrated with the global economy (discussed in Chapter 2). The global community's commitment to eradicating poverty was renewed in the Millennium Development Goals (MDGs). Globalization underpinned poverty eradication endeavors and led to measurable improvements (discussed in Chapter 2).

However, these positive achievements of globalization do not conceal its negative and marginalizing aspects. If globalization creates opportunities for accelerating growth in participating economies, it can pose myriad challenges to and impose constraints on policy makers. It has created a litany of national, regional and global economic problems. First, it is correctly blamed for the uneven distribution of the benefits from globalization. These are badly skewed within and between countries. A good deal of evidence shows that the poor are affected disproportionately when globalization-driven crises are precipitated, while they are not able to share equitably during globalization-driven upswings.[5] A group of economies did not benefit from the contemporary globalization (Chapter 1, Section 2.2). Income and job insecurity has risen, particularly for unskilled labor. Second, while foreign direct investment (FDI) and portfolio investment soared markedly, they disproportionately went to the mature industrial economies and EMEs.

Third, while integration of global markets generally spawned welfare gains, in some markets, like the financial markets, integration became a source of value-destroying volatility. The frequency of financial crises increased with the growth of trans-border capital flows. Crises in the large Latin American economies during the early 1990s, the Asian financial crisis of 1997–8, instability in Russia and Turkey towards the end of the decade, the sub-prime mortgage crisis of 2007–08 in the United States (US) and the sharp decline in the value of the dollar, among other things, demonstrated that the economic and social costs of such crises have tended to be high. In mid-2008, the US economy was teetering on the brink of a recession. These financial crises led to a high incidence of bankruptcies, unemployment, poverty and reduction in essential social and public services. The ultimate result was an increase in social stress, as well as fragmentation and acute deterioration in quality of life. Closer integration of financial markets, while enormously beneficial, also had a downside. It resulted in contagions and recessionary effects. Both the Asian crisis and the sub-prime mortgage crises testify to the detrimental effect of globalization, as do the other events. They demonstrated that the complex – and opaque – financial instruments developed in the recent past became instrumental in spreading the influence of "risky investments across continents, institutions and markets" (UNCTAD, 2008d, p. 4). The Union Bank of Switzerland (UBS), whose core business was staid wealth management, lost $38 billion on American mortgage-backed assets. Fourth, offshore outsourcing of white-collar and services sector jobs on the one hand and outsourcing of components and routine manufactured products and sub-assemblies on the other to EMEs affected unemployment rates in the mature industrial economies. The outcome was the attrition of the middle class and social distress, which has soured the attitude of the industrial countries towards globalization. Fifth, information and communication technology (ICT), which is regarded as a strong sinew of contemporary globalization, is highly unevenly distributed globally. This disparity is termed the digital divide.

In a globalized world economy, crises have a penchant to turn global quickly. During 2007 and 2008, grain prices on world markets soared by 60 percent in a year. Rice, maize and wheat prices in the international markets reached a record level in the first quarter of 2008.[6] Wheat alone shot up by 130 percent. In Asia, rice prices doubled. The principal causal factors included increasing demand in a lot of rapidly growing countries, such as China and India, soaring energy prices that made it much more expensive to produce food and increasing use of food crops as a fuel source. Drought in Australia and floods in West Africa were the other sources of loss of many crops. A small contribution was made by panic buying, hoarding, some countries closing their markets and lastly, speculation. While its sources were localized, the spike in the price of food crops became a global quandary. Food riots took place in 32 developing countries and we witnessed the first ever globalization of a humanitarian crisis (Bartiromo, 2008). Second, during the same period, petroleum prices rose precipitously and globalization was once again made out to be the villain. Third, the collapse of the housing bubble in the US mutated into a global phenomenon. The US housing market slump, the worst since the Great Depression, was transmitted to Europe without delay. Real estate prices collapsed in a synchronized manner in the United Kingdom (UK), Spain, China and India. Even the Baltic economies were not spared. Thus viewed, the list of collateral damage from globalization is not trivial by any measure.

There is another perspective coming from academic economists who straddle both beliefs and take a yes-but attitude.[7] While conceding the welfare effects of globalization, this group of analysts asserts that the power structure of national and supranational institutions is such that the potential benefits of globalization cannot be realized. This group of economists believes that the conviction that globalization leads to welfare gains is based on the assumption that markets function optimally, in a competitive manner, while in reality they do not, but suffer from imperfections. This group contends that the failure of globalization is caused by its governance. While they are not averse to the theoretical link between globalization and welfare gains, they see clear flaws in its management. It is because of this limitation that globalization has turned into "a perverse malign force hurting millions" (Stiglitz, 2003a, 2005 and 2006). They take a nuanced approach and see adherence to globalization as an incomplete

strategy that needs to be complemented by adopting eclectic policies
tailored to the individual realities of each economy (Rodrik, 2007a).[8]

2. ANTAGONISTIC PERSPECTIVES ON GLOBALIZATION

Politicians of various persuasions often find that they get more mileage
out of being globalization skeptics than out of being its proselytizers. The
political payoff from opposing globalization is high in both the European
Union (EU) and the US.[9] Opinion pieces and articles in the news media
and journals have begun questioning the need for and sustainability of
global economic integration. In general, the global policy environment in
2008 was not globalization-friendly. That the Doha Round of multilateral
trade negotiations (MTNs) was allowed to languish is a proof of disillusionment with and estrangement from globalization.[10] An attempt to
resuscitate it was made by the World Trade Organization (WTO) in July
2008, but it collapsed in acrimony.

Ironically, some of the most trenchant assaults on the consequences
of globalization came from the industrial economies, the very architects
and builders of the contemporary phase of globalization. Protectionist
sentiments in the EU and the US have been on the rise; inward FDI and
immigration have become issues for policy makers as well as of rancorous
popular concern (Abdelal and Segal, 2007). A stronger anti-globalization
sentiment is also to be found in African and Latin American countries,
where people feel that they are the losers from globalization. A 2008
opinion poll, conducted in 34 countries, found that while there was general
support for globalization (positive replies outnumbered negative by two
to one) there was unease about globalization and its pace. Of the 34 000
respondents, 50 percent considered that economic globalization was
moving too fast. This proportion was 57 percent in the Group-of-Seven
(G-7) countries. A majority (64 percent) of those polled also believed
that the gains and losses from globalization were distributed unevenly.[11]
The benefits and burden of globalization were asymmetrically shared;
therefore it was believed to be an unfair phenomenon.

Tangible gains from globalization accruing to the EU, Japan and the
US have been sizeable. Income boosts, employment generation and GDP
increases in the three economies have been substantive (Chapter 2, Section
4). Yet, pressure for a policy shift has been strengthening in both the
EU and the US. Its essential source is the economic adjustment that the
ongoing globalization calls for in these economies. If feelings, perceptions
and opinions towards globalization continue to be negative, protectionist

pressure as well as calls for a policy shift will build up further. Social and political antagonism will rise. Eventually, instead of facilitating ever deeper global integration, this environment will significantly slow or modify the process of globalization. Positions taken up by trenchant critics cannot be dismissed out of hand because it cannot be denied that not everyone has benefited from the onward march of contemporary globalization. Also, in many cases, adjustment costs have tended to be high and have had both economic and social dimensions. Although one cannot regard all the denigration as objective, logical and valid, globalism does have a downside.

In search of higher returns on their investments, several EMEs and the six Gulf Cooperation Council (GCC)[12] economies have established Sovereign-Wealth Funds (SWF). Due to negative perceptions about globalization, financial protectionism has begun to affect the operations of the SWFs. These are funds owned and run by the government of a sovereign nation that manages national savings, budget surplus and excess foreign exchange reserves by investing them globally in corporate stocks and bonds and other financial instruments. As of June 2007, the total foreign exchange reserves of the developing countries added up to $3.2 trillion, which was 23.6 percent of their GDP. These reserves were highly concentrated, with the largest five reserve holders accounting for 68 percent of the total (World Bank, 2008b).

These foreign currency assets of the developing economies are managed separately from the official reserves of the monetary authorities. However, whether these foreign assets are a part of the reserve assets of a country is hitherto ambiguous. SWFs funnel capital into investment vehicles other than low-yielding US Treasury securities. Their essential objective is to improve returns on investments for sovereign governments. Financial markets and analysts have been concerned about these large sources of global capital which are owned by governments in the EMEs and the GCC.

The US Department of Treasury estimated that the aggregate assets of the SWFs range between $1.5 trillion and $2.5 trillion (US Treasury, 2007). The IMF estimates the range to be between $1.9 trillion and $2.9 trillion (IMF, 2007a). Deutsche Bank Research (2007) put the number a tad higher, at $3 trillion. This is a mammoth amount of capital and SWFs from the EMEs can find investment opportunities in their own economies, or at least in their respective regions.

In spite of the large volume of their operations, the SWFs managed by and large to remain low-key and obscure for a long while. Only occasionally in the last three or four years, have they become a source of argumentative debate, even sour controversy, when they tried to make a large and conspicuous acquisition in the industrial economies. The popular and financial media did not begin copious discussions regarding the operations of the SWF until the last quarter of 2007, when they acquired considerable eminence (Mallaby, 2007; DeLong, 2007, Tassell and Chung, 2007 and Farrell and Lund, 2008). The Financial Times and the Wall Street Journal have started covering SWFs extensively and a new class of SWFs experts has emerged. Esteemed institutions like Deutsche Bank, Morgan Stanley and Standard Chartered began publishing well-researched pieces on SWFs. In rapidly globalizing financial markets, the growing role and activities of SWFs also began to attract a great deal of attention from central bankers and finance ministers in the industrial economies. In the G-7 meeting held in October 2007, the leaders of industrial economies had expressed concern about the investments made by the SWFs, disapproving, in particular, of the lack of transparency in their operations.[13] The Senate Banking Committee in the US repeatedly held lengthy hearings on the SWFs in October and November 2007.[14] In mid-November, the IMF convened its first annual roundtable on sovereign assets. For the first time, the US Treasury discussed SWF operations in its *Semi-Annual Report on International Economic and Exchange Rate Policies*, published in June 2007. The industrial countries felt uncomfortable about the operations of SWFs. China's CNOOC's failure to buy the US oil company Unocal is one example of financial protectionism raising its head in the US. The prolonged Dubai Port World saga was another similar case in point.

Academic researchers and policy mandarins have paid a great deal of attention to the issue of the impact of globalization on poverty alleviation, domestic income distribution and global income disparities (Das, 2004a and 2004b). There are distinct possibilities of globalization hurting the poor. It has been observed that the lower the skill level of the people, the greater is the probability of being adversely affected by the onward march of globalization. Globalization causing the closure of businesses and rising rates of unemployment aroused a strong adverse emotional response in many people and societies. Although in some instances, these could be essentially short-term and exclusive phenomena, there are strong arguments against certain policies that are frequently recommended by the supranational economic institutions for advancing globalization, for instance, the so-called Washington Consensus[15] (Stiglitz, 2005 and 2006). There are recent instances of economies like those in Latin America, which embraced the Washington Consensus unreservedly, on balance suffering from this set of policies. Argentina is one recent tragic example of Washington Consensus-led globalization (Rodrik, 2007a).[16]

We cannot possibly overlook the academic analysts who straddle both the opposing beliefs on globalization.[17] While admitting the welfare-enhancing effects of globalization, this group of analysts contends that the power structure of national and supranational institutions is such that the potential benefits of globalization cannot be realized. It is largely because of this limitation that globalization has turned into "a perverse malign force hurting millions". Stiglitz believes that globalization is driven by a "special privilege" agenda, therefore, fundamental problems underlying globalization have not been addressed. He found it particularly disturbing that, "while we were talking about how wonderful globalized financial system is in addressing the problem of risk, the developing countries were left to carry the burden interest rate and market volatility. This has had enormous *(negative)* consequences for the developing countries" (Stiglitz, 2003b).[18]

3.   DETRACTORS OF GLOBALIZATION

Anti-globalist research and writing have had the upper hand. They outnumber those that advocate globalization. Among lay persons, there is no scarcity of those who are completely and intransigently opposed to globalism and globalization and are certain of their perverse and malevolent contributions. Protracted protests, both peaceful and violent, by detractors of the globalization process have become commonplace. They were blamed for the debacle of the Third Ministerial Conference of the WTO in Seattle in 1999. This collapse left a lasting impression on the minds of TV viewers globally. It was far from the first manifestation of anti-globalization opposition, which had continued all through the 1990s and gathered momentum in the closing years of the decade. The street theatre and protest marches of the anti-globalization activists continued.

3.1   Targets They Home in on

The Bretton Woods twins and the WTO are frequently the targets of those who disapprove of globalization because they see them as the principal perpetrators or arch villains. In December 2005, during the Sixth Ministerial Conference of the WTO, pitched battles took place between anti-globalization activists and the Hong Kong police. Large parts of the host city had to be closed down because the police came under heavy attack from the demonstrators, particularly indignant South Korean rice farmers who were dead set against free trade in rice. During the Turin Winter Olympics in February 2006, the anti-globalization mob vented their wrath by attacking the Olympic flame, because they regarded the large expenditure on it as grossly and ostentatiously wasteful. Anti-globalization activists' protests and rallies against economic and corporate globalization have grown louder and are frequently violent. The annual meetings of the IMF and the World Bank have become a routine target of disruption for the detractors of globalization.

Often it is unclear whether the grievances of the detractors are directed more against big business in general than against global integration of the world economies. One common feature of these protests is strong passion, with a touch of clouded judgment. In one of the recent World Bank annual meetings, I saw a banner paradoxically reading, "World-wide Movement against Globalization". This ironic banner reflected the intensity of the passion. Although they are motley groups, the detractors of globalization essentially include three basic categories of people. The first comprises the incorrigible enemies of market capitalism, big business and large transnational corporations (TNCs), those of an anti-establishment disposition. The majority of this group is not open to serious thinking, analysis or logical dialogue. The second large category comprises well-intentioned but ill-informed young idealists living in industrial countries. This is a proactive group that does not realize that ignorance about such a major policy area can indubitably have perilous consequences. If anything, it can defeat the objective for which they are demonstrating.

The third group comprises well-informed, highly educated groups of left-of-center well-wishers of the have-nots in the world. They are not only knowledgeable people, capable of clear thinking, but also provide wholesome policy percepts. Their thinking, analytical prowess, bearing, comportment and behavior pattern are those of seasoned professionals. This group operates largely through its membership of non-governmental organizations (NGOs). A large majority of them has emerged as avowed critics of globalization per se, or of its various consequences. They hold globalization, in particular the operations of big business, TNCs and supranational institutions, responsible for many of the economic woes of the developing economies, and in general for the misery of the global poor. Their intentions are noble. According to them, globalization has resulted in a rapid pace of expansion of big business corporations and TNCs. These, in turn, have glaring exploitative tendencies because profit maximization is their *raison dêtre*. They firmly believe that the supranational institutions, in particular the Bretton Woods twins and the WTO, do not really understand what grass-roots economic development is really about. According to these antagonists, the supranational institutions are in a state of institutional denial regarding their professional capability. Being limited to theoretical precepts, their developmental strategies are misguided. In their view, the poverty alleviation methods adopted by these institutions are in fact deepening and worsening the plight of the global poor. They were highly critical of the handling of various EMEs' financial crises by the IMF in the 1990s and early 2000s. They were sure that the IMF's crisis management was a debauched operation. In particular, they found numerous faults with the IMF's analysis and perception of the Asian crisis as well as with its management. They considered it erroneous on theoretical grounds but also complained that it lacked what they called a "human face". Their denigration successfully influenced the crisis management formulae of the IMF.

The critics of globalization believe that the activities of big business organizations and TNCs have expanded far too rapidly and that they have become economically too powerful, garnering a disproportionate proportion of global resources. This process has been termed "transnationalization" of the global economy. Antagonists contended that in their manufacturing facilities in the developing economies TNCs exploit labor as well as the host country in various devious ways. These manufacturing facilities are nothing more than sources of high profits for big business and the TNCs.

3.2 Surging Corporate Profits

Rising corporate profit upsets the detractors. It vindicates their globalization-is-a-villain view. The upsurge in corporate profits in the US was monotonic; profits were higher in 2007 than at any time in the last half century. The benefits of globalization went asymmetrically to the owners of capital. Roach (2006, p. 1) called it "a veritable bonanza for the return to capital – pushing the profits share of national income in the major countries of the industrialized world to historical highs. . .". Normally productivity growth in an economy is correlated with growth in real wages. But over the 1996–2001 period, this relationship did not operate in the US. Only the top 10 percent of income earners enjoyed a growth rate of real wages or salary equal to or above the average rate of productivity growth in the economy. Median real wages and salaries barely recorded an increase, albeit the average wage and salary continued to grow apace with productivity growth in the economy. As almost half of the income gains went to the top 10 percent, the remaining 90 percent was left with little (Dew-Becker and Gordon, 2005).

In the past, labor unions would have reacted strongly to this trend, but in the globalizing world economy of the 1990s, the labor unions had become feeble. However, politicians have espoused the cause of labor in the industrial economies; there have been strident calls to assuage and moderate globalization and promote protectionism. This penchant is strong in the US and several West European economies, namely, Germany, France, Italy and Spain. In Australia and Japan, it is moderately high. In many of these countries, the squeeze on labor income, which has altered the income distribution in many of these societies, became one of the most passionate, energetic and acrimonious political issues. Recent presidential political campaigns in France and the US assigned a great deal of significance to it. To court the workers and attract their votes, Mme Ségolène Royal rejuvenated several pro-labor formulas of yore during her presidential campaign. Although the powerful forces of globalization cannot be stopped in their tracks, the body politic in many industrial economies has tilted leftward, toward the interests of the working classes. They are the losers from globalization. This leftward tilt is not limited to the wealthy industrial world. The critics are certain that globalization is an instrument of immiserizing the developing economies as well, particularly the low-income groups in them. Convinced that it is a villainous economic force, they contend that globalization threatens employment and living standards everywhere and that it is a means of thwarting social and economic progress the world over.

3.3 Asymmetric Income Distribution

That income distribution in many economies, particularly in the wealthy industrial economies, was unfavorably affected is another glaring social malaise caused by the advent of globalization. A large and conspicuous disparity has become obvious between the return to capital and rewards of labor during the contemporary phase of globalization. For the detractors this is a serious and valid affront and a limitation of globalization. Although after 1980 income distribution in the industrial economies did become genuinely skewed, this was not due to global integration. In the US, the share of national income of the top 10 percent between 1947 and 1980 hovered around 31 percent. Thereafter it began to rise and in 2004 it rose to 44 percent (Piketty and Saez, 2006). This trend was observed in all English-speaking countries, but not in Europe and Japan. In the late 1970s, top wage and salary earners' income began to increase. It accelerated in the early 1990s. Consequently, top salary earners, or the so-called working rich, replaced capital income earners at the top of the income distribution in English-speaking countries (Atkinson and Piketty, 2006).

Globalization is often squarely blamed for being the causal factor of this asymmetry in income distribution, although numerous other obvious reasons were also responsible for widening income asymmetry in the US and the EU, particularly in the English-speaking countries. Levy and Temin (2007) assigned a great deal of responsibility to economic institutions. In the early postwar period when US income distribution was not so uneven, this was due to active institutions like strong labor unions. A negotiating framework set within the Treaty of Detroit was established and taxation was progressive. Besides, in real terms, minimum wages were high. All these institutions and regulations were instrumental in broadly distributing the gains from productivity and economic growth in the society. The role of these institutions and practices changed with the passage of time. They slackened, even reversed, during the recent decades.

Technological development was another major factor causing income inequality. As discussed in Section 5.1, during the recent decades, it became increasingly skill- and factor-biased and adversely affected both the income of blue-collar and low-skill workers as well as income distribution. Another recent relevant change was acceleration in the compensations of senior and top corporate managers since the early 1990s, which widened income inequality. The highly trained and accomplished top managers' market value rose in English-speaking countries for reasons that had no relation to global integration. Inflated compensations of business executives were due to domestic market-based considerations rather than globalization. One of the reasons was that many of these top income earners succeeded in determining their own market values. The current trend of relating CEOs' compensations to the performance of firms or to the stock market also contributed to the steep rise in their compensation packages. Stock options became an increasingly common part of compensation.

The domestic political climate, conservative policy dominance and changing tax structure were also responsible for rising incomes for those in the top income brackets, resulting in exacerbating income inequality (Krugman, 2007b). Therefore, globalization and expanding international trade with the EMEs and developing economies can only be "seen as factors operating within this broader institutional story", not as the exclusive causal factors behind worsening income inequality (Levy and Temin, 2007, p. 12). Basing his analysis on factor content of imports as well as the rising sophistication of imports, Lawrence (2008, p. 80) deduced that rapidly expanding trade with the EMEs and the developing economies had "little to do with global forces that might be expected to especially affect unskilled workers" in the industrial economies. While counterintuitive and surprising, this inference does seem logical.

4.　GLOBALIZATION AND SURGING INCOME INEQUALITY

Global income inequality, that is, income inequality among countries, has increased dramatically over the last two centuries, albeit much of this increase had taken place before 1950. It almost exploded in the 19th century, which is historically regarded as the worst period of worsening income inequality in the world. Global income inequality has not worsened significantly since 1950. If anything, the contemporary phase of globalization has witnessed a slowing down in the secular trend toward growing global inequality among countries. This was essentially due to the partial convergence of GDP per capita in a sub-group of developing economies toward that of the industrial economies. This sub-group comprises the rapidly globalizing East Asian economies, China and the other EMEs. Another sub-group of countries that joined in income convergence is the GCC. In stark contrast to this convergence, many rapidly globalizing economies, both developing and industrial, demonstrate widening domestic or within-country income inequality, which has been alluded to in Section 3.

An empirical study of Latin American economies presented compelling evidence of within-country income inequality being higher for periods when globalization progressed and when domestic economies were relatively more open. During periods when policy makers ignored globalization and kept the domestic economy closed, income inequality was markedly lower in this sub-group of economies. This result was empirically tested and found to be robust under four different definitions of openness (Baten and Fraunholz, 2004). Some of the most conspicuous cases that conform to this trend during the contemporary phase of globalization are China, India, Japan, the UK and the US. Over the preceding three decades, income inequality worsened noticeably in the US, much of the blame for which is frequently put at the door of globalization (Bernanke, 2007). A striking feature of the inequality data in many economies was that the income gap widened more between the top and the middle of the income distribution, but remained stable between the middle and the bottom (Wilson, 2007).

The Gini coefficient, a statistical measure of the inequality of the distribution of income, has starkly deteriorated in economies that were either globally integrated, or were doing so rapidly.[19] The value of the Gini moved closer to 1 (or 100 percent, depending upon the scale) for the rapidly globalizing economies, implying increasing inequality in the distribution of disposable income. A rising Gini stands for worsening income inequality. Recent calculations of the Gini coefficient show that over the 1985–2005 period the Gini rose in most regions of the global economy, including the East Asian economies, the EMEs and the mature industrial economies. Conversely, it has declined for sub-Saharan Africa and the Commonwealth of Independent States (CIS) (IMF, 2007b). In the industrial economies globalization influenced the Gini coefficient adversely through several causal factors discussed in Section 3. Apart from a greater inflow of unskilled labor and pressure from low-price imports from the EMEs, rising competition from foreign suppliers who supplied their goods and services to importing firms in the industrial economies through off-shore outsourcing and global production network channels also affected the wages and income of low-skill workers. Increasing income inequality in the industrial economies is largely explained by a rise in earnings inequality (Atkinson, 2000).

Under the auspices of the General Agreement on Tariffs and Trade (GATT) and subsequently the WTO, various multilateral rounds of trade negotiations took place and trade and non-trade barriers manifestly declined sharply. Consequently, trade, one of the principal channels of globalization, has expanded at an accelerated rate, particularly since the early 1980s. Its long-term (1980-2006) average annual rate of growth was 7.1 percent. In a generation, multilateral trade sextupled. The share of multilateral trade in world GDP increased from 36 percent to 55 percent (Jaumotte, 2007). In the process, the EMEs increased their share in multilateral trade from 25 percent to 37 percent over the 1990–2005 period (Braeuninger, 2008). Many of them grew into significant exporters of manufactures, and some commercial services. Taking all the developing economies, which includes the EMEs, the share of trade in total multilateral trade went up from 28 percent in 1990 to 43 percent in 2005. In this case, the data for the recent years have been influenced by high commodity prices, which includes petroleum. The share of exports of manufactures from developing economies in total manufactures trade also shows a significant increase (Section 5.2).

An important characteristic of the accelerated integration of the global economy through the trade channel during the 1990s was the entry of former socialist economies into the global trading system and many developing economies, particularly those in Asia, dismantled their trade barriers. Most trade theories stress that expanding trade leads to increased specialization. It also leads to increased competition in global markets. These two aspects of trade coalesce and lead to gains and prosperity from trade. This trade expansion opened new markets for industrial country firms. Their ability to specialize was increased considerably by offshore outsourcing and global networked production, two idiosyncratic features of contemporary globalization. These firms also exploited scale economies, which in the long run, became a source of large and lucrative gains. The largest gains from this channel of globalization accrued to consumers who benefited from lower prices and greater variety in goods and services.

However, there was a downside to this channel of globalization. Large risks were created for firms and workers that were producing low-technology and labor-intensive products. Competitive pressure rendered them out of business. The lower-skilled part of the workforce in the industrial economies suffered wage stagnation and dislocation. In the US, the lower-skilled workforce is declining, while in EU economies, they faced increased risk of unemployment. These households not only failed to share the benefits engendered by globalization, but were also faced with declining incomes and seriously damaging economic plight. No quick resolution could be found for this segment of the labor force. If less-skilled workers do not flexibly learn to shift to higher-skilled and higher-productivity occupations, they will run the risk of remaining vulnerable to ongoing globalization. The same observation applies to firms that have been unable to compete in the newly evolving global industrial structure.

Notwithstanding the fluctuations, FDI, another important channel of globalization, has accelerated since the early 1990s. It is known to have become a virtuous circle, that is, firms that had made a high level of FDI, recorded better than average financial performance, which in turn encouraged them to invest more globally. Firms with a high level of FDI are defined as those earning more than 25 percent of revenues globally or having more than 25 percent of employees outside their home country. Such firms learned from their global ventures and took a more sanguine view of global production; consequently their confidence and risk-taking propensity increased. Despite a slowdown in the US economy in 2007, global FDI inflows were $1.76 trillion, above the previous record level of $1.4 trillion achieved in 2000.[20] As global integration gained momentum, FDI accelerated. This had an analogous impact on the worsening of income inequality. In the host developing countries, FDI increased demand for highly qualified and highly skilled workers. In tandem with that, outward flows of FDI in the industrial economies led to a reduction in demand for relatively low-skilled workers.

To worsen the situation further, the supply of unskilled labor has exceeded demand in the global economy since the early 1980s. On average, the Gini coefficient of disposable household income for the OECD economies climbed from 29.3 percent to 31 percent over the 1985–2000 period; this meant a worsening of Gini by almost 6 percent. Far more of the increase took place over the 1985–94 period than during the 1995–2000 period. One reason for a steady Gini over the latter period was labor market reform in OECD economies (Bumiaux et al., 2006). After 2000, the Gini coefficient again began to climb for the OECD economies, reflecting the end of the New Economy boom, and the consequent rise in unemployment rates. Above average inequality continued in Italy, Spain, the UK and the US, while the rise in the Gini coefficient was relatively less in Germany and the Nordic economies. Over half a century ago, Simon

Kuznets (1955) suggested that income inequality may follow an inverse-U curve, that is, first rising with globalization and then declining. It is likely that the Kuznets relationship still holds and time may tell when we enter the declining phase of income inequality with advancing globalization.

4.1　China: A Case Study of Escalating Income Inequality

If the long-term trend is analyzed, in terms of income inequality, China displayed a U-shaped pattern. When the Maoist reforms began in 1953, the Gini coefficient of household disposable income was as high as 56 percent, an alarmingly high level, making China a country with among the most unevenly distributed income. However, after the era of socialist reforms, the Gini sharply declined to 26 percent in 1975. This represented a rather egalitarian society, albeit large regional disparities existed. As this egalitarian society had exceedingly low per capita income, there existed an equality of poverty using international poverty lines, which millions lived on under $1 a day. In 1978, China adopted its now-renowned *Gai Ge Kai Fang,* or "change the system, open the door" strategy. The Gini coefficient at that point stood at 32 percent. The economic reforms began with rural households and spread to other sectors of the economy. They transformed China both economically and socially.

Before 1978, China was an autarky. Since the early 1980s, it has turned into an epitome of global integration. Trade (exports plus imports) accounted for 69.4 percent of GDP in China in 2005; the corresponding proportion was 39.6 percent in 2000.[21] This is but one indicator of its rapid pace of global integration. A vertiginous long-term GDP growth rate and global integration increased China's per capita income. In 2005 it was almost six times its 1985 level (Wan, 2008). Quickening of economic growth was first accompanied by a modest surge in income inequality, but it rose rapidly after 1985. In 1988, the Gini was 38 percent. After 1990, as GDP and per capita income rose, income inequality worsened at a higher rate; in 1995, it was 43 percent and in 1998, it declined marginally to 41 percent (Gustafsson and Zhong, 2000). The rapid increase in income inequality can be traced to a widening of the rural-urban gap, which in turn was driven by urban-based industrialization and export-led growth, which was made feasible by the rapid growth of special economic zones (SEZs) situated in the coastal provinces.[22]

The rise of China is regarded as globalization-powered. The rapid outer-oriented GDP growth that China was able to sustain for a long time without any period of major decline, coupled with focused efforts by the government to reduce rural poverty, which started in 1980, led to remarkable poverty alleviation. Absolute poverty in rural areas declined from 250 million in 1978 to 26.1 million in 2004 (OECD, 2005b). This is regarded as the largest single contribution to global poverty reduction in the global economy. Large-scale poverty alleviation in rural areas owes a great deal to the rural production responsibility system, which is often referred to as the "second land reform". Under this system, land was not only decollectivized but allocated to individual rural households. This ensured that early growth in China was pro-rural, which led to a reduction in rural income inequality as well as a narrowing of the urban–rural income gap. When, in the mid-1980s, the emphasis of reforms shifted to urban China, inequality in China stopped declining. Since then, as testified by the rising Gini, little official attention has been paid to equity concerns until recently. By 2008, China's Gini coefficient reached as high as 46.9 percent, in that it was ranked below India (36.8 percent), Indonesia (34.3 percent), the Republic of Korea (31.6), the Russian Federation (39.9 percent) and Turkey (43.6 percent). However, China was still better off than countries like Argentina (51.3) and Brazil (57.0); these are the EMEs with the most uneven income distribution (UNDP, 2008).

Rapid global integration, sustained brisk growth and breakneck industrialization created a middle class of some 400 million, who are a little higher up the income scale. They own their apartments and some have even bought their first car. There is a small super-rich class, albeit there is no Chinese billionaire in Forbes 2008 list of the 20 richest people in the world. The same phenomenon made a tangible contribution to poverty alleviation endeavors. However, concurrently China's income inequality rose steadily to a high level. Also, a striking spatial gap has emerged in China. Export-oriented industrialization essentially took place in the coastal provinces of southern and eastern China, where the majority of SEZs are located (Das, 2008c). It passed the other half of China by, which included those in the urban areas who were not part of this veritable economic revolution and rural inhabitants.

Spatially, the northern and eastern provinces lagged behind in the race to prosperity. On the one hand, you see glittering airports and six- or eight-lane highways. The view from Shanghai's Bund across the Huangpu River to the towers of the new financial district of Pudong is world class and breathtaking. Beijing's concentric ring roads are full of elegant modern cars. On the other hand, stark urban and rural poverty still visibly exists. While it exists all over China, its magnitude is higher in the North and the West of the country. The *nouveau riche* class that benefited from the economic revolution comprises those workers, professionals and entrepreneurs who succeeded in joining the export-oriented economic expansion and being part of the global integration of the Chinese economy. Goodman and Zang (2008, p. 5) regarded the emergence of a well-off social class as "a consequence of globalization", so did Chow (2006, p. 271). Their higher incomes skewed income growth in favor of those who were skilled, well-trained and were the owners of capital. This explains the high value of the Gini in 2008. While trickledown may take place, it is a time-consuming process.

5. GLOBALIZATION AND EMPLOYMENT INSECURITY ANGST

The globalization-employment-insecurity nexus has compelling and damaging implications for societies. In the mature industrial economies, this nexus fermented something of a popular movement against globalization. It has received strong support from the popular press, which has piled up large anecdotal evidence to validate this viewpoint. It has received a lot of empathy and proactive backing from political parties because workers are voters.

This nexus has stimulated a vigorous debate in the industrial economies. Representing the pro-globalization side of the motion, Gregory Mankiw of Harvard University has fervently contended that globalization of labor markets, which includes offshore outsourcing, is a long-term plus for the industrial economies. It also implies a larger benefit for the EMEs, making it a win-win proposition for the two sides. He regards the eventual qualitative impact of globalization on the industrial economies as comparable to intensified multilateral trade. However, Alan Blinder of Princeton University, who took a position against the motion, held that labor market globalization has had a major impact on the industrial and employment structures in the industrial economies. As in the short run it has negatively influenced wages and labor turnover, it should matter to policy makers. It has serious economic and social ramifications. This is Blinder's justification for the adoption of a protectionist strategy (Blinder, 2007; Leamer, 2007). However, it must be emphasized that he did not refute the basic economic gains from globalization of labor markets.

That some workers, particularly at the lower rung of the skill and technology ladder, lost their jobs due to increasing global integration through the trade channel as well as through the global integration of labor markets cannot be denied. Due to wage rigidities, job losses were much higher in the EU economies than in the US. Therefore, labor forces in the mature industrial economies, particularly in the EU, the US and other Anglo-Saxon countries, have demonized globalization for apparently legitimate reasons. They regard it, first, as a job killer and, second, as the cause of wage stagnation in their respective economies. Sizeable job losses did occur in some manufacturing and services sectors. Blame for higher unemployment rates in general and for the slowing down in the rate of employment creation was put at the door of globalization in labor markets. Since 2001, workers' wages in the EU-15 economies and the US have languished. Particularly in the US, real wages grew less than half as fast as productivity. If these allegations are true, globalization must be spurned.

Does global integration of labor markets deserve this allegation? An honest answer cannot be categorically negative. The rationale behind this acerbically negative perception of globalization as a job destroyer evolved in the following manner: with progress in the integration of labor markets, the labor forces in the East European economies, China, India and the Russian Federation have been incorporated into the global production system. There are no historical antecedents for this development. By joining the global labor force, millions of workers in these and other EMEs have won a chance to eschew the poverty and squalor they endured for a long time. In terms of per capita incomes, these economies are still at a much lower level than the industrial economies. As the wage gap, adjusted for productivity, between the two sets of economies is large, these econo- mies stand to gain significantly from trading with the industrial economies. Assisted by advances in ICT and modern technology, globalization of labor in several sectors has gathered momentum since the early 1990s. *Pari passu*, firms in the mature industrial economies find themselves in the fortuitous situation of having an oversupply of labor in the global labor market. This in turn has led to intensified competition in labor markets. For firms in the industrial economies, in several industrial and services sectors foreign workers not only became available in plenty but also at much lower wages, in many cases at a fraction of the prevailing wages in their own economies. Therefore, their profits soared. Booming corporate profitability in the industrial economies has attracted a great deal of attention. The flip side of this coin was falling income for some workers and other low-income households in the industrial countries. Krugman (2006) noted that, even in good years, the incomes of most non-elderly households failed to keep up with the rate of inflation and that the number of Americans in poverty rose. Blue-collar workers in the US were financially worse off in 2006 than in 2000. Labor markets in the industrial economies, particularly the US, became polarized into high-wage and low-wage workers. While the former flourished, the latter languished (Autor et al., 2006).

Thus viewed, if workers in the industrial countries believe that globaliza- tion of labor markets roiled labor markets in their economies and caused employment insecurity and adverse pressure on their wages, they are not wrong. Labor's share of GDP in the industrial economies fell steadily, and came down to historic lows (Rose, 2007). At the same time, a rising share of capital in GDP has become the latest trend (Thirlwell, 2007b). As labor market globalization accelerates in the foreseeable future, more and more workers will be exposed to foreign competition. Blue-collar workers and middle-class office workers perceive themselves as the principal casualty of globalization. They clamor for protection, as set out in Section 3.2, making globalization of labor markets into a politically sensitive issue.

This view of the globalization of the labor market as a source of unemployment runs counter to what economists assert, that is, integration of the labor force globally is a source of long-run welfare gains for both the domestic economy as well as for the global economy. It is a win-win situation for both the firms in the industrial economies and the labor-exporting EMEs and developing economies; it matters little what mode of labor export is chosen. The modern theory of international trade posits that factors of production are used far more efficiently when they are mobile than when they are static; labor mobility increases long-run welfare gains. Thus globalization of labor forces results in tangible benefits in the long run (Chapter 2, Section 1). Empirical evidence is available to demonstrate that offshore outsourcing did not account for a meaningful part of the job losses in the recent downturn in the US and the slower rebound of the labor market. If anything, empirical evidence suggests that increased employment in the overseas affiliates of US multinationals was associated with more employment in the parent firm at home rather than less (Mankiw and Swagel, 2006). Also, productivity increases due to offshore outsourcing and a rise in profitability may lead firms to increase domestic hiring, leading to net employment generation. A large survey in the UK of firms that routinely imported services from abroad found such firms to have faster employment growth than those that did not (Hijzen et al., 2007).

Obviously, those workers who lose jobs in the industrial economies are not impressed by the possible long-term welfare gains to their economies nor by net employment gains. Their innate and instinctive concern is the short-term loss of income, which leads to personal distress and deprivation for their families. If it happens to (i) a lot of workers and to (ii) those who have aged in a particular profession and are relatively older, then it turns into large-scale social distress for a society. It is easy to see why these categories of workers regard globalization as a villainous phenomenon that intrudes into their lives and that of their families and therefore should be shunned, or at least controlled, at all costs.

5.1 Factor-Biased Technological Development

A factor that had little relation to globalization but had the same impact of worsening the Gini coefficient and increasing employment insecurity was biased technological development over the preceding three decades. It made globalization a scapegoat. The newly evolving technologies increased unemployment and spurred the domestic income gap, particularly in the industrial economies. They were skill-intensive and increased the premium on skills. They had an obvious factor bias. The new technologies reduced demand for unskilled workers, while increasing that for skilled workers. Advances in ICT, which became a robust engine of economic change, intensified this trend. They contributed to the worsening of the plight of low-skilled workers in the industrial economies. *Au contraire*, those with higher skills and superior education benefited markedly from this development. ICT-led as well as ICT-enabled automation and the transition to flexible production processes not only boosted productivity but also caused a shift from labor-intensive to capital- and skill-intensive production methods. The result was that those who owned neither capital nor skills became the losers. Income flows became skewed in favor of better qualified and higher-skilled workers. The newly evolving technology also accelerated the replacement of lower-skilled workers by physical capital.

Although expanding trade by the industrial economies with the developing economies, particularly the EMEs, which are low-cost producers of manufactures and services (Section 5.2), had an adverse impact on the lower-skilled labor segments and their wages in the industrial economies, biased technological development harmed them more (Lindert and Williamson, 2005). According to an empirical estimate, while globalization contributed 20 percent to wage stagnation and depression, ICT was responsible for 60 percent (de la Dehesa, 2006). Some large EMEs, like China, have begun to have the same effect on the labor force in the large developing economies. Thus, global integration has been wrongly accused of the problems facing lower-skilled labor, which, for the most part, emanated from the idiosyncratic technological evolution.

5.2 Gloomy Side of Globalization

The contemporary phase of globalization has led to swift movements of firms from mature industrial economies to developing and emerging-market economies, wherever they could find a market-friendly investment environment and a high quality labor force. As globalization progressed, this movement of firms became swift; with the inward movement of firms, jobs were created and with outward movement, they were readily shed. Samorin in Slovakia, a relatively new member of the EU, epitomized this trend. Slovakia is a cheerleader of globalization and public opinion enthusiastically supports it. Samorin is ideally located near a four-way border, where Slovakia, Hungary, Austria and the Czech Republic meet in a cat's cradle.

It had the advantage of location as well as an industrial base. In the 1990s, it was full of low-wage, experienced workers with a 20 percent unemployment rate. It attracted firms from Western Europe and even as far away as the US, where wages were high and labor markets highly regulated. EU officials explained that these movements of manufacturing activity were in keeping with the current trend in globalization and that this process made the EU economy more competitive.

For Samorin, this trend spelled a veritable economic boon, which led to a sharply declining unemployment rate, rising wages and a segment of the skilled labor force migrating to other EU countries. What people in Samorin did not see was that the same trend could move the incoming firms to other places for the same set of reasons. Since early 2000, many large firms decided to move on to China and Vietnam, shedding large numbers of Samorin workers. Also, as supply chains break into ever smaller sections, jobs are lost in one place and created in different parts of the globe. A typical example of globalized movements of firms and jobs is a German lighting firm that had moved to Slovakia which recently sent its manufacturing operations to China and its R&D back to Germany, shutting down its facility in Samorin. Similarly, a large Hong Kong textiles manufacturer that had set up manufacturing operations in Latvia shifted its production to Macedonia and Vietnam. In both these examples, the earlier locations lost a large number of firms and jobs. Prosperity that had come to Samorin turned into gloom. In a globalizing world economy, firms behave like citizens of the world.[23]

5.3   Four Horsemen of the Apocalypse

Little wonder that (i) import competition from low-income, low-wage developing countries and the EMEs, (ii) technologically assisted offshore outsourcing, (iii) global production networks and (iv) immigration of skilled and unskilled workers are regarded as the Four Horsemen of the Apocalypse by labor forces in the industrial economies. Both in the EU economies as well as in the US, imports from the EMEs and other low-wage developing countries increased steadily. In the EU-15,[24] the proportion of imports from these economies almost doubled. They soared from 2.7 percent of GDP in 1990 to 4.9 percent in 2004. In the US, this increase was a trifle more, from 2.2 percent of GDP to 4.4 percent over the same period. Another telling measure is the increase in imports from this country group as a proportion of total imports. For the EU-15 economies, they rose from 12.4 percent of total imports to 18.7 percent between 1990 and 2004. For the US, they soared from 24.4 percent to 33.7 percent.[25]

In the past, imports of manufactured goods into the EU economies as well as into the US were sourced from both the EMEs and other low-wage developing countries and other industrial economies. In the late 1980s, this trading pattern began to change and exports for manufactures from the former groups of countries to the industrial economies began to rise and its share almost doubled (Bivens, 2007a). Until the late 1980s many of these developing-country exporters were small and their exports of manufactured products were small in both relative and absolute terms. This is no longer true at the present time. Not only did they grow large but their number also increased. The steady increase in their exports of manufactures to the industrial economies led to a greater income distributional effect than in the early 1990s, when the exports of manufactured products were not large. The exporting economies were low-wage economies; hourly wages in these economies were only 3 percent of the US level. This transformation in the trading pattern suggested that "the distributional effects of trade may well be considerably larger now than they were in the early 1990s" (Krugman, 2008b, p. 4).

A large empirical study undertaken using a panel of 18 industrial countries over the period 1960–2000 inferred that while productivity growth increased labor's share of national income until the mid-1980s, after this point it became biased towards capital and increased profits. Both globalization and trade with low-income, low-wage, developing economies had a negative impact on labor's share of national income in the industrial economies after the mid-1980s. This was in accordance with the Heckscher-Ohlin theory. The role played by the ICT revolution is relevant in this context; ICT favored higher-skilled workers at the expense of low-skilled ones. Also, in keeping with the Heckscher-Ohlin theory, the industrial economies tended to specialize in skill-intensive industries, which *a fortiori* benefited workers with higher skills. Thus, the declining share of labor in the national income of the industrial economies was more of a structural or equilibrium factor, rather than a cyclical one (Guscina, 2007). This tendency is supported by the standard theoretical Stolper-Samuelson model (1941), which emphasizes that the trading pattern has a strong influence on income distribution. As this kind of trade pattern evolved with advancing globalization, the textbook analysis suggests that lower-skilled workers in wealthy countries were going to bear the brunt. Trade with labor-abundant economies causes a reduction in the relative price of labor-intensive goods in high-income industrial economies. This should *ceteris paribus* have an adverse effect on the wages of low-skilled and less-educated workers, in both absolute and relative terms.

Several categories of jobs that are frequently outsourced offshore at present were regarded as immune to international competition until recently. Increased import competition, technologically assisted offshore outsourcing, global networked production and the movement of skilled professionals in some high-technology production activities have created a new trend in global commerce during the contemporary phase of globalization. These are justifiably regarded as its characteristic features. The innovative trends are here to stay. If anything, they are likely to evolve and develop further. These trends have long-term implications for the global economy and will continue to influence employment security and the relative wages of workers in the mature industrial economies. This applies *a fortiori* in the short term. That said, empirical studies reveal that quantitatively the impact on wages was not trivial, but neither was it sizeable (Section 5.4).

5.4   A Flawed Line of Logic?

Most economists concur that in the long run, globalization, including that in labor markets, will have a beneficial economic impact in both industrial economies and their partner economies, be they developing economies or EMEs (Coe, 2008). Yet, towards the end of the decade, even those who considered that globalization would eventually have beneficial implications became concerned about the short-term income and wage disruptive impact in the wealthy industrial economies. To some, it started to appear larger than earlier envisaged; for political reasons, it soon became an overly sensitive issue. The revisionists gave two reasons for this: first, trade of the industrial economies with low-income, low-wage, countries continued to increase at a rapid pace (Section 5.2). Second, due to fragmentation of the production process and global networked production, workers in industrial countries had to compete with workers in the developing economies. This applied more in labor-intensive tasks than in capital- and technology-intensive ones (Krugman, 2008b).

However, this line of logic is not without its basic flaws. First, globalization is not limited to employment-shrinking and wage-stagnating imports in the industrial economies. It significantly increased exports, which tends to create jobs for a different category of workers, including blue-collar jobs. It went unnoticed that the exports that are generated are in higher-technology, higher-value-added, sectors. Therefore, the new jobs that are created are higher-wage jobs and result in far greater gains in the industrial economies than the losses incurred due to job losses. Second, not all the allegations of an increasing income gap in the industrial economies can stand close scrutiny. Lawrence (2008) measured the income gap between white-collar and blue-collar workers in the US and concluded that it did not widen markedly over the 1990–2006 period. Also, wages of the least-skilled workers improved in comparison to those of middle-skilled workers. On analyzing recent US wage statistics, Lawrence (2008, p. 10) found "wages in the 50th percentile rising more slowly than those in the 10th percentile and . . . the wages of high-school dropouts rising as rapidly as the wages of high-school graduates". Third, in many industrial economies, the labor force has been undergoing a transformation in that the proportion of white-collar workers in these economies has been on the rise while that of blue-collar workers is in decline. This is the natural outcome of these economies moving further up the technological ladder.

Scrutiny of recent research on this politically sensitive economic issue points to the fact that the culpability of globalization on this count can not be substantiated. Several empirical studies have concluded that "globalization does not appear to have had a *major* influence on the US labor market" (Blanchflower, 2000, p. 50 emphasis added).[26] Other studies using more current statistical data came to a more credible and realistic conclusion. They demonstrated that globalization was partly responsible for the wage and income gap between skilled and unskilled workers in the US and other industrial economies. Saito and Tokutsu (2006) concluded that while the effect of globalization on wages in industrial economies was statistically significant, it was small in magnitude. Its influence was limited, ranging between 10 percent and 12 percent. Most studies blamed skill-biased or factor-biased technological progress for the greater part of the wage gap.[27]

No doubt the EU economies or the US could stop all imports of manufactures from China and other low-income countries and produce them domestically using capital-intensive production methods. When imports are reopened, for sure they would displace workers in these economies, but without substantially widening wage inequality. However, a caveat is essential here. This is not to deny that the share of income going to a small segment of high-income earners in the workforce in the US has increased substantially since 2000. This small class comprised highly and professionally trained people, having PhDs, JDs, MBAs and MDs. They recorded a sharp inflation-adjusted increase in their take-home incomes.

6. GLOBALIZATION AND FINANCIAL VOLATILITY AND MACROECONOMIC INSTABILITY

Although integration of global financial markets is widely regarded as healthy for the global economy, recurrent financial crises have become its inevitable by-products. Global integration is held responsible for macroeconomic as well as financial instability. Numerous financial crashes in the EMEs in the recent past and the 2007–08 sub-prime mortgage crises in the US were blamed, partly or wholly, on financial globalization. They have had high economic and social costs, which vividly epitomized the downside of globalization. As for the plausible relationship between globalization and financial crises, to financially globalize governments are pressured to relax restrictions and regulations on domestic financial markets. The slackening or absence of restrictions and regulations makes feasible the financial crises that were precipitated during the 1990s and 2000s. Therefore, often these crises and financial market volatility are treated at the cost of financial globalization.

Going by simple logical proposition, financial globalization was to augment savings and investment in the developing economies that needed capital and underpin their growth endeavors, through direct and indirect channels. Intensive research found little evidence supporting this line of logic (Kose et al., 2006). Global financial flows failed to promote even risk sharing or consumption smoothening. Kose et al. (2007) found only modest evidence of risk sharing, which was nowhere near the level predicted by theory. Furthermore, during the contemporary phase of globalization, only industrial economies were able to attain to any degree a risk-sharing outcome. The developing economies were shut out of this benefit of financial globalization. Interestingly, even the EMEs, which participated in large cross-border capital flows, experienced little change in their ability to share risk.

Early in the 1980s, it was believed that the costs of macroeconomic volatility caused by liberalization of trade and financial markets in terms of long-term economic performance were minor. However, this view changed as more macroeconomic and financial crises occurred in the 1990s and early 2000s. Some of the economies that were struck by serious volatility had a meritorious record of growth and were regarded as well-managed economies, among them, the Asian economies that were struck down by crises in 1997–8. These crises reduced long-term growth and had a large welfare cost, leading to a serious adverse impact on the poor in crisis-affected economies. The Asian financial crisis roiled not only the crisis-affected Asian economies, but also the entire region (Das, 1999; Das, 2005b). Costs of these crises were borne "overwhelmingly by the developing world, and often disproportionately so by the poor", who were the most vulnerable groups (Nissanke and Thorbecke, 2007b, p. 2). This reinforces the oft-repeated allegation that globalization not only did not benefit the poor but also inflicted harm on this vulnerable group. In the post-Asian crisis period, central bankers began to regard financial globalization as being volatility-prone. To defend themselves from the vacillation and fickleness of financial markets and high-cost macroeconomic and financial crises, the EMEs began to self-insure by accumulating large foreign exchange reserves. China's foreign exchange reserves reached \$1.81 trillion in July 2008, the highest for any economy in the world (PBC, 2008). Other EMEs, particularly those in Asia, also accumulated sizeable amounts of forex reserves. This defensive strategy was self-defeating because massive reserves have low yields. This means that the social opportunity costs for economies with high reserves is large, often close to 1 percent of GDP.

6.1   Financial Volatility and Growth Performance

Economic and output volatility wrecks the investment climate and reduces investment in an economy. It is usually followed by a credit crunch in the economy, which affects long-term growth. Infrastructure and long-term investment projects are usually put on hold, if not shelved completely. Openness of financial markets was found to increase volatility of output. DiGiovanni and Levchenko (2006) employed industry-level panel data to prove that openness also results in higher sectoral volatility. Kose et al. (2005) documented that countries subject to higher output volatility show worse growth performance on average than those that are more stable. A 1 percentage point increase in the standard deviation of output growth is associated with a 0.16 percentage point decline in the average growth rate of a developing country. A caveat is essential here. An economy's structural characteristics, as well as the nature and origin of volatility, have a good deal of impact on the empirical relationship between volatility and growth. Many of the financial crises in the EMEs coincided with sudden stops in financial inflows, which exacerbated macroeconomic volatility and worsened the intensity of the crisis. These sudden stops work as financial shocks and tend to be costly for EMEs that are well-integrated into the global financial markets (Becker and Mauro, 2006).

Before the current (2007–09) global financial crisis erupted, financial volatility in the global economy had dampened. Developing economies and the EMEs have not suffered a financial crisis. The reason for their resilience in the face of financial turbulence was not the large mountains of liquidity amassed by them. Many have been running trade surpluses and lending capital to the rest of the world, particularly to credit-parched economies like the US. Rodrik (2007c, p. 8) pointed to the irony hidden in the reversal of the direction of capital flows. That is, in order to protect themselves from "the whiplash of financial crises", developing countries have been forced not only to shun the benefits of financial globalization, but also to make large capital transfers to rich countries. Has financial globalization caused a paradoxical and perverse flow of capital from the low-income developing to the high-income advanced industrial economies? This is a travesty of neoclassical economic thinking.

6.2   Question Mark over Global Capital Inflows and Rapid Growth

The proposition that financial globalization, or capital flows from economies with high capital-labor ratios to those with low capital-labor ratios, are normal and that they lead to rapid growth in the latter group of economies has been challenged. While prima-facie correct, this proposition deserves to be analyzed in depth, bearing in mind the current climate of financial flows. Correlations between the growth rate and current account balance over the period 1970–2004, analyzed by Bosworth and Collins (2003) and Prasad et al. (2007), are positive.[28] This implies that developing economies that did not rely on capital inflows grew more briskly, or those that depended less on global capital inflows grew faster. When Lowess regressions of economic growth on the current account for the entire sample of developing countries were computed for four sub-periods, a positive correlation for the first period, the 1970s, was not found. For the other three periods, correlation was uniformly positive and robust. When the sample of developing economies was divided into four groups based on whether (i) their ratios of investment to GDP and (ii) current account balance to GDP were above or below the median, it was observed that countries with higher investment achieved superior growth rates of GDP per capita than those with lower investment. This does not appear to be counterintuitive. However, a noteworthy observation was that the developing economies that had *higher* investment ratios as well as *lower* reliance on global capital inflows, which was reflected in their smaller current account deficits or larger surpluses, grew at a brisker rate. This group of developing economies had an approximately 1 percent higher GDP growth rate than those that had high investment but relied more on global capital finances. Economies do not grow at a brisk pace when they rely on external capital for investment. This is a crucial result for policy mandarins.

The reasons for weak GDP growth in the presence of global capital inflows may be credit and product market imperfections in the developing economies. Weaknesses in financial markets and macroeconomic distortions are endemic in the developing economies. Given these systemic flaws, they are generally not able to use external capital for growth in an efficient manner. Gourinchas and Jeanne (2006) concluded that, for many of them, lower productivity and a higher level of distortions are the principal factors determining GDP growth, not scarcity of capital. These difficulties limit their ability to absorb external capital.

7. TEXTBOOK GLOBALIZATION IS AT VARIANCE WITH REAL LIFE GLOBALIZATION

Proselytizers for globalization focus on its theoretical form, which is pristine and immaculate, and shows it to be a benign mechanism, ideal for building up total factor productivity (TFP), enhancing welfare gains and improving the economic lot of the impoverished groups of populations (Chapter 2).[29] To this end, market forces need to be freed. In reality, its operations and management are not precisely what the theory indicates. The potential gains from global integration are not always delivered in the manner indicated by economic theory. If contemporary globalization and its actual operation are closely examined, one can find that its negative aspects have been somewhat overlooked and consequently it was oversold à la Stiglitz (2005).

Those who have closely analyzed its unfolding have pointed to its potential weaknesses and asserted that many of its benefits are conditional (Rodrik, 2007a). They pan out only when certain macroeconomic policy prerequisites are present. For instance, it is vitally important that in the economies that benefit from globalization, market forces are perfectly operational. Furthermore, markets need to function in a competitive manner. That being said, some economies that are regarded as epitomes of successful globalization by its proponents, such as the four newly industrialized Asian economies (NIAEs),[30] China and lately India and Vietnam, did not play the game according to the orthodox neoclassical economic rules for appropriate and orderly global integration. China and Vietnam became WTO members late, years after achieving sustained high growth rates. This means that they could subsidize their exports and impose quantitative restrictions on imports. Trade liberalization in China, India and Vietnam was significantly delayed; tariff and other barriers were reduced well after the onset of rapid economic growth. Rodrik (2007c, p. 2) emphasized that Japan, Korea and China "combined orthodoxy on some (mostly macroeconomic) policy fronts with a good bit of heterodoxy on others (especially in microeconomic policies)". Each one of these economies "played by very different rules than those enunciated by the guardians of orthodox globalization – multilateral institutions such as the World Bank, IMF and GATT/WTO and by Western-based academics".

This successful group of Asian economies did not follow the full range of Washington Consensus strategies either. This proves that the problem essentially is not with globalization but with its implementation and management. Accepting the phenomenon of globalism uncritically for its strengths, while ignoring its limitations, can turn out to be a disadvantageous proposition for the economy in question, *a fortiori* when the weaknesses are left unattended to by policy mandarins in individual economies. No doubt the so-called Washington Consensus and its emphasis on deregulated markets can have a welfare-enhancing impact; national policies based on the basic realities are of crucial importance for eschewing the negative consequences of globalization. The process of globalization needs to be based on a *sui generis* strategic structure.

Although the potential benefits of competently managed global integration are obvious (and have been dealt with in Chapter 2), it is often not proficiently managed. The role of supranational institutions of global governance, particularly the IMF, in this regard has come in for frequent criticism. Besides, "the rules of globalization have been determined by the advanced industrial countries, for their interests, or more precisely for the interests of special interests" in their countries, which not only made the operation of globalization complex but also more skewed in favor of the industrial economies (Stiglitz, 2005, p. 228). There is a lot of insight and logic to what Stiglitz contended. Democracies in the industrial economies have functioned for a long time; consequently their systems of checks and balances have evolved and normally work well. For the most part, these systems try to balance commercial interests, which assume a great deal of importance, vis-à-vis other social interests such as labor, consumers and the environment. In a strategic decision-making process, they are regarded as significant in their own right. In contrast, the system of global economic governance is relatively young and lacks a checks and balances mechanism. The supranational organizations were designed as professional institutions in their respective areas of expertise, which made their vision and focus narrow. The agendas of the IMF and the World Bank are run by central bankers and finance ministers of member countries, while in the WTO, trade or commerce ministers call the shots. The resulting near-sightedness and limited vision of these institutions often leads to sub-optimal decisions. Their policies have often shown a strong imbalance in favor of economic variables. Non-economic variables are ignored, sometimes at a high cost to societies.

The failure of globalization is routinely blamed on corrupt and incompetent governments in the developing countries, particularly their failure to launch macroeconomic reforms and complete lack of transparency in governance. No doubt these problems exist and the allegations ring true. It is imperative for developing economies to address these damaging and costly irritants and to implement much-needed macroeconomic reforms. However, this is not an explanation of the negative aspects and impact of ongoing globalization. Even if corruption is eradicated and transparency in governance is achieved, globalization can, and does, have a detrimental effect on developing economies. The Argentinean crisis is one case in point. Currency depreciation by its principal trading partners, while it followed a fixed exchange rate regime, was enough to drive it into a crisis situation. Privatization, the IMF-suggested remedial measure, caused the situation to deteriorate further. Thus, blaming developing economies for the problems created by globalization is not always correct.

Accepting the wisdom of the Washington Consensus only partially has resulted in rapid growth with poverty alleviation for the East Asian economies, China and lately India and Vietnam. An inconvenient truth is that this group of economies flouted several policy guidelines of the Washington Consensus with impunity, devised their own development strategies, taking into account their own economic realities, and eventually had wholesome, even meritorious, results to show for it. Paradoxically, these economies succeeded despite their heterodox strategies. A good question to ask is whether they succeeded due to them.

There are many clear examples of this behavior. The Washington Consensus prescribed rapid deregulation, liberalization of trade and financial sectors in these economies, which progressed only at a snail's pace. All of them had elaborate government-designed economic and industrial plans, and the strength of their private sector grew, but again gradually, in short steps. As noted above (in this section), lowering trade barriers and opening up of the domestic economy also advanced rather slowly. Most importantly, the financial sector was kept closed for a long period, particularly to short-term capital inflows. Both China and India still have not fully liberalized their capital account (Das, 2006). While these economies had no illusions regarding the contribution of the Washington Consensus, as well as the value of global integration, they managed and crafted their macroeconomic policies according to their own exclusive needs and ensured that on balance they work to their advantage.

China's case is particularly enlightening in this regard. Its rapidly globalizing economy is a testimony to the fact that economies can productively and energetically integrate globally, even after violating every rule in the book of the proselytizers for globalization. Significant trade liberalization began late in China, particularly when the economy was gearing up for WTO accession. The dual value of the renminbi yuan was also unified late, in 1994. China persistently delayed its liberalization of financial markets. The most striking incongruity in this regard is China's deferred adoption of private-property rights; the property law was adopted by the National People's Congress in 2007 and came into force in October 2007. A large number of its gigantic state-owned enterprises (SOEs) have still not been privatized; they are merrily if wastefully chugging along. It continues to be a glaring weak spot of the economy. China's road to privatization has been long and winding (Das, 2008c). An extraordinary feature of the Chinese economy is that it managed to achieve a high degree of global integration despite the fact that it ignored the rule-book. The Chinese policy makers were pragmatic and earnest, and realized that "the solution to their problems lay in institutional innovations suited to the local conditions – the household responsibility system, town and village enterprises (TVEs), special economic zones (SEZs), partial liberalization in agriculture and

122   *Two faces of globalization*

industry – rather than in off-the-shelf blueprints and Western rules of good behavior" (Rodrik, 2007a, p. 239).

Two earlier success stories of dynamic growth and global integration, those of Korea and Taiwan, point in the same direction. During their early growth periods, they made use of high tariff barriers, import quotas, local-content regulations. These policy measures go counter to the grain of neoclassical economics, are regarded as anathema by proselytizers of globalization and are prohibited under WTO regulations. Furthermore, both the dragon economies strictly regulated capital flows until the early 1990s. Likewise, India has begun a lucrative integration with the global economy and recently upped its GDP growth rate to a much swifter rate than ever in its post-World War II economic history. In achieving this growth performance, its competitive services sector was of help. Until recently, India had one of the most protectionist and irrationally restrictive trade regimes in the world. Its financial markets and capital account were liberalized quite late and hesitantly. Several controls still remain in place (Reddy, 2007).

In contrast to East Asia, China and India, many developing countries and EMEs liberalized trade and capital flows in a hurry, in accordance with the policy prescription of the Washington Consensus. They were soon rewarded with financial crises and poor macroeconomic performance. One country group that stands out is Latin America. Several large economies from this region that adopted the globalization agenda over-credulously were unpleasantly surprised at the unexpected outcome. They recorded growth rates which were far lower than their long-term averages and their income distribution worsened. Their economies also suffered from repeated bouts of volatility. Their GDP growth performance during the period 1990–2003 was much poorer when compared to those of East and South Asia. While East Asian economies grew at an average annual rate of 6.4 percent and South Asia at 3.3 percent, Latin American economies grew by a measly 1.0 percent over this period.[31]

Theoretically, integrated financial markets were going to be a boon to the global economy. They were expected to effortlessly facilitate channeling of capital from where it was to where it was needed and could be productively utilized. High saving economies like China, Japan, the other East Asian economies, Germany and the members of the GCC began investing in the US, where the fiscal deficit was high and the economy had suffered from a chronic deficit in the balance of trade in goods. The US economy needed external capital. One could treat this scenario as innocuous and take it as representing mere claims from "intertemporal trade" in goods and financial services (Cordon, 2007, p. 363). Alternatively, it can be couched in neutral terms of saving and investment imbalance in the economy. However, as it transpired, in a short span of time, huge current account imbalances in the global economy developed. They were an unforeseen consequence of financial globalization. By 2006, the build-up of macroeconomic imbalances began to pose a serious threat to the global economy. Based on the US fiscal and trade policies of the 2000–05 period, this deficit was projected to grow to 10 percent of GDP in 2010; at that point, US debt was projected to reach 60 percent of GDP. It was projected to cross 100 percent of the GDP by 2015 (Buira and Abeles, 2006). A disorderly unwinding of these imbalances could mean rapid dollar depreciation, a sharp increase in US interest rates, which in turn could have serious consequences for global financial markets and eventually global GDP growth. A hard landing for the global economy, and a prolonged recession, were well within the realm of possibilities. However, assisted by an IMF-backed process of multilateral consultation, an abrupt unraveling of the imbalances was avoided. The imbalances peaked in 2007. In early 2008, they began to narrow. Slower growth and a sharply depreciated dollar led to a decline in the US current account deficit. Also, the surplus economies made some progress in implementing policies made under the IMF-sponsored program to bring down their ever rising surpluses (Faruqee, 2008).

8.   PLAUSIBLE SHAPE OF THINGS: WILL THE GENIE GO BACK INTO THE BOTTLE?

A century ago, the erstwhile wave of globalization fell victim to a backlash in 1913, and went into reverse. This was partly provoked by distributional consequences. The question whether the present phase of globalization is likely to meet the same fate is increasingly being pondered. It is widely acknowledged that the ongoing global economic integration has a downside and that it needs to be addressed by policy mandarins at national level thoughtfully and clairvoyantly. Will the problems spawned by contemporary globalization derail it? Could they reverse some forms of global economic integration and undermine the progress achieved from globalization so far?

   An educated and considered answer to the first question will have to be in the negative. So long as the world economy succeeds in keeping away from a major armed conflict or a steep recession, the realistic probability of a full-fledged globalization backlash in the latter half of 2008, comparable to the one that occurred approximately a century ago, was not strong. That being said, there could be harmful ramifications from globalization fatigue. Problematic issues associated with globalization and its negative public perception (Chapter 4) are capable of undoing some forms of global economic integration and undermining the progress achieved thus far.

The present core of institutions of economic governance has succeeded in laying down a reasonably sound institutional foundation for globalization. For instance, the WTO regulations that oblige member countries to keep their markets free of tariff, non-tariff and other barriers to multilateral trade have evolved quite well, and this process is continuing in fits and starts. The WTO has a more solid institutional and political base than its predecessor, the General Agreement on Tariffs and Trade (GATT), and a much firmer structure of rules and regulations (Das, 2007d). The objective of the WTO regulations is to lay down a foundation for multilateral trade so that economies can exploit their comparative advantage, and trade in goods and services so that they can produce at lower opportunity costs than their trade partners. Second, demands from manufacturing industries for protection are muted. Third, the technological advances of the preceding three decades cannot be abruptly undone. Boeing 747 and Airbus A-380 will not be grounded. Fourth, barring the unforeseen, the technological revolution that supported the current phase of globalization is likely to continue. Fifth, costs of transport and communication are also likely to continue their downward movement, enabling business corporations to expand their business operations globally. Sixth, global trends in networked production have become increasing intricate and cannot be undone in a short span of time. The same applies to global R&D, designing, marketing and financial networks, which have also become shock resistant to an extent and therefore likely to persist. Seventh, talent movements have also gained significant momentum, particularly those of technologically trained professionals. These factors debilitate the case for a globalization backlash, or a complete reversal of the contemporary phase of globalization.

However, given the problems spawned by the onward march of globalization, discussed in the preceding sections, resistance to global integration has been on the increase in the advanced industrial economies. Competition for resources, particularly energy, has become intense and has been affecting global growth. In future, the probability of further intensification is strong. If one takes a level-headed view of the pros and cons, a plausible course of action could well be as follows: barring a serious crisis, the probability of a reversal of backlash of globalization was not high. A major global financial crisis did occur (2007–09) and globalization, particularly financial globalization, did go into reverse gear. After the recovery from the crisis, the process of globalization would start, albeit its pace would be retarded.

To some of those who have been examining this process closely, forewarnings of a slowdown in the pace of globalization have become increasingly obvious for some time. If the negative consequences of global integration are not adequately and imaginatively addressed by national governments, this slowdown may be prolonged. If that comes to pass, globalization is sure to wane as a powerful transformative force in the global economy. Stagnation in some forms or channels of global economic integration may occur. In addition, the welfare gains that global integration has made feasible thus far may well be undermined.

It is apparent that a great deal will depend upon the abilities of national policy makers to resolve the challenging economic issues. No doubt some will manage them deftly and in so doing ease the onward movement of global economic integration. Others may not be able to do so and may cause a policy backlash. Can some pragmatic policy measures be taken to ward off the slowdown in global integration? There is prudence in taking the following two-tier precautionary measures. Domestically, a creative and upright approach would be to emphasize the benefits of the current phase of globalization to wary constituents, make sure that those benefits materialize and then to ensure that those benefits are distributed in as equitable a manner as possible. At the global level, creating an overarching structure of rules with the involvement of the supranational institutions like the Bretton Woods twins, the WTO, the Organization for Economic Cooperation and Development (OECD) and empowering them to advance and manage globalization in accordance with those multilateral rules, in an even-handed manner, without undue interference by any monolithic power, could be a pragmatic way out. It would lead to the creation of systemic strength to administer and manage globalization.

9. SUMMARY AND CONCLUSIONS

Some economists and other social scientists regard contemporary globalization as a source of serious problems. There are others who, logically or illogically, consider it a negative, harmful, destructive, marginalizing and malevolent influence on economies and societies. Populist views on globalization frequently tend to be on the negative side. Anecdotal accounts often draw a downbeat and damaging image of ongoing globalization. No doubt, globalization can create opportunities for accelerating growth for participating economies, but it can also pose myriad challenges to and impose constraints on policy makers. It has created a litany of national, regional and global economic problems. In addition, it is correctly blamed for the uneven distribution of the benefits from globalization. These are badly skewed within and between countries.

Virulent criticism of globalization often comes from politicians, largely because they get more mileage out of being globalization skeptics than out

of being its proselytizers. Opinions and writings in news media and journals
have begun to question the need and sustainability of global economic integration. In general, present (in 2008) global policy environment is far from
globalization-friendly. That the Doha Round of MTNs was allowed to
languish is a proof of disillusionment with and estrangement from globalization. Not all deprecation is unwarranted. There are distinct possibilities
of globalization hurting the poor. It has been observed that the lower the
skill level of the people, the greater is the probability of getting adversely
affected by the onward march of globalization. It has caused the closure of
businesses and worsening rates of unemployment, which aroused strong
upsetting emotional responses in many people and societies. Also, there
are strong arguments against certain sets of policies that are frequently
recommended by the supranational economic institutions for advancing
globalization, for instance, the so-called Washington Consensus.

Among lay persons, there is no scarcity of those who are completely
and intransigently opposed to globalism and globalization and are convinced of their perverse and malevolent contribution. Protracted protests,
both peaceful and violent, by detractors of the globalization process
have become commonplace. The WTO and the Bretton Woods twins
have become frequent targets for those who disapprove of globalization
because they see them as the principal perpetrators or arch villain. Also, it
is often unclear whether the grievances of the detractors are more against
big business in general than against the global integration of the world
economies. The critics of globalization believe that the activities of big
business organizations and TNCs have expanded far too rapidly and that
they have become economically too powerful, garnering a disproportionate proportion of global resources.

Rising income inequality, as measured by the Gini coefficient, is held
to be another weakness of globalization. Many rapidly globalizing economies, both developing and industrial, demonstrate widening domestic or
within-country income inequality. Rapidly expanding multilateral trade
and FDI have exacerbated this intra-economy increase in income inequality. A case study of China, which globalized at a rapid pace, emphatically
proves this point.

Import competition from low-wage EMEs, technologically assisted
offshore outsourcing, global production networks and the immigration of
skilled and unskilled workers are regarded as the Four Horsemen of the
Apocalypse by labor forces in the industrial economies. That globalization
creates unemployment is another ubiquitous angst, particularly in wealthy
industrial countries. The globalization-employment-insecurity nexus has
compelling and damaging implications for societies. In the industrial
economies, this nexus has instigated something of a popular movement

against globalization. That some categories of workers, particularly those on the lower rungs of the skill and technology ladder, have lost their jobs due to the advancing global integration of labor markets cannot be denied. Therefore, labor forces in the EU, the US and other Anglo-Saxon countries have demonized globalization for seemingly legitimate reasons. However, this view of globalization of the labor market as the source of unemployment runs counter to what economists assert, that is, the integration of the labor force globally is a source of long-run welfare gains both to the domestic economy as well as to the global economy. Also, while increasing trade with the EMEs and developing economies has affected the labor force, particularly low-skilled workers, more at present than in the past, quantitatively this impact is still modest.

Proselytizers for globalization focus on its theoretical form, which is pristine, immaculate and streamlined, and show it to be a benign mechanism, ideal for improving TFP and enhancing welfare gains and, thereby, improving the economic lot of impoverished groups in populations. In reality, its operations and management are not precisely what the theory indicates. The potential gains from global integration are not always delivered as indicated by economic theory. If contemporary globalization and its actual operation are closely examined, one finds that its negative aspects have been somewhat overlooked and consequently it has been oversold as a policy instrument.

Those who have analyzed its operation comprehensively have pointed to its potential weaknesses and asserted that many of its benefits are conditional. They pan out when certain macroeconomic policy prerequisites are present. For instance, it is vitally important that market forces are perfectly operational and that markets function in a competitive manner. Interestingly, some economies that are regarded as the poster babies of globalization by its proponents, such as the four NIAEs, China and lately India and Vietnam, did not play the game according to the orthodox neoclassical economic rules for appropriate and orderly global integration. Nor did this successful group of economies follow the full range of Washington Consensus strategies. This proves that many of the basic problems lie not with globalization but with its implementation and management.

NOTES

1. See for instance Bhagwati (2004), Wolf (2005b) and Thirlwell (2007b).
2. The term industrial country has become a misnomer, because some of the emerging-market economies, like China, have become extensively industrialized. The contribution

of the industrial sector to their GDP is larger than that in the wealthy countries of the developed world, whose economies are overwhelmingly dominated by the services sector. These countries have become large exporters of manufactured products as well.
3. See Note 4, Chapter 2.
4. The reference here is to Lou Dobb's 6 o'clock news on CNN.
5. For a literature survey, see, Nissanke and Thorbecke (2007a).
6. In May 2008, after staying at their peak, grain prices declined.
7. Nobel Prize-winning economist and former Senior Vice President of the World Bank, Joseph E. Stiglitz, is one such academic analyst.
8. See Stiglitz (2005) also.
9. For instance, several important European countries, including France, voted against the EU's constitutional treaty. Mittal Steel's successful bid to acquire Arcelor was initially blocked by the French and Luxembourg governments.
10. After the crucial Group-of-Four (G-4) meetings of June 2007 in Potsdam, Germany, when multilateral convergence seemed tantalizingly close because the components of an interim agreement had been identified, which was to become a launching pad for the rest of the Doha agreement. Negotiations broke down once again; disarray in the Doha Round continued. There was a discernible rise in protectionist sentiment in industrial economies after this point (Das, 2008d). This was taken as an indicator of the reversal of the current phase of globalization.
11. This survey was conducted for the BBC World Service by the international polling firm GlobeScan, in collaboration with the Program on International Policy Attitude (PIPA) at the University of Maryland in January 2008. See "Widespread Unease about Economy and Globalization", available at http://www.worldpublicopinion.org/pipa/articles/btglobalizationtradeera/446.php?lb=btgl&pnt=446&nid=&id=. World Public Opinion, Washington, DC; posted on February 7, 2008.
12. The Gulf Cooperation Council (GCC) was established in 1981. Its members are Bahrain, Kuwait, Oman, Qatar, Saudi Arabia and the United Arab Emirates (UAE).
13. This G-7 meeting was hosted by the US Treasury Secretary Henry Paulson and Federal Reserve Chairman Ben S. Bernanke in Washington, DC, on October 22. Aside from the US, members of the G-7 include Japan, Germany, France, Britain, Italy and Canada.
14. Several noted scholars, including Kenneth Rogoff, Patrick Mulloy and Edwin Truman, participated in these hearings. Christopher Cox, the Chairman of Securities and Exchange Commission, expressed his concern regarding the operations of the SWFs in a speech at Harvard University on October 24, 2007.
15. John Williamson reasonably argued that the set of policy reforms that would serve the developing economies, particularly those of Latin America, should encompass the following ten propositions: emphasis on fiscal discipline, a redirection of public expenditure priorities toward fields offering both high economic returns and the potential to improve income distribution, such as primary health care, primary education and infrastructure, tax reform (to lower marginal rates and broaden the tax base), interest rate liberalization, a competitive exchange rate, trade liberalization, liberalization of FDI inflows, privatization, deregulation (in the sense of abolishing barriers to entry and exit) and secure property rights. Its emphasis was on deregulated markets.
16. Rodrik (2007a), see chapter 9.
17. For example, Joseph Stiglitz.
18. Emphasis in original.
19. The Gini coefficient can assume any value between 0 and 1 (or 0% to 100%). The closer the value is to 1 (or 100%), the more unequal is the distribution. This implies that only a small section of society possesses an overwhelmingly large proportion of income.
20. The sources of these statistical data are EIU (2008a) and EIU and CPII (2007).
21. The source of these statistical data is the World Bank (2007).
22. Das (2008c) provides a meticulous analysis of how this urban–rural inequality developed and intensified in China.
23. See *The Economist* (2008d), pp. 52ff.

24. The EU-15 comprised the following 15 countries: Austria, Belgium, Denmark, Finland, France, Germany, Greece, Ireland, Italy, Luxembourg, Netherlands, Portugal, Spain, Sweden and the United Kingdom. This was the number of member countries in the European Union prior to the accession of ten countries on 1 May 2004.
25. These statistical data come from OECD STAN Bilateral Trade Database for 2008.
26. Both Blanchflower (2000) and Slaughter (2000) provide extensive reviews of research papers on this issue.
27. Other noteworthy writings include Pierce (2001), Amiti and Wei (2005a), Goldin and Katz (2007) and Reynolds (2007).
28. A negative current account balance indicates a net capital inflow, while a positive current account balance indicates just the opposite, that is, net outflows of capital.
29. Total factor productivity (TFP) measures the use of better technology and improvements in the quality of labor and capital. TFP explains between half and three-quarters of economic growth. Differences in TFP account for most of the differences in output growth rates among countries.
30. They are the Hong Kong SAR, the Republic of Korea, Singapore and Taiwan.
31. Sources of these statistics are various issues of the World Bank (2007).

4. A vituperative anti-globalization movement

1. ANTAGONISTS OF GLOBALIZATION

Many people from different walks of life and with diverse disciplinary and ideological backgrounds regard globalization as a malevolent phenomenon. They regard globalization with deep-seated skepticism and hostility. Together, they succeeded in launching a fairly successful anti-globalization movement. Evidence of trenchant and unyielding opposition to globalization is endemic. Its manifestation in diverse forms is widespread. When venerable scholars like Joseph Stiglitz (2003a, 2003b, 2005, 2006), with priceless academic credibility, write critical books like *Globalization and its Discontents*, they are avidly read by a large readership of academics, policy makers and business decision makers. Award-winning journalists like Naomi Klein (2000, 2002)[1] write articles and books discrediting globalization, in particular the business practices of large business houses and transnational corporations (TNCs). Op-ed and editorial pages of major news dailies are filled with frequent criticism of different facets of globalization. The extreme views on globalization have attracted a great deal of attention, particularly in the popular media and the economic and business press. The information age has provided the movement against globalization with many more instruments to spread its disapproval of globalization than were available in the past.

The protagonists and antagonists hold viewpoints that are frequently diametrically opposite. So much so that they interpreted the gruesome terrorist attack of September 11 on the World Trade Center from two opposite angles and read into it vindication of their own respective positions. The antagonists were certain that it was a justification of their belief that global integration had widened the gap between the haves and the have-nots and created a great deal of resentment among a large number of people. The destruction of an icon of global business was a manifestation of this resentment. Conversely, the message that those in favor of globalization drew was that the cure for such a large gap between the haves and the have-nots was more not less globalization, which could strengthen the economic base of the global economy, benefit the have-nots as well as spreading the values of freedom and civil conduct worldwide.

The objective of this chapter is to study the anti-globalization movement. We trace its birth, delve into its proclivities and activities and the process by which it gained strength over the years. As globalization progressed, the concepts and mindset of the activists underwent a steady transformation. What they found acceptable and what they totally rejected went on changing over the years. These transformations and adjustments in their approach, attitude and outlook is the focus of this chapter. The activists were not lightly brushed aside by the international institutional and governmental establishments. The rationale behind this has been examined. Several influential non-governmental organizations (NGOs) are an ingrained part of the anti-globalization movement. They not only played a meaningful role, but also contributed to its strength. The antagonists have not always been correct; they made several conceptual mistakes. Towards the end, we try to see whether the present phase of globalization is in jeopardy of stalling or reversing because so many question and disapprove of it.

1.1 Anti-globalism

The antagonists blame globalization for a litany of global economic problems, although they accept some of the assertions of its supporters. Although fundamentally they were passionately disinclined to support the policies of economic neoliberalism,[2] numerous diverse causes also became associated with anti-globalism. Anti-globalists regarded the majority of consequences of globalization as harmful. Downward pressure on wages and increasing unemployment in some manufacturing and services sectors were some of their principal grievances. In particular, in their discontent, they link concepts of capitalism and the behavior of large business firms. Anti-globalists have been completely averse to the policies of supranational institutions that are responsible for global economic governance. They are sure of the erroneous, if not downright ignorant, ways of these institutions. In addition, they believe that the activities of large business houses and the TNCs have expanded far too rapidly and that they have become economically too powerful for comfort. As TNCs politically superseded governments and garnered a disproportionate proportion of global resources, old nationalistic resentments began to be directed against them.

There is no gainsaying the fact that the ongoing phase of globalization, a source of dynamic economic growth, has created both winners and losers. It is often not an unambiguously and uniformly beneficial process, leading to win-win outcomes. It cannot be denied that, notwithstanding the unprecedented benefits of globalization over the preceding three decades, some socio-economic groups have suffered damaging economic and social consequences. Also, its benefits are glaringly asymmetrically distributed. Incongruously, benefits went asymmetrically to those at the higher end of the income and wealth spectrum, whereas costs were largely borne by those at or close to the bottom. A large and conspicuous disparity has become obvious between the return to capital and the rewards of labor (Chapter 3, Section 3.3). An ironic fact in this context is that globalization has been out of favor with large population groups in the countries it has benefited most, namely the advanced and high-income industrial countries.

A seemingly unbridgeable chasm has been created between economic evidence and popular gloomy and downbeat views on globalization. The principal reason for this difference in the two perspectives is that increased trans-border flows of goods and factors of production (including labor) can have adverse results when there are domestic market failures or regulatory weaknesses (Chapter 3, Section 1). Both of these need to be dealt with directly, with the help of appropriate domestic policy measures. They will indeed reduce the costs of globalization. If the appropriate policy measures are not adopted and implemented without delay, the danger of a globalization backlash looms, which could stall, defer or reverse some forms of global economic integration. The ultimate effect would be the undermining or loss of the economic progress that has so far been achieved. Second, anti-globalism is also promoted by improved global communications and the reach of television and broadcasting. While a beneficial phenomenon, it has a downside. It has enhanced global awareness of differences between rich and poor economies. The poor were less aware of this disparity in the past, albeit the differences did exist.

1.2   Change in the Zeitgeist

Public attitudes in the late 1980s and early 1990s were changed by some of the negative consequences of globalization. Many of the grievances aired by the anti-globalization movement were legitimate. A broad populist movement developed during the 1990s. As stated above, while essentially this was a movement against economic neoliberalism, it was also a cynical mélange of several issues about which groups of people were disgruntled. For instance, protestors for protectionism, ecological, national, native culture, democracy and human rights-related issues coalesced and became a part of the anti-globalization movement. Judging by the number of articles and books produced on this theme, anti-globalization has also been the focus of a good deal of academic research. As alluded to above, several noted contemporary scholars, such as Joseph Stiglitz, Dani Rodrik, Francis Fukuyama, Samuel Huntington and Stephen Korbin, have contributed seminal thoughts on these and related issues, although none can be regarded as part of the populist anti-globalization movement. Their analysis of the failings of globalization is of a thought-provoking and academic nature (Chapter 3, Section 1). Opponents of globalization believed that globalization tends to interpret and analyze the world in narrowly economic term. This majestic stand of economists was regarded as counterproductive and became a source of indignation for those who saw many flaws in the onward march of globalization.

The new public outlook of the 1990s was quite distinct from the earlier celebration of victory by free-market forces that ushered in globalization. This change in the *zeitgeist* was manifested in the speeches and writings of influential global opinion leaders. Financial leaders like George Soros attacked great wealth, wanton money-making, the irresponsible behavior of investors, and the "unsound and unsustainable capitalist system". Soros warned against the profit-maximizing behavior which "ignores the demands of morality" (Soros, 2005, p. 123). Concern about the negative influences of globalization was publicly expressed by revered public opinion leaders like Pope John Paul II, who was once an ardent supporter of globalization.[3]

The allegation of asymmetric distribution of benefits of globalization is decidedly correct. Countries on the continent of Africa benefited relatively less from the favorable influences of globalization. A large majority failed to take advantage of the dynamic growth impulses provided by globalization. Consequently, the incidence of poverty rose in this region during the contemporary phase of globalization. The number of people living at or below $1 a day, measured in PPP and inflation adjusted, doubled in Africa between 1981 and 2001, increasing from 164 million to 313 million (Nissanke and Thorbecke, 2007c). This poverty line was recently updated to $1.25 a day in 2005 PPP (Ravallion et al., 2008). There were many other countries that failed to globalize and join this benign economic movement. One measure of their failure to globalize is their declining trade-to-GDP ratio. Almost 50 countries fall into the category of non-globalizers. Apparently, this large group, with a population of some 2 billion, did not benefit from globalization. They were the bystanders of globalization. If anything, these economies became more marginalized. Collier (2007) identified a sub-group of economies which he referred to as "trapped" countries. This sub-group of countries has been in steady economic decline. Approximately 980 million people live in this sub-group, which includes countries like Bolivia, Cambodia, Haiti, Laos, Myanmar, North

Korea and Yemen. Over 70 percent of these bottom billion live in Africa. Stagnation and poverty is their common fate.

2. GENESIS OF THE ANTI-GLOBALIZATION LOBBY

The anti-globalization lobby or movement was born at an early stage in the current wave of globalization. Its inception took place around the late 1980s. During the 1990s, the movement had a highly visible presence. It began to wane after September 11, 2001 (Section 7). At the beginning, the movement was broad and simple in its anti-globalism. This was a period of declining influence of organized labor in the industrial economies as well as popular nationalist movements in the developing economies. This decline was one of the basic impulses behind the emergence of the anti-globalization movement. Besides, this was also the period when China had rejected Maoism and turned to what it called "market socialism", and the Former Soviet Union (FSU) and the East European economies, having rejected Marxism, were turning to embrace the market-economy system. The latter group of countries frequently appeared to be in total chaos, in a state of lawlessness. Anecdotal accounts of gangster capitalism in this set of economies frequently appeared in the international media. This contributed to a negative impression of contemporary capitalism.

Anti-globalization sentiments were subsequently buttressed by a spate of corruption, financial, accounting and sex scandals in Belgium, Britain, France, Italy and particularly the United States (US), during this period. The image of the US business and financial world suffered a serious blow because of corporate crimes – which went undetected and unpunished for a considerable length of time – in multi-billion dollar corporations like Enron and WorldCom. Many financially average families lost their life's savings in these scandals. These major financial and corporate scandals sullied the image of the US, which was regarded as a pioneer of enterprising buccaneer capitalism. It engendered a high degree of public distrust of the governing as well as social elites, which found themselves on the defensive. In contrast, the steady progress of China's market-oriented reforms was admired by many. However, it was seen as an inhuman form of capitalism by some Western commentators. Its environmental and social side-effects were widely disapproved of and it was believed that China's rapid growth was coming at a high social cost (Das, 2008c).

This mindset fed the anti-globalization movement, which grew in an atmosphere of self-doubt, moral turpitude and consternation, as well as of general disorientation among governments and ruling elites in the industrial countries.[4] Reacting in a confused manner, governments and elites supported the youthful idealism of the anti-globalization activists and tried to accommodate and incorporate them into quasi-governmental organizations. This strengthened the anti-globalization lobby, making activists bolder than ever before in their disapproval of the process of globalization, free-market forces and liberal neoclassical economic precepts. They took the moral high ground, while the political leadership of the capitalist world struggled to save face.

3. SUCCESS OF THE ANTI-GLOBALIZATION MOVEMENT

The anti-globalization movement was particularly opposed to the agendas and actions of supranational organizations of economic governance that are perceived to proliferate and advance the cause of globalism (Section 1.1). At the annual meetings and conferences organized by the United Nations (UN), the International Monetary Fund (IMF), the World Bank and the World Trade Organization (WTO), the Group-of-Seven (G-7) summits and after 1994, G-8[5] summits, participants, delegates and world leaders found themselves pilloried by vocal groups of activists and protesters. While they were the most visible targets of the anti-globalization lobby, they were only the tip of the iceberg. Small-scale local rallies were organized in as many as a hundred cities in the world on the days earmarked for large demonstrations. Many of the activists were generally well-informed and most were well-intentioned. However, the large groups of anti-globalization activists also contained closet anarchists; therefore, their peaceful protest marches frequently turned violent, fierce and occasionally, even vicious, which often caused an image problem for the anti-globalization movement.

Broadly speaking, while the summiteers and conference participants of the largest industrial economies and the institutions of global economic governance were essentially committed to globalization, free markets and liberalization of domestic economies, the anti-globalization activists promoted and demanded a halt to globalization and the strait-jacketing of market forces. The two sides had polar viewpoints. The antagonists trenchantly protested against what they regarded as the sell-off of the global commons. The success of these critics of globalization was greater than was justified by their social weight. The social base of the anti-globalization lobby comprises the middle classes, essentially in the industrial economies, and the NGOs, based in both developing and industrial countries. The principal reason for their more than expected success was that the anti-globalization sentiments of the protestors outside the ornate conference halls and their call to regulate market forces in *part* reflected the premonitions and gut feelings of at least some of the summiteers and conference participants inside those elegant halls. That said, the anti-growth sentiments of the anti-globalization movement were the proposed alternative to globalization. They were not soundly premised. When examined more closely, the zero-growth concept of economic development did not go very far. Growth is imperative for development and poverty alleviation. There are multiple paths to achieve growth; zero growth need not be one of them. Rapid-growth achievers like China and Chile had little in common. The same applies to the growth strategies adopted by Botswana and Singapore.

The simplicity with which the anti-globalization movement started changed in the early 2000s, when it became more subtle and discriminating. The anti-globalizers grew less broadly opposed to globalization in general. They no longer sought un-globalization or the dismantling of global networks of economic and other linkages. The anti-globalizers began to differentiate between different kinds of globalization and accept some, while rejecting others. For instance, there were those that were clearly and steadfastly against what they referred to as corporate globalization, while there were others who went all out to establish global social justice. Thus, from a unified broadside against globalism, this movement turned into a branched opposition to different kinds of globalism. Those in the academic community who opposed globalization in the past, more recently have attempted to stake out different models of globalization, while not rejecting the basic premise of globalism. Academic scholars began to propose changing the emphasis of globalization, as well as making use of policy compromises in implementing it.

Information and communication technology (ICT) helped make the anti-globalization movement stronger and activism widespread. The anti-globalization movement relies heavily on electronic communication. Email and text messaging enabled activists to marshal large number of members and launch hard-hitting campaigns, resulting in real-time social action. The 2003 protest against the G-8 Summit in Genoa and the 2006 protest in Prague against the Bank-Fund annual meeting were large in terms of the sheer accumulation of activists. They seemed like a global movement, with representatives from several European and North American countries and organizations, dressed appropriately to flaunt their national origins.

In the developing world, the backlash against globalization has been strongest in Latin America. Their disenchantment with globalization is due to the disappointing economic performance of the regional economies after 1990, when they adopted neoliberal strategies to integrate with the global economy. They opened up their economies, particularly to capital inflows. In several Latin American economies, disastrous crises were precipitated during the 1990s, culminating in serious recessions. Argentina, Ecuador and Mexico are some of the cases in point. These economies suffered from double-digit unemployment rates as well as serious economic contractions in their post-crises periods. Bolivia and Venezuela also manifested strong anti-globalization sentiments, followed by political upheaval. The only exception was Chile, a small country with a population of 16 million, that liberalized its economy to trade and capital flows and embraced globalization with zest. Its average GDP growth rate between 1990 and 2004 was 5.6 percent, the highest in the region (Mishkin, 2006). For good reason, it is called the "only Asian economy of Latin America".[6]

3.1 Anti-globalization Movement in the Advanced Industrial Economies

After benefiting from globalization during the contemporary phase of globalization, and after convincing the developing economies of its large economic payoff and high value, the mature industrial countries were, and continue to be, in two minds about their commitment to globalization. How was it that distrust towards globalization was born in the industrial economies? The changing *zeitgeist* and its impact on the general public mindset was explained in the preceding section. Furthermore, as globalization progressed and new vigorous economies like China, India and other emerging-market economies (EMEs)[7] slowly came to the fore, they began influencing the *mise-en-scène* of the global economic stage. Consequently, the global geo-economic – and therefore geo-political – balance of power underwent a subtle but certain transformation. *En masse* these large EMEs have begun to function as a new engine of growth for the global economy (Nayyar, 2008; IMF, 2008b). Thirlwell (2007a, p. 5) went so far as to assert that some opponents of globalization in the industrial economies were worried about it "creating powerful new competitors in the global markets, while others are spooked by the security implications of the consequent redistribution of economic power" in the world.

Some of the other evident causal factors firing anti-globalization sentiment included the charge of rising income inequality and a *pari passu* worsening Gini coefficient in the industrial economies. This was being squarely blamed on globalization. Also, expanding multilateral trade, including trade in services, with large populous economies like China, India and the other low-wage EMEs resulted in short- and medium-term employment losses in the industrial economies. Layoffs in several large manufacturing and services sectors made eye-catching headlines in the newspapers and exacerbated anxiety about the damaging influences of globalization. Employment growth in many large industrial economies, like Germany, was painfully slow. Workers in several categories of employment felt exposed to competition from these economies and they felt threatened. For these reasons, the anti-globalization movement grew far stronger and the debates more heated in the industrialized world than those in the developing countries.

As alluded to earlier (Section 1), globalization has benefited many economies and some population groups within them have gained from it, but there were others who lost out as a result of its progress. Therefore, several constituencies came into being in the industrial economies that proactively, often violently, opposed globalism. Rather than looking for the source of their economic problems in specific domestic policies, they blamed globalization in general for their plight. Consequently, politicians resorted to protectionist rhetoric and called for legislative action to protect the interests of their voters. Politicians are sensitive to the globalization-related views of voters for good reason. In the 2006 Senate and House of Representatives elections in the US, many incumbents were defeated by challengers who called for a new approach towards trade and globalization (Teixeira, 2007). This was in contrast to what transpired in the 1970s and 1980s, when it was the developing economies that castigated the international economic order and called for what became known as a New International Economic Order. They fought for an equitable and fair international trade and financial regime. The tables have been turned during the current period and the excoriation of globalism has come from the countries that were the original conceptualizers, cogent supporters and engineers of contemporary globalization.

Antipathy towards globalization is not confined to lay persons, who form a strong anti-globalization constituency. The economic and financial media and international affairs journals have also been full of well-intentioned writing on the sustainability of globalization as it was unfolding. Ironically, failures of globalization like the Asian crisis of 1997–8 or the sub-prime mortgage crisis of 2007–08 and the credit crunch did not fan the flames of the current anti-globalization movement, albeit financial globalization and its mismanagement were directly blamed for them. It was largely the celebrated successes of globalization that created adjustment strains in the industrial economies and ignited a widespread anti-globalization movement. To this must be added some noted economists and thoughtful analysts, who hold the view that globalization, a benevolent force of dynamic economic change, is being mismanaged because the supranational institutions of economic governance (the Bretton Woods twins and the WTO) and policy mandarins at national level have only a superficial understanding of its intricate mechanics. The adherents of the anti-globalization movement regard them as arch villains and vent their rage against them.

That there has been a steady and monotonic upsurge in corporate profits over the past two decades cannot be denied. These were higher in 2007 than at any time in the last half century. This implied that the benefits of globalization went asymmetrically to the owners of capital. Roach (2006, p. 1) called it "a veritable bonanza for the return to capital" (Chapter 3, Section 3.2). These trends provoked the ire of the antagonists, who grew certain that globalization was an instrument of immiserizing the poor economies, particularly the low-income groups in them. They are certain that it has had a detrimental impact on income inequality both within and between countries. They also blamed globalization for job destruction (discussed in the following paragraph) in the industrial econo- mies. Convinced that it is a villainous economic force, they contend that globalization threatens employment and living standards everywhere and that it is a means of thwarting social and economic progress.

Anti-corporate sentiment and activism became more intense due to the elimination of good jobs by large brand-name multinational firms. Over the preceding three decades, their focus shifted from manufactur- ing products and services to producing brands and strengthening brand image. TNCs focused their resources, energies and expertise upon market- ing. The production side of their enterprises gradually became dominated by offshore outsourcing. They went on refining this mode of production, while paying a lot of attention to their brand image. Phil Knight, the CEO of Nike, succinctly put this new business philosophy as follows, "There is no value in making things any more. The value is added by careful research, by innovation and by marketing".[8] In accordance with this philosophy, many TNCs, like Nike and Levis, moved their manufactur- ing operations from the high-wage industrial countries to manufacturing facilities throughout the world, and in the process strengthened brand promotion. They went on shutting down their domestic plants, laying off a large number of their existing labor force. As the innovative global production process caught up, in advanced industrial countries, both manufacturing activity and the labor force became significantly devalued. Meanwhile, free trade zones (FTZs) and export promotion zones (EPZs) in developing economies began to grow briskly. They manufactured goods strictly for export and became important tools of export-oriented growth. A large number of them exist in East and Southeast Asia, Latin America and lately, in East European countries. In 2007, there were 3700 FTZs and EPZs in 130 countries, employing 66 million workers (Engman et al., 2007). China, and more recently India and Russia, also expanded their EPZs by adopting new EPZ legislation to respond to this trend in global manufacturing and trade. A good number of developing economies, particularly the EMEs, became the new producers of manufactured and consumer goods. China grew into one of the largest exporters of these products. Rapid growth in the Chinese EPZs and of manufactured products, with a steady high-technology orientation, turned it into the second largest exporter in the world, after Germany, in 2007. Considering China exported only half the amount of manufactured goods as the US in 2001, this expansion of manufactured export was striking and impressive (Das, 2008c). It is increasingly moving up the technology ladder and competing with the industrial economies in areas like ICT, aerospace, biotechnology and advanced electronics.

3.2 Some Misguided Beliefs

The rationale behind some of the criticism of globalization by the antagonists is simply incorrect. Often critics took up conceptually flawed arguments (Krugman and Obstfeld, forthcoming).[9] In a caustic reaction, Mishkin (2006, p. 15) remarked, "Anti-globalizers have it completely wrong". Many campaigners are poorly informed about the relevant economic annals, the theoretical premise of growth potential that global integration offers and the valuable contribution it has made thus far. When groups of left-leaning do-gooders declare their rancorous anti-globalization sentiments, they do not realize that in the present economic setting, to be anti-globalization is to be anti-poor in the world, which is a morally indefensible position. Embracing global economic integration and thoughtfully implementing neoliberal strategies in a proper sequential manner may well enable developing economies to reach their full potential. This in turn will help eradicate poverty. In today's global economy, the main losers are not those who are exposed to globalization, but those who have been left out. A fierce backlash could put paid to many of the real welfare gains that globalization has achieved.

Anti-globalizers suspected the TNCs, many of which are gargantuan business entities and economically and financially more powerful than many of the developing economies they operate in (Section 1), of wrongdoing. The business ethics of many of their practices in the developing countries are questioned by the antagonists. As these TNCs are answerable to no one but their shareholders, they get away with a lot of unethical corporate conduct. They have been accused of living beyond the reach of the law. The antagonists contended that through their manufacturing facilities in the developing economies, which produce products for affluent markets in high-income industrial countries, the TNCs exploit labor by paying low wages and making their employees work long hours under stressful conditions, as well as exploiting the host country per se in different ways.[10] These manufacturing facilities are regarded as nothing more than sources of high profits for big business and the TNCs. They have been accused of a profits-first people-last mentality. While some would believe that TNC operations have been "transnationalizing" the global economy, the antagonists have perceived them as mere economic exploiters. Anti-globalizers unearthed cases of low wages and poor working conditions in numerous TNC manufacturing facilities around the globe and publicized them.

In the 1990s, the anti-globalization movement attracted many adherents on university campuses in high-income industrial countries, protesting against the disturbing corporate practices of TNCs. Essentially due to these practices, the anti-globalization movement took an anti-corporate turn. Indeed, the anti-globalizers tended to amalgamate – mistakenly or deliberately – their anti-corporate concerns with globalization. While a stressful working environment and sweatshop conditions cannot be justified by any stretch of the imagination, if workers are coming to work in the manufacturing facilities run by TNCs, these jobs must be valuable to them. Also, low-income economies are also low-wage economies. There is a possibility that while wages are low, or very low, compared with industrial-country norms, they are normal by the standard of the host developing countries where these manufacturing facilities are located. Lastly, to rectify corporate malpractices, it is the individual TNC or malpractice that needs to be attacked. A broadside against globalization will not cure them.

A false belief, in fact a consensus among anti-globalization activists, is that there has been a disturbing increase in world poverty during the present phase of globalization. Economists have devoted a lot of energy to measuring poverty trends. Not only has the latter half of the 20th century proved to be a period of unprecedented increases in global per capita income, but also poverty alleviation during the present era of globalization has been noteworthy. This issue has been seriously analyzed in several empirical studies and a large literature has grown up on poverty and its measurement. These studies have emphatically concluded that global poverty has been in decline. Some of the influential studies include Bourguignon and Morrisson (2002), Sala-i-Martin (2006) and Chen and Ravallion (2007). The international reference line of poverty, that is, $1 a day, measured in PPP and inflation adjusted,[11] shows a sharp decline in global poverty over the last three decades. The second internal poverty line of $2 a day confirms this trend. This was discussed in Chapter 2 (Section 3).

Globalization was blamed for a slowdown in job creation in the corporate world as well as for job destruction in the industrial economies (Section

3.1). Job creation in traditional jobs did slow down because of the increasing trend of using part-timers and freelancers, which helped to keep costs down in an intensely competitive business environment. Also, many service sector jobs tended to be filled by part-time experts, who often work at two or more such jobs. However, one would be remiss to ignore the newly growing high-technology sectors that created a larger number of high-paying jobs. High-technology companies like Apple, Intel and Microsoft are known not only for creating a large number of such jobs but also for scores of young millionaires, because of the lavish stock options made available to them. Many high technology firms have grown accustomed to a two-tier workforce. Around their core groups or inner circles of permanent, full-time, highly-paid employees works an orbit of temporary workers. While those in the orbit do make high salaries, they do not have pension benefits or generous stock options. They are not even considered official employees.

Another flawed argument that is frequently made by antagonists is that espousing neoliberal economic policies to globalize is wrong for developing countries because such a strategy (say, lowering tariff barriers) led country A to economic doom. There is usually a cause-and-effect mix-up here. Antagonists make an error of logic known as *post hoc ergo propter hoc*, meaning after it therefore due to it. External or domestic economic shocks always affect economic performance. If an economy is hit by one such shock soon after its adoption of economic reforms and liberalization, to an untrained eye, the resulting recession appears to have been caused by economic liberalization or policy reforms. Also, most economies make a large number of policy choices spread over several economic dimensions, like fiscal or monetary policies, exchange rate or banking regulations, and so on. Their trade policy choice represents only one dimension. It would be erroneous to think that, just because the GDP growth rate dipped after an economy implemented trade policy reforms and opened up, the economy was wrong to liberalize. It could well be that the beneficial impact of trade policy liberalization was negated by bad policy choices on another dimension, or offset by policy errors in other areas. While there may be occasional cases, a recession in a developing economy need not be caused by liberalization to globalize.

4. ACTIVISTS OR LOBBYISTS?

Given the circumstances of the birth of the anti-globalization movement, anti-globalization activists and protestors were treated more as lobbyists by heads of governments and supranational institutions of global governance than as a mere protesting mob. To be sure, there was a favorable side to these anti-globalization activists. Against the backdrop of major scandals (Section 2) affecting a large number of ordinary people, many of their protests had drawn attention to government oversights and spurred timely and appropriate reforms. As noted in Section 3, with a change in mindset during the early years of the current decade, anti-globalization activists no longer had an entrenched antipathy towards globalization per se or global economic integration, but they took a strong view of government oversights, macroeconomic malfunctioning, financial malfeasance, corporate crimes and environmental degradation.

With the passage of time, the reaction of influential political leaders and heads of supranational institutions towards the stance taken by the anti-globalization lobby changed. They began to be treated with a degree of deference, perhaps even with indulgence. Notwithstanding the fact that their demonstrations frequently turned violent, these lobbyists were never summarily dismissed as ignorant anarchists and radical rebel-rousers. Numerous instances are available to show that public leaders not only succumbed to their demands but also tended to agree with many of them. For instance, when the anti-globalization lobby demanded debt cancellation of the public debt of low-income developing countries in 1999 at the time of Cologne G-8 summit, Tony Blair proposed a debt-easing package. The Seattle Ministerial Conference of the WTO in 1999 was a high-water mark for the anti-globalization movement. During the conference, Bill Clinton cautioned the international trade negotiators and advised them not to ignore the "legitimate concerns of legitimate protestors" outside the conference hall. While members of the anti-globalization movement were angrily protesting outside, Mike Moore, Director General of the WTO, a former labor union leader, was saying in his address (2000) that he was of the same mind as many of the antagonists and that he agreed with their views on most issues.[12] The views of peaceful demonstrators were supported by the Swedish authorities at the time of the Göteborg summit, when the heads of state of the European Union (EU) met at the European Council summit, held in 2000.

James Wolfensohn, the two-term president of the World Bank, who had earned a reputation for being the plutocrat for the poor, routinely invited representatives of the protesters for serious discussions when they gathered outside in their thousands at the time of the Bank-Fund annual meetings to protest against the "follies" of the ways of the IMF and the World Bank. Irish Rock star Bono, of U2 fame, who has a rare ability to build trust and empathy across an eclectic group of influential people, frequently attended the Bank-Fund annual meetings as a representative of "civil society". He is a generous philanthropist as well as a fund raiser for humanitarian causes. His viewpoint and position on development-related issues is respectfully considered by the participants, many of whom have unreservedly endorsed them. There is plenty of evidence available to show that the views of NGOs were not dismissed by top political leaders and heads of supranational institutions as the thoughtless and shallow notions of non-serious and poorly informed people. During the Prague Annual Meeting of the IMF and the World Bank in 2006, Wolfensohn told an audience of finance ministers and central bankers, "Outside these walls, young people are demonstrating against globalization. I believe deeply that many of them are asking legitimate questions, and I embrace the commitment of a new generation to fight poverty."

The rapid growth of the anti-globalization movement, particularly during the 1990s, was supported strongly by college and university students in high-income industrial countries. Broadly speaking, globalization fell foul of the younger generation, known as the generation X, the generation following the baby boomers, which overwhelmingly dominates the anti-globalization activists and has contributed to its strength. Idealists in this generation felt that capitalism as a system could never address the question of social justice. These are young people, born between 1965 and 1980, who are typically fairly well educated, under-employed, private and unpredictable. They were brought up on TV and PCs and are usually highly ICT-savvy. They are regarded as less concerned about class, status and material wealth, but are more fitness, environment and socially conscious than the baby boomers. For them, peace of mind is more important than leisure time. When they think they are right, Xers are not afraid of challenging authority. They are not anarchic but realistic and thinking people. Therefore, they recognize that it is usually unrealistic to directly confront issues, but better to get around them by lobbying and protesting. Identifying the downside of globalization and protesting against it came naturally to them. They regard globalization as capitalism run amok. They accuse it of many social and economic limitations. Nothing upset them more than environmental degradation, for which they hold globalization responsible. Many of them are earnest and sincere about their causes.

5.   NON-GOVERNMENTAL ORGANIZATIONS AND ANTI-GLOBALIZATION LOBBY

In general, NGOs include altruistic charitable "civil society" aid organizations, philanthropic groups and voluntary policy-oriented citizens' advocacy groups. In wider usage, the term NGO can be applied to any non-profit organization which is independent of government. NGOs are quasi-independent entities, which are value-based, task-driven and organized at local, national and international levels. They are operated by like-minded people with common perspectives, interests and objectives. They are not directly affiliated with any national government but often have a significant impact on the social, economic and political activity of the country or region involved. Their presence and role has grown in recent years. They are consulted by governments as well as international organizations. NGOs are generally respected for their strong grass-roots links, field-based knowledge of economic development and the ability to innovate and adapt policies. They perform a variety of functions and carry citizens' concerns to governments, TNCs and supranational bodies. They monitor policies and encourage participation, essentially through the provision of information.

Although the NGO sector has become increasingly professionalized over the last two decades, the principles of altruism and voluntarism continue to be its strategic defining characteristics. The World Bank defines NGOs as "private organizations that pursue activities to relieve suffering, promote the interests of the poor, protect the environment, provide basic social services, or undertake community development" (Operational Directive 14.70). Their orientation is sometimes economic and business-related, while on other occasions non-economic and non-business-related. They have a high degree of interest in the developing economies and growth-related issues, including globalization and its socio-economic impact.

Some of the large international NGOs, like Oxfam, retain subject area experts and possess a significant stock of knowledge. Funded either by governments or charities, some of them also have deep purses. There are now tens of thousands of them in the world, operating in most countries. Aided by ICT-driven global networking, NGOs and their activities have expanded fast. They are highly media-savvy. Above all, they make use of television in a skillful manner. Cognizant that their campaign could have an enormous impact when covered by the modern mass media, NGOs have devoted a lot of energy and attention to using the media and have become increasingly powerful at local, national and global levels.

5.1 NGOs and Supranational Organizations

NGOs interested in influencing global economic policies and financial architecture take twin routes of direct public demonstrations and indirectly approaching national representatives. The NGO-based class of experts, noted in the preceding paragraph, has worked its way into the UN system and other supranational institutions. Many NGOs have become capable of having high quality dialogues with supranational institutions, which has enabled them to have an impact on international agreements and supranational institutions' policy-making process. This has become their mode of successfully influencing their globalization-related positions. NGOs have played a pivotal role in their respective areas of operation. For instance, their impact on the formation of the North American Free Trade Area (NAFTA), the Rio Earth Summit (or the United Nations Conference on Environment and Development), on the Marrakesh Agreement establishing the WTO, and subsequent biennial Ministerial Conferences of the WTO, is widely acknowledged to be significant.

There are area- and issue-specific NGOs, for instance, the Berlin-based Transparency International is an NGO that maps global corruption and keeps an eye on kleptocracy. Its data compilation capability and activities have expanded significantly during the past decade. Readership of its annual publication on corruption in different countries and the index of corruption has grown at an exponential rate. There are many others with significant expertise in their areas of focus, like environmentally sustainable development, human rights or women in development, and the like. During the 1990s, NGOs began influencing the operations of supranational institutions in a meaningful manner. A United Nations (UN) Working Group report, published in July 1996, encouraged and accepted the role of NGOs in the UN system. The Economic and Social Council (ECOSOC) of the UN formalized the rules for NGO participation in the policy-making process in the UN system.

The World Bank is now officially committed to an open dialogue with civil society organizations, that is, NGOs that are involved in growth and development-related issues, which includes globalization. The World Bank has also dedicated a website to their activities. Following in its footsteps, the regional development banks have set up full-fledged divisions to liaise with the civil society movement. Those large industrial economies which are members of the G-8 also created NGOs in important functional areas. For instance, the G-8 created the Financial Action Task Force (FATF) in 1989 as an international regime against money laundering. The FATF set up practices and procedures that affected global banking supervision and regulation norms as well as enforcement guidelines. It coordinated international cooperation to prevent money laundering. The FATF practices were codified and have strong support from institutions like the IMF and the World Bank. It is widely hoped that NGOs will provide meaningful support in accelerating global policy convergence in different economic, financial, environmental and other areas.

5.2 NGOs and the Developing Economies

Several large and resourceful NGOs became self-appointed intermediaries between the industrial and developing economies. They perceived themselves as the representatives of the have-nots in the impoverished developing world. Paradoxically, this sometimes pitted them against competing bodies in the developing economies, even against developing country governments. Although their activism led to a great many constructive and positive results, not all was well with the NGOs' developing country operations. There were instance of their clientele having strategic disagreements with them and the very poor people they were claiming to assist and save did not agree with the course of action taken or recommended by them. Often fundamental disagreements surfaced between those who benefited from their operations and the NGOs. One well-publicized case of differences in opinion concerned the views of local leaders who supported the resettlement and recreation packages that were devised for those affected by the Narmada Valley Project in India and the objections of large NGOs to the project per se. Similarly, the National Authority in Palestine found that its functions as a state were often in competition with many European NGOs functioning in Palestine. The local leaders bitterly complained publicly.

Many NGOs played a proactive role in the globalization–anti-globalization debate. They are dead set against what they regard as "destructive" globalization. They have compared some of the strategies that come under the rubric of globalization to "imperialism" and "feudalism". In the past, NGOs wholeheartedly supported the concept of the Tobin Tax. This was a proposal by Nobel laureate James Tobin to tax all speculative financial transactions. However, they soon shifted equally unreservedly to a general target of "democratizing the global financial institutions" (Wood, 2004).

Often NGOs gave the impression of having a bone to pick with globalism per se and with the phenomenon of globalization. Not everybody concurs and supports this stand taken by the NGOs. Some large NGOs are not transparent regarding their financial operations and therefore have invited criticism. Cooper (2004, p. 45) blamed American and European NGOs for

> their lack of transparency of funding operations and choice of issues and their tendency to speak on behalf of the world's poor without consulting them. Western NGOs and developing world's NGOs often hold diametrically opposed views on issues such as extension of WTO authority on global labor and environmental standards. Yet, largely due to better funding wealthy NGOs based in Europe or the US get most of the attention and often make their cases directly to intergovernmental organizations, bypassing national constitutional processes set up to facilitate compromise among diverse interests in pluralistic societies.

Hindsight reveals that, disagreements apart, some of the globalization-related causes picked up by the NGOs were indeed worthy.

5.3   NGOs and Transnational Corporations

It is widely acknowledged that NGOs frequently took a strong stand against big business organization and TNC operations in developing countries. They were absolutely convinced that big business and TNCs' manufacturing operations in developing economies represented the seedy side of globalization. Therefore, TNCs became a prime target for NGOs in their anti-globalization movement. While they may not always be right in this contention, NGOs are credited with influencing the behavior of big business and TNCs, particularly their developing country operations. Levis, McDonalds, Monsanto, Nike, Shell and several others came under frequent pressure and were often under heavy attack from them. Aware of the vulnerability of their image and brand name in the face of NGOs' protests, TNCs were not in a position to ignore their viewpoint. NGOs' anti-sweatshop activism found an outlet in opposition to some of the practices followed by TNCs in their manufacturing facilities located in developing countries. Anti-corporate or anti-TNC protesters treated large business and TNCs as generic targets that signified their multiple global ills. By protesting against them, the anti-globalization movement was fighting for global labor rights, against environmental degradation, and on behalf of other comparable policy objectives of global significance.

In their eagerness to appear as responsible actors in a globalized economic world, big business and TNCs took several measures in response to NGOs' protests. Their investment in corporate governance increased significantly. They were also made to develop codes of conduct and codes of practice to be followed by their developing country facilities. In their international operations, TNCs were made to put "people before profits", as the slogan went. There were instances of TNCs donating technology to the host developing economy as charity. Thus viewed, NGOs did make a positive contribution to economic globalization.

Another encouraging result of NGO activism is that presently big business and TNCs organize sub-cultural events to demonstrate that their presence in the host developing economy aims to improve people's lives, not merely to make large profits. Positive results of this kind of self-regulation are truly praiseworthy. After the September 11 attack on the World Trade Center (Section 2), the environment changed and so did the manner of NGO protests against the TNCs. Direct attacks on them were mellowed. In general, the intensity of protests against the corporate targets declined because NGO protestors wanted to distance themselves from any resemblance to the attackers of the World Trade Center.

6. IS GLOBALIZATION IN JEOPARDY?

If many disillusioned people are averse to it and regard it as a *bête noire*, the contemporary wave of globalization could stall or even reverse. This happened not too long ago in the past; could it happen again? The most recent reversal of globalization occurred during the inter-war period. That was an era known for dismantling the earlier phase of globalization. Its circumstances have been discussed by several analysts. There were two reasons that accelerated the inter-war deglobalization: first, the Great Depression and, second, those economies that were losers from the operations of free world markets came under public pressure to protect their economies. An environment of trade wars was generated in a short time span. Is the current anti-globalization sentiment as critical as that during the post-World War I period? The forces responsible for the setback to global integration during the 1930s included hostility among the erstwhile large and leading economic powers, an increasingly protectionist inclination, the dominance of anti-liberal ideas, economic instability and economic rivalry.

As pointed out in Chapter 3 (Section 2), a 2008 opinion poll, conducted in 34 countries, found that while there was general support for globalization (positive replies outnumbered negative by two to one), there was unease about some facets of globalization, in particular its pace of advancement. This discomfort was relatively higher in the advanced Group-of-Seven (G-7) countries. Of the 34 000 respondents, 50 percent considered economic globalization as moving too fast. This proportion was 57 percent in the G-7 countries. In the US, 58 percent of those polled believed that globalization was bad for the economy and only 28 percent were positive about its benefits. A majority (64 percent) of those polled in the G-7 countries also believed that gains and losses from globalization were distributed unevenly.[13] People felt that the benefits and burdens of globalization were asymmetrically shared; therefore it was believed to be an unfair phenomenon. Also, rising unemployment among low-skilled and unskilled laborers and problems faced by sunset industries in the G-7 countries due to ongoing globalization created similar political pressures. In addition, the Doha Round for multilateral trade negotiations (MTNs) progressed with difficulty before being suspended. This led to increased interest in regionalism among WTO member economies. Bilateral trade agreements also proliferated. There was reasonable concern in some quarters that the political consensus supporting globalism might evaporate, causing a backlash.

To progress, globalization indispensably needs political support. Political argument supporting globalization is changing and has begun

to be aligned with public opinion. Candidates in the 2008 US presidential campaign showed increasing skepticism about free trade. Nicolas
Sarkozy favored what he called "community preferences", implying that
higher tariff barriers need to be imposed against imports from non-EU
economies. While his argument did not win many European enthusi-
asts, the re-election of Silvio Berlusconi may change this environment.
Although China is a one-party state, its government did seem anxious
about some of the consequences of globalization and brisk growth. These
include the rural–urban income gap, high inflation and threatening levels
of environmental degradation. Regional income disparities may increasingly make global capitalism a hard sell in China. The BJP lost the 2004
election in India, partly because of mistakes made in globalization-related
policies. Indian farmers and the underprivileged classes found themselves
economically stagnant, saw themselves as the losers in globalization and
voted heavily against the BJP. The "India Shining" campaign of the BJP
fell flat with these large groups of voters. Rising world food prices were
also blamed on globalization. Political leaders around the world have to
come to grips with these pressures. The consensus that made adoption
of neoliberal strategies possible in the past had significantly dwindled
by the latter half of 2008 (Rachman, 2008). Unless corrective economy-
specific policy measures are put in place, the progress of further integration of the global economy may be retarded by an escalation in political
opposition.

As alluded to above, spiraling protectionist sentiment during the
inter-war era proved toxic for the previous wave of globalization. It was
instrumental in disintegrating the global economy. The US economy,
the largest during that period, adopted a protectionist posture, which
culminated in the enactment of the Hawley-Smoot Tariff Act of 1930.
The US's strong protectionist tendency encouraged other economies to
do the same in retaliation. It advanced the breakdown of the erstwhile
global integration. Global trade architecture has evolved considerably
since then. After eight rounds of multilateral trade negotiations (MTNs)
under the sponsorship of the General Agreement on Tariffs and Trade
(GATT), the trade and economic world of today is strikingly different
(Das, 2007d). A Hawley-Smoot Act-like relapse into protectionism looks
impossible. Besides, TNC operations and networked production have
integrated the global economy far more at present than in the former
era of globalization. Broadly spread out production networks entailing
inter- and intra-firm production have produced intricately enmeshed
relationships among business firms. These networks have elaborate
horizontal, vertical and diagonal links. They form multidimensional lat-
tices of production and economic activities. Transnational production

networks operate at national, regional and global levels (Dicken, 2007). Most modern firms have global business interests. As they take a broad cosmopolitan view of their businesses, the managements of large firms generally do not collaborate with unions and ignore their protectionist demands. Developing economies, in particular the EMEs, have been endeavoring to attract foreign direct investment (FDI) and participate in regional and global production networks. In such an economic environment, traditional protectionist interest groups become irrelevant. With the expansion of service sectors in most high-income economies and the shrinking of the manufacturing sector, the proportion of the labor force adversely affected by the expansion of multilateral trade fell. Consumers became accustomed to imported products and regarded them as a means to improve their life style. These trends helped reduce the power of the unions and unskilled workers, consequently protectionist pressures during the present phase of globalization are not as intense as they were in the past.

The groups who team up to protest against globalization existed during the earlier era of globalization also. They converged around two basic themes, namely, "radical socialism and racially-defined nationalism" (Wolf, 2005a, p. 5). During that era, the antagonists demanded restrictions on the powers of the state over the economy and the supremacy of the collective over the self-seeking individual. Conversely, the anti-liberal movements of the present period are not so narrowly based in terms of ideas. They decry institutions of economic governance and TNCs as well as banding together against environmental degradation. As noted in Section 1.1, these heterogeneous groups also include activists who espouse national, native culture, democracy and human rights-related causes as well as anti-poverty and development lobbyists and left-leaning do-gooders. Spurred by diverse and wide-ranging motives, these groups oppose globalization. They neither adhere to party politics nor have an alternative concept of running an economy. As noted above, the anti-globalization movement has lost the thrust and passion of the 1990s since the 9/11 attack (Section 7). Even if it had not, the various groups were

> split in their objectives. (Although) part of what some protesters say – notably on the hypocrisy of advanced countries and the plight of the poor – is valid. But a political movement cannot beat something with nothing. A movement that offers only protest is unlikely to triumph. (Wolf, 2005a, p. 6)

Some of the factors that played an important role during the deglobalization of the inter-war period are not relevant or menacing for the

contemporary wave of globalization. Besides, the economic policy repertoire of the contemporary period is far superior and can shield the losers of
globalization better than during the earlier phase of globalization. Also, it
is widely acknowledged that during the preceding three decades the depth
and scope of globalization has spread much more deeply and widely than
during the earlier phase. In addition, the egregious macroeconomic and
monetary policy errors made during the inter-war period are well known
and widely recognized in the economics profession. The economic history
of that period has provided today's policy makers with invaluable lessons.
As regards afflictions like the rising unemployment rate of low-skilled
and unskilled laborers in advanced industrial economies, economists and
policy mandarins concur that the principal causal factor has been skill-
biased technological change. Factor price equalization through the expansion of trade, à la Heckscher-Ohlin theory, did not have much to do with
it. This implies that prima facie there is much less risk of a backlash of the
kind that took place during the inter-war period. More likely would be a
partial backtracking or slowing down of the ongoing globalization, which
could be caused by "the leftward tilt of the body politic in the industrial
world" (Roach, 2006, p. 2).

7. WANING OF THE ANTI-GLOBALIZATION MOVEMENT

The September 11 attack on the World Trade Center took the wind out
of the sails of the anti-globalization movement. Holms (2008, p. 15) called
it a "dizzying setback" to the anti-globalization movement. It cooled the
ardor of the activists. Gathering to protest suddenly began to seem a much
more sinister activity than before. Seattle-style shenanigans became anathema in an atmosphere of injured patriotism. The activists woke up to the
fact that there were larger threats and more important issues to protest
against than Starbucks and Nike. The outrage and horror caused by the
9/11 attack made the anti-globalization movement look self-indulgent. In
some countries, like the United Kingdom, where May 1 was devoted to
anti-globalization parades, these rituals were called off. The attention of
the popular media switched to the much more sinister and threatening war
on terror.

The Fund-Bank annual meetings began to attract much reduced
numbers of protesters. The anti-Fund-Bank slogan of "Fifty Years is
Enough" mellowed to a rather conciliatory requirement, asking for
reforms of these institutions in lieu of their abolition. A consensus
emerged regarding the strategies for growth that needed to be reviewed

at both national and global level. Homogenized or one-size-fits-all policies have increasingly been rejected. Likewise, the villainous properties of the WTO began to appear tolerable, albeit after some modification. The institutional acceptance of this was reflected in the Doha Development Agenda of 2001 (Das, 2005a). A belief took hold that the multilateral trade regime could be reshaped to serve the interests of the developing economies and the poor. At the September 2003 Cancún Ministerial Conference of the WTO, the developing economies joined hands as the Group-of-Twenty (G-20) for the first time. Although this Ministerial Conference failed to achieve its objectives, the developing economies succeeded in influencing the multilateral trade negotiation (MTN) process. As a group, they were able to make their presence felt (Das, 2003).

The street theatre and protest marches of the anti-globalization activists weakened and slowed, but they continued in new places and on new occasions. For the nth time, the members of the anti-globalization movement went on the rampage at the seaside resort of Mar Del Plata, Argentina, in November 2005. This time the event was the Summit of the Americas. While some 10 000 anti-globalization demonstrators, a much smaller number than before, marched peacefully in the morning, expressing their concerns by way of slogans and placards, by the afternoon the tenor had changed. A few thousand plucky activists began to protest violently. They smashed shop windows and hurled Molotov cocktails and rocks at the local police force, who retaliated with tear gas and water cannons. When the G-8 summit took place in Hokkaido's main city of Sapporo, Japan, in July 2008, just over a thousand demonstrators came from all over the world. The campaign of the malcontents was understandably targeted at rising global food prices, fuel prices and the financial credit crunch, which were fast becoming menaces of universal proportions. However, the proceedings outside the adorned conference hall were more subdued and lackluster than inside, and were ignored by the visual news media (*The Economist*, 2008c). Press coverage of the anti-globalization movement during this G-8 summit was conspicuous by its absence.

On the one hand, much-needed political support for an advancing neoliberal policy structure and advancing globalization has recently been in decline (Section 6); on the other, the anti-globalization movement has not been as vigorous and violent. Although the latter has lost its primacy and the thrust it had during the 1990s, it is still continuing in a restrained, subdued and muted manner. Activists have lost a good deal of their zeal and passion for the assortment of causes they were committed to, but rumors of the death of the anti-globalization movement are exaggerated.

8.   CONCLUSIONS AND SUMMARY

Notwithstanding its successful outcome in terms of the income convergence of the global economies, many people from diverse backgrounds
have focused on some of the negative aspects of globalization and regard
it as a malevolent phenomenon. Public attitudes in the 1990s changed
and the earlier celebration of the victory of free-market forces that had
ushered in globalization and economic prosperity in many economies
began to be replaced by the perception of globalization as a villainous
force. A broad populist anti-globalization movement developed, which
was noisy, raucous, sometimes violent, but in part successful and meaningful. The decade of the 1990s is well known for it. The antagonists
blamed globalization for a litany of global economic malaise. In particular, in their discontent, they linked the behavior of large business firms
and TNCs with the concept of anti-globalism. While fundamentally this
was a movement against the policies of economic neoliberalism, it was
also a cynical mélange of several issues about which groups of people were
disgruntled.

During the decade of the 1990s, anti-globalization sentiment was buttressed by several global trends and incidents, gaining strength towards
the end of the decade. This chapter discusses the global events and trends
which caused a great deal of embarrassment to the political and economic
establishment. This mindset fed the anti-globalization movement, which
grew up in this atmosphere of self-doubt, moral turpitude and consternation, as well as general disorientation among the governments and ruling
elites in the advanced industrial countries.

The anti-globalization movement was particularly opposed to the
agendas and actions of supranational organizations of economic governance, which were perceived to proliferate and advance the cause of globalism. In particular, it trenchantly protested against what it regarded as
the sell-off of the global commons. Some other causal factors that evidently
fired anti-globalization sentiment in the industrial countries included the
charge of rising income inequality and a *pari passu* worsening Gini coefficient in the industrial economies. The success of these critics of globalization was greater than was justified by their social weight. The social base of
the anti-globalization lobby comprises the middle classes, essentially in the
industrial economies and the NGOs, based in both developing and industrial countries. The general simplicity with which the anti-globalization
movement started changed in the early 2000s, when it became subtle and
discriminating. The anti-globalizers grew less broadly opposed to globalization. They no longer sought un-globalization or dismantling of global
networks of economic and other linkages. The anti-globalizers began to

differentiate between different kinds of globalization and accept some, while rejecting others.

Several developing economies have benefited from the onward march of economic globalization. The success of China, India and other low-wage EMEs resulted in short- and medium-term employment losses in the industrial economies. This fanned anti-globalization sentiment. The rising trend in corporate profits in the industrial economies had the same effect. Globalization changed the *modus operandi* of the TNCs significantly. Over the preceding three decades, their focus shifted from manufacturing products and services to producing brands and strengthening brand image. Anti-corporate sentiment and activism became more intense due to the elimination of good jobs by large brand-name multinational firms.

Not everything was perfect with this movement; it was based on some misguided beliefs. The rationale behind some of the criticism of globalization by the antagonists was simply incorrect. Often critics took up conceptually flawed arguments. For instance, anti-globalization activists suspected the TNCs of wrongdoing and declared that this was a limitation of globalization.

Given the circumstances of the birth of the anti-globalization movement, anti-globalization activists and protestors were treated more as lobbyists by heads of governments and supranational institutions of global governance than as a mere protesting mob, with anarchist notions. To be sure, there was a favorable side to these anti-globalization activists. The movement was supported by large and resourceful NGOs, which added to its strength. Several large NGOs played a proactive role in the globalization–anti-globalization debate. They were dead set against what they regard as "destructive" globalization. They even compared some of the strategies that come under the rubric of globalization to "imperialism" and "feudalism". The September 11 attack on the World Trade Center took the wind out of the sails of the anti-globalization movement. It marked the waning of the anti-globalization movement.

With so many disillusioned people averse to it and regarding it as a *bête noire*, the contemporary wave of globalization may stall or even go into reverse. Popular opinion does not support it and is against several of its aspects. Lately, political opinion has begun to turn against it. The consensus that made the adoption of neoliberal strategies possible in the past had been significantly weakened by the latter half of 2008. Political leaders around the world have to come to grips with these pressures. Unless corrective economy-specific policy measures are put in place, the progress of further integration of the global economy may be retarded by an escalation in political opposition. Although stalling or reversal of the present phase of globalization, as occurred in the previous era of globalization, does not seem likely, its advancement may indeed be slowed by political and populist pressures.

NOTES

1. After publication of these books Klein became an official spokeswoman of the anti-globalization movement.
2. As explained in Chapter 1 (Section 3.4), the meaning of the term neoliberal has been in dispute. It is used more by the opponents of neoliberalism than by its supporters. I use it to convey that globalization necessitates the adoption of free-market policies.
3. As Archbishop of Cracow in Poland, Pope John Paul II was a passionate supporter of globalization. But as the 1990s wore on, the Pope became increasingly uneasy about "unbridled capitalism". He traveled extensively and expressed his disapproval of globalization in his Apostolic Exhortations to the Catholic Church in different parts of the world.
4. The term industrial country has become a misnomer, because some of the emerging-market economies, like China, have become extensively industrialized. Contribution of industrial sector to their GDP is larger than that in the wealthy countries of the developed world, whose economies are overwhelmingly dominated by the services sector. These countries have become large exporters of manufactured products as well.
5. The members of the Group-of-Seven (G-7) are Canada, France, Germany, Italy, Japan, the United Kingdom and the United States. Together this group of matured industrial economies accounts for about two-thirds of the world's economic output. The leaders of these largest industrialized democracies have met annually since 1975 to discuss major economic and political issues related to the global economy. The participants at the first meeting in Rambouillet, France in November 1975 were France, West Germany, Italy, Japan, the United Kingdom and the United States. Canada joined, at the 1976 Dorado Beach, Puerto Rico Summit, what came to be known as the G-7. Ever since, the site of the yearly summit of leaders has rotated among the seven countries. The Group-of-Eight (G-8) comprises the G-7 nations plus Russia. Russia began to participate in a portion of the meetings at the 1994 G-7 Summit in Naples. Russia officially became the eighth member at the 1997 Denver, Colorado, "Summit of the Eight". While Russia is a G-8 member, it does not participate in financial and economic discussions, which continue to be conducted by the G-7. It is the smallest economy of the G-8. G-7 Finance Ministers meet four times a year to review developments in their economies and the global economy, and to develop common approaches on global economic and financial policy issues. The G-7 Central Bank Governors join the Finance Ministers at three of these meetings.
6. See Mishkin (2006), chapter 1, for a detailed discussion on the disappointment of the Latin American countries with the current phase of globalization.
7. See Note 4, Chapter 2.
8. Cited by Segerstrom (2005), p. 7.
9. See chapter 11, where globalization and anti-globalization movement are discussed.
10. A crystallizing event took place in 1996, when it was discovered that the clothes sold in Wal-Mart with a fanfare and chic advertising were tailored by exceedingly low-paid workers in Honduras.
11. This international poverty line was recently updated to $1.25 a day in 2005 PPP (Ravallion et al., 2008).
12. "If people, especially young people, say unemployment is too high, they are right. If unions want better wages and conditions for working people, they are right. If

environmentalists say that growth must be sustainable – and not destroy the planet's ecological balance – they are right. When developing countries say that they are not getting fair access and economic justice, they too are absolutely right." This excerpt comes from the opening address to NGOs at the Seattle Symposium on International Trade, on 29 December, 1999. It was published in the *Social Development Review* (2000) 3 (4), pp. 88–106.

13. This survey was conducted for the BBC World Service by the international polling firm GlobeScan, in collaboration with the Program on International Policy Attitude (PIPA) at the University of Maryland in January 2008. See "Widespread Unease about Economy and Globalization", available at http://www.worldpublicopinion.org/pipa/articles/btglobalizationtradeera/446.php?lb=btgl&pnt=446&nid=&id=. Washington, DC, World Public Opinion, posted on February 7, 2008.

5. The smiling face of globalization: the market-driven ascent of the dynamic South

A barrage of statistics shows that economic power is shifting away from the 'developed' economies towards emerging ones, especially in Asia . . . The West, and hundreds of millions of people in developing countries, has benefited from emerging-world growth. Globalization is not a zero-sum game.

The Economist, 2006

As a consequence of trade liberalization and other economic policy reforms, economic growth has accelerated in most of the developing world, with the most rapid growth in the countries whose reforms have gone the farthest.

Anne O. Krueger, 2008

1. GLOBALIZATION AND THE CHANGING ECONOMIC GEOGRAPHY

The contemporary phase of economic globalization picked up pace and widened its scope during the twenty-first century. One of its prominent constructive achievements is that it succeeded remarkably in benefiting and upgrading one group of developing economies more than others. As set out in Chapter 2, led by the four newly industrialized Asian economies (NIAEs), or the so-called East Asian dragons,[1] a not-so-small group of robustly growing developing and transition economies effectively reformed and restructured their economies.[2] This subset of dynamic developing economies has evolved better than the others and is continuing to do so. Their GDP growth rate has also been much higher than that of the advanced industrial economies. This unprecedented growth performance has dramatically changed the global economic landscape. It caused a gradual shift in global economic power from the advanced industrial economies to a subset of emerging economies of the dynamic South (EEDS), or simply the emerging-market economies. The Economist (2007c, p. 11) called it "the biggest revolution in history". Their interconnection with the mature industrial economies by way of global production networks and other channels is a first. Some members of this group of economies have acquired a noteworthy niche on the global economic stage. The People's Republic of China (hereinafter China) is indubitably the most significant example of this phenomenon (Das, 2008b).

The term 'South' used above needs brief explanation. It was used by economists and other social scientists for the developing economies of Africa, Asia and Latin America. In this terminology, the high-income industrial economies are referred to as the 'North'. This geographical designation was born of the fact that most economically advanced, high-income industrial countries are located in the North, while most of the low- and middle-income developing economies were in the South. It is economic characteristics that decide whether an economy is part of the North or the South. According to the *World Development Indicator 2008* (World Bank, 2008c), the South comprised 47 low-income countries with average per capita income of $578 in 2007 and 95 middle-income countries, with average per capita income of $4437. The middle-income countries were further subdivided into 54 lower-middle-income countries, with average per capita income of $1887 and 41 upper-middle-income countries, with average per capita income of $6987. In contrast to this group, the North comprised 27 of the 30 OECD economies – the so-called rich-man's club – with average per capita income of $37 566 in 2007.[3] The 15 Euro area countries, with average per capita income of $36 329 are part of the North.

To integrate with the global economy, several developing and transition economies made concerted efforts to undertake macroeconomic reforms, which facilitated their transition to a smoothly functioning market economy. As global transaction costs declined with improvements in transportation and communications, they were able to globalize their economies. The other driving factors that initiated and brought about this change in economic geography was expanding and deepening trade and financial linkages. Since 1990, the volume of multilateral trade has tripled and the volume of cross-border financial flows soared nine-fold. At this point in time, a broad class of global investors began to take an interest in this group of economies. Also, there has been an unremitting increase in the cross-listing of stocks, cross-border ownership and control of exchanges as well as banks and securities settlement systems. These economies were perceived by the global investing community as having strong, if unrealized, growth prospects. At the same time, they were somewhat peripheral to the mainstream of global economic functioning. They were instrumental in globalizing contemporary financial activity. Stock ownership grew increasingly global. According to the statistics compiled by the Federal Reserve Board, outside the US, 15 percent of the assets in private equity portfolios were in foreign equities in 1997; the corresponding proportion rose to 24 percent in 2007. For the US, the comparable proportion grew from 9 percent of total equity portfolios to 19 percent over the same period (Kohn, 2008).

160 *Two faces of globalization*

These transformations in the economies were of a fundamental nature and spurred dramatic changes in the location of production and demand for goods and services. Equally remarkable were the developments in global financial markets and the growth in cross-border trading of financial assets. As these profound transformations continued to take place in the volume, location and direction of trade and capital flows, global economic geography began to assume a new shape. The pace of the emergence of this new economic geography has been unprecedented. The evolution, spread and strengthening of completely new methods of trade, like outsourcing and integrated production networks, took place during the contemporary phase of globalization. Owing to these developments, the role of policy mandarins in reshaping the global economy by allowing their domestic economies to exploit their comparative advantage has become more crucial than ever.

The subset of dynamic developing and transition economies, noted above, has played a crucial role in the evolution of global economic geography. We shall see in this chapter how a steady rise in the economic prominence of these EEDS contributed to the changing *mise-en-scène* of the global economy. Any ambiguities about this fact were dispelled with the advent of the twenty-first century. The EEDS seem to be on the cusp of a new era in which they, as a group, are likely to play an increasingly important role in the global economy, parallel to the one played up till now by the advanced industrial economies, particularly the US. The rapid rise of the economies of the dynamic South, in particular the large economies like China and India, has begun impacting not only the global economy but also the advanced industrial economies (Winters and Yusuf, 2007; Das, 2006). Until not too long ago, both of these economies were autarkic and in a self-imposed isolation. As brought out in Section 2.1, this group of economies has been contributing to global growth; they could well become the new engines of growth in the foreseeable future.

1.1   Fluid Nature of Classification

The simple question of what countries can be called EEDS is difficult to answer because of the multiplicity of classifications. Institutions of global financial governance and large investment banks have propounded their own nomenclature, so has the *Economist*, which has closely monitored this subset of economies on a weekly basis since the early 1990s. Each of the following institutions has its own definition of EEDS and taxonomy:

1.   Institute of International Finance, Washington, DC;
2.   International Finance Corporation (the World Bank), Washington, DC;

3. International Monetary Fund, Washington, DC;
4. J.P. Morgan, New York;
5. Morgan Stanley, New York;
6. *The Economist*, London.

The number of economies in each classification varies marginally. One can take solace in the fact that, in spite of some variations, many countries are common to these lists. Only one country classification, by the FTSE Equity Committee, of the *Financial Times*, divides this group into two. The first it calls 'advance emerging' and includes Brazil, Israel, Korea, Mexico, South Africa and Taiwan. The second group it calls 'secondary emerging' and includes all the other EEDS. My own categorization of EEDS (given in Table 5.1) is eclectic. Many of these countries are common to all the classifications and are included in the list in Table 5.1.

Some of the above-mentioned members of the dynamic South have now grown into large economies of a significant size. In Table 5.1, they have been ranked according to the size of the GNI, indicating their gross national incomes.

Interestingly, four of the largest economies of the dynamic South have four different economic strengths. China has emerged as a strong manufacturing hub of global significance, Brazil's strength lies in agriculture and agro-processing, Russia has become one of the largest producers of oil and gas and India has been exploiting the ICT and ICT-enabled services sectors to a remarkable degree. The EEDS have also developed global brand equity in several areas of manufacture and services. Also, in crucial areas such as food and energy security, the EEDS "are becoming major players as producers and consumers in the global markets" (UNCTAD, 2008a, p. 2). The NIAEs have achieved a higher stage of economic development than the other economies of the dynamic South, with comparative advantage in high-technology industrial sectors. This country group is regarded as the first tier of recently industrialized countries, which have development lessons for the other developing economies. Many developing economies took a leaf or two from their book in devising their own economic strategies.

2. EMERGENCE OF THE DYNAMIC DEVELOPING ECONOMIES

The developing economies lacked not only capital, skills and a sound macroeconomic policy framework but also technology during the early postwar period. Both developing and transitional economies made grave macroeconomic policy errors during this period. Consequently, they paid

Table 5.1   Members of the dynamic South: global ranking and gross national income in 2007 (billions of $)

Economy	Rank in the global economy	Gross national income
China	4th	$3120
Brazil	10th	$1133
Russian Federation	11th	$1070
India	12th	$1069
Republic of Korea	13th	$955
Mexico	14th	$878
Turkey	17th	$592
Taiwan	20th	$395
Poland	21st	$374
Saudi Arabia	22nd	$373
Indonesia	23rd	$373
South Africa	28th	$274
Argentina	30th	$238
Hong Kong SAR	32nd	$218
Thailand	33rd	$217
Malaysia	37th	$173
Israel	38th	$157
Colombia	39th	$150
The Czech Republic	40th	$149
Singapore	41st	$149
The Philippines	42nd	$142
Pakistan	43rd	$141
Chile	44th	$139
Egypt	50th	$119
Hungary	52nd	$116
Peru	53rd	$96

Sources: World Bank (2008c); Council for Economic Planning and Development (2008).

the price of languishing at low economic levels for decades. However, this state of affairs has changed and over the past three decades several of them carried out market-oriented macroeconomic policy reforms, as elaborated in Section 2.2. They adopted a so-called outer-oriented economic regime, à la Anne Krueger, and liberalized their economic structure to trade and foreign direct investment (FDI), and making determined and concerted attempts to integrate with the global economy during the contemporary phase of globalization (Section 2.2). These developing economies started to be referred to as 'emerging' or 'dynamic' when they began to record substantial and sustained economic growth, essentially based on productivity gains and technological advancement. A group of transition economies joined this sub-group of economies. Not only have these economies been industrializing rapidly but they have also been experiencing rapid informationalization. The role and importance of these EEDS have changed substantially over recent years. They are no longer dependent on external capital as they were in the past. Due to rising commodity and energy prices and expanding exports of manufactures, many of the EEDS have significant current account surpluses. In the past, they used to import capital from the global capital market to finance their current account deficits. Many of these economies have now turned into capital exporters. Firms from these EEDS have become competitive in many products and services in the global markets and are making their presence felt. At this stage in their development, the EEDS can be regarded as being in a transitional stage between developing and advanced industrial economies.

The interest and participation of developing economies in the global economy grew in the mid-1980s. As their membership of and participation in the General Agreement on Tariffs and Trade (GATT) system increased and several of them ingeniously adopted export-led growth strategies, several developing economies began strengthening their external sector and exporting more than they had done in the pre-Uruguay Round (1986–94) period. They also initiated supply-side improvements in their economic structures. Recent export growth rates of developing economies were faster than the rates of exports of multilateral trade. Therefore, their share in multilateral trade has been growing. Developing countries' share of multilateral trade in total multilateral trade increased from 20 percent in 1970 to 29 per cent in 1996 and further to 37 percent in 2006, but declined in 2007 to 34 percent (WTO, 2008).

In the arena of international trade, developing economies that are part of the so-called dynamic South are led by China, which was the third largest trader in 2005 but surpassed the US in 2007 to become the second largest trader in the world. The dynamic South also includes other important trading economies. Korea is the 11th largest exporter, the Russian Federation the 12th, Hong Kong SAR the 13th and Singapore is the 14th largest exporter in the world. They are followed by Mexico (15th), Taiwan (16th), Saudi Arabia (18th), Malaysia (19th), Brazil (23rd), the United Arab Emirates (24th), Thailand (25th), India (26th), Poland (28th) and the Czech Republic (30th). All of these developing economies were included in the 2007 World Trade Organization (WTO) league table of leading exporters because they are significant exporters of merchandise. Among them China (7th), India (11th), Hong Kong SAR (12th), Singapore (14th), Korea (15th), Russian Federation (25th), Taiwan (26th), Thailand (27th),

Poland (28th), Malaysia (29th) and Turkey (30th) have also become substantial exporters of commercial services.[4]

As alluded to in Section 1, the four NIAEs were the initial trail-blazers. They in turn were followed by Southeast Asian and other economies. China's is by far the most noteworthy and educative illustration in this context. It joined this group of dynamic Asian economies after 1978, when it launched a comprehensive program of market-oriented economic reforms and restructuring. Until this time, China was a near autarky (Section 1). Since 2005, China has been the fourth largest economy in the world. It was projected to be the third largest in 2008. In August 2008, the Industrial and Commercial Bank of China (ICBC) became the largest bank in the world; at this point, three of the largest five banks in the world are Chinese. It is in no way surprising that after almost two decades of explosive growth, China's manufacturing sector has developed into a powerhouse and is making its presence felt globally. The era of producing labor-intensive manufactured products has receded into the background. It competitively produces medium- and high-technology products. There was little element of astonishment when, in 2004, China's electronics sector overtook the US's as the world's largest exporter of advanced-technology products like laptop computers, information technology products, cellular phones and digital cameras. Many of China's exports were computer-related equipment. In 2003, the US was the global leader in this category, with exports of $137 billion, followed by China with $123 billion. In 2004, China notched up another first. It exported $180 billion worth of high-technology equipment in 2004, compared to US exports of $149 billion, making China the leading global economy in exports of high-technology products (OECD, 2005a).

China's exports of computer-related equipment were significantly based on imports of electronic components from the other Asian economies. Both export-oriented information and communication technology (ICT) products and those required by the domestic market attracted large FDI. In 2005, $21 billion of FDI went to ICT-related manufacturing. China's export performance continued and by 2005, China's high-technology exports had reached $220 billion (EIU, 2007). This was a veritable land-mark in China's technological up-grading and industrial diversification. It moved up the ladder from being a country of low-technology sweatshops, to one with sophisticated electronics factories. China's total trade (imports plus exports) in both advanced-technology and ICT products in 1996 was $35 billion. What has been particularly impressive is the speed of China's emergence as an exporter of high-technology products. Growing at the rate of 38 percent a year, it soared to $329 billion in 2004 (OECD, 2005a). Also, value-added per worker in foreign-affiliated ICT enterprises went on rising steadily. Foreign investing firms have been shifting technically complex activities, such as design, testing and R&D, increasingly to China (OECD, 2006).

2.1 Increasing Economic Vigor

Principal economic indicators reveal that, for the most part, the majority of the EEDS are on a sound economic footing. For over two decades, their GDP grew at a brisk pace. Average annual GDP growth rates of this subset of economies have been higher than for other developing economies and much higher than for advanced industrial economies. During the 2000–07 period, the average growth rate of the EEDS hovered around 7 percent. In 2006, it rose to 7.4 percent, while moderating somewhat to 7 percent in 2007. As a group, the EEDS have emerged as a major determinant of global growth and prosperity. Measured in purchasing power parity (PPP) terms, according to Kose et al. (2008b), the EEDS accounted for 40 percent of global GDP in 2007, up from 25 percent in 1990. Due to sustained more rapid GDP growth rates, this subset of economies became a major contributor to global growth. Noteworthy is the fact that in 2007, China's contribution to global GDP growth alone, measured at market exchange rate, was larger than that of the US. Over the 2000–07 period, this group accounted for the bulk of global growth. This unprecedented growth dynamics enabled the EEDS to weather the recent global financial disturbance caused by the sub-prime mortgage crisis in the US. Also, by strengthening their financial trade and linkages with the global economy, "they helped keep advanced economies from slowing down" (Johnson, 2008, p. 54).

Since the late 1990s, the EEDS have emerged as large holders of foreign-exchange reserves. At $1.76 trillion in April 2008, China held the largest foreign-exchange reserves in the world. Foreign liquidity reserves of this group of economies exceeded $3.5 trillion and they own three-fourths of global foreign exchange reserves. This has generated a fervent debate in the profession about the justification for holding such large amounts of capital in reserves. Also, large reserves of foreign liquidity led to sharp exchange rate appreciation in some countries.

Many of the EEDS run large current account surpluses, which became their main source of foreign currency earnings. This is in stark contrast to the early 1990s, when their principal source of foreign currency was capital inflows. Their aggregate current account surpluses grew and were more than double their net private capital inflows in 2007. However, some EEDS went against the grain and recorded current account deficits. Hungary, India, South Africa and Turkey came into this category;

external capital inflows continued to finance their current account deficits. One important implication of large current account surpluses is that these economies are far less vulnerable to external shocks and abrupt cessation of external capital inflows known as "sudden stops". As a group, they do not need external capital resources. Their external debts were in decline. As a group of economies, they are net creditors.

As many EEDS carried out their market-oriented reforms and adopted an outer-oriented economic strategy (Section 2), their net exports continued to increase and contributed sizeably to aggregate demand and economic growth. This applies most to the NIAEs, China and the other Southeast Asian EEDS. The contribution of external demand has fallen for the EEDS in Europe since 2005 but remained positive. It also fell for the EEDS in Latin America, but turned moderately negative. Strong domestic demand supplanted the weakness of the external sector and played a crucial role in sustaining growth. Investment demand was also strong in many EEDS, in particular in Europe, China and Latin America; it helped underpin rapid growth in these economies.

With one exception, their budget deficits were either manageable or enviably small. Disturbing levels of budget deficits has remained a chronic problem in India. In general, fiscal consolidation and improved budget management have improved the economic resilience of EEDS. Inflation, another important indicator of economic performance, remained generally low during the preceding ten years. It has hovered around 3.5 percent since the late 1990s, although a small number of EEDS presented a minor problem in this regard. In some EEDS, concerns were expressed regarding rising levels of inflation. Argentina and the Russian Federation are prominent among them. In India and Mexico, inflation rates did cross target levels. In India, 2006 and 2007 continued to be years when inflationary rates shot above the central bank's medium-term comfort zone. Compared to other EEDS, China's inflation rate was low, but it picked up in 2007. In a majority of EEDS, currencies were not overvalued. If anything, they were somewhat undervalued. Between 2004 and 2007, over 10 percent real currency appreciation took place in Korea, Malaysia and Thailand. In Brazil, this was much higher, at 34 percent. The *Economist* (2007c) reported that, during 2007, all the 32 EEDS that were tracked by the *Economist* recorded positive growth rates. This was a first. In every previous year, at least one economy recorded a negative growth rate, or a recession. However, the flip side of the coin is that none of them so far is a high per capita income economy. Also, the EEDS are better integrated with the global economy in terms of trade in goods and some services; the same can not be said about their degree of financial integration. The banks and financial institutions in the EEDS grew more cautious after the financial crises of the late 1990s (Johnson, 2008). It was essentially for this reason that the EEDS were not badly mangled by the sub-prime crisis.

2.2   Metamorphosis in Global Economic Geography

This is the story of the changing geography of the world economy during the contemporary phase of globalization and of the emergence of the so-called dynamic South, which is leading to startlingly rapid changes in the geographical locus of global economic activity (Fischer, 2006). The contemporary phase of globalization is not only sustaining and advancing the emergence of the dynamic South but also promoting *partial* economic convergence. It is also restructuring and rearranging multilateral trading and international financial systems.

One of the reasons why this group of developing economies has performed better than other developing economies is that, over the past three decades, these developing economies successfully carried out market-oriented macroeconomic reforms and restructuring and adopted resilient domestic policy frameworks, which contributed to strong domestic economic performance. A small number of developing economies – particularly the East Asian economies – has managed sustained growth since the 1960s. By the late 1980s and early 1990s, several more developing and transition economies had learned how to run their economies with sustainable budget deficits or occasional budget surpluses and moderate inflation, while preventing currency overvaluation. Many of them successfully brought in institutional improvements, including in the investment environment, along with political stability. One important outcome of these policy measures was rapid growth in these economies, which was sustained, almost without a break, for a substantial length of time. In their economic restructuring period, they showed a clear preference for outer-oriented economic policies (see Section 1.1), which in turn resulted in an increase in their export-to-GDP ratio. Global economic and financial integration measures were an integral part of this outer-oriented strategic stance. Greater integration with the global economy enabled these economies to grow rapidly.

This group of economies is characterized by their movement towards an open market economy, as well as by transparency and efficiency in the capital market. In particular, they endeavor to reform their exchange rate regimes, because a stable currency builds confidence in an economy. This is also an indispensable condition for attracting foreign direct and portfolio investments. An idiosyncratic feature of this group of economies is their ability to attract capital from global financial markets, both direct and portfolio (Section 4). Inflows of external capital denote, first, that the economy has come into its own and that the global investing community feels confident about investing in it. Second, these capital inflows serve to enhance the volume of domestic equity markets in the EEDS. Third, these inflows also increase investment in long-term infrastructure in the economy, resulting in steady gains in total factor productivity (TFP).

Another essential characteristic of the EEDS is their proactive and conscious endeavors to integrate globally, which has lent a helpful hand to this group of economies (alluded to in Section 2). To that end, the EEDS erred on the side of keeping their exchange rates somewhat undervalued. It is difficult to determine whether this was ultimately a good idea, although this strategy did contribute to strong GDP growth for a short period. Their endeavors to integrate in the global economy helped them in poverty alleviation and rapid pace industrialization, thereby markedly improving the living standards of their people in the short span of two generations. As the confidence of the global investing community and entrepreneurs, including transnational corporations (TNCs), grew in these economies, they began expanding their business activities in them by establishing joint ventures or building greenfield plants. For the recipient EEDS, this entailed benefits like employment generation, refinement in managerial skills and sharing in the transfer of technology, which had long-term implications. Ultimately, the effect would be rising production levels of goods and services, augmenting GDP, leading to a reduction in the gap between the EEDS and the advanced industrial economies.

This subset of developing economies also undertook the difficult task of up-scaling their productive capacities and structurally diversified their economies. In the process, they exploited their traditional strength in labor and natural resources and, using the available technology, generated significant production capabilities. This process contributed to a steady improvement in domestic economic performance and TFP. With the passage of time, they climbed to the higher rungs of the technology ladder and turned into EEDS. Towards the end of the twentieth century, these economies began to produce high-technology products and compete in the global marketplace. There was a rapid and sustained technological upgrading in the product and export composition of developing countries (Mayer, 2003). What is new in this regard is integrated networked production, which is responsible for the bulk of high-technology exports from the EEDS (Srholec, 2007). A caveat is essential here. While EEDS began producing high-technology products, the technological level of these economies is far from uniform. A fair degree of diversity exists in them.

In this sequence of developments, the Asian crisis of 1997–8 was an important time for the EEDS. Large economies in Latin America, the Russian Federation and Turkey also fell victim to macroeconomic and financial crises in the late 1990s. The recovery from crises was swift and taught many invaluable lessons to public policy makers. One important lesson was that, after liberalizing their economies to financial flows of diverse kinds and different maturities, they needed to carry larger foreign exchange reserves than they had done in the past. Consequently, between 1998 and 2008, Asian economies quadrupled their reserves. Even if China is excluded, these reserves doubled in nominal terms during the stipulated period. Such a large build-up of reserves exposed the Asian economies to the accusation that they were building Noah's ark, not saving for a rainy day. After recovery from the crises, increased emphasis was placed by the EEDS on further improving macroeconomic policy frameworks and implementing more growth-enhancing structural reforms. Against the backdrop of the crisis, the adoption of a flexible exchange rate regime became a crucial policy measure. Fiscal discipline was tightened and achieving a current account surplus was made into a priority objective. Also, the banking and financial sectors became more conservative and less adventurous than before. The country ratings of the EEDS reflected these improvements and changes in stance. Between 2000 and 2007, the average credit rating of the economies included in the EMBI global index improved from BB- to BB+ (Maier and Vasishtha, 2008).

The evolution of the dynamic South would lead to three immediate consequences: first, as the balance of economic prowess in the world shifts, the balance of political power follows suit. That is not to say that the dynamic South will form a political bloc. Given the diversity of these countries and their interests, cultures and histories, the possibility of the formation of such a bloc seems far-fetched, albeit several regional and sub-regional groups may emerge. However, these geo-economic and geo-political transformations will engender new economic and political relationships and the alignments that evolved during the latter half of the foregoing century will need to change materially. Second, as the contemporary phase of globalization has progressed, the collapse of the Soviet bloc brought some 760 million workers into the global labor market, while the opening up of the Chinese and Indian economies added a further 760 million and 440 million, respectively, to the global labor pool (Venables, 2006). This doubled the global labor pool. A direct consequence of this was that the return to capital was boosted, which richly rewarded its owners. Third, impressive GDP growth in this group of emerging economies has been driving growth in the global economy (IMF, 2008b). As these newcomers to industrialization become better integrated in the global economy in the foreseeable future, this impetus to sustained global growth can reasonably be expected to be maintained.[5] This implies a healthy reinforcement of the global economy.

Although the EEDS have been growing at a more rapid rate than high-income industrial economies since the early 1980s, this became more noticeable in the late 1990s because the difference in the growth rates of the two groups widened at this point in time. More importantly, after the early 1990s, several EEDS became progressively integrated into the global economy, in particular through integrated production networks. In addition, during this period, global trade and capital flows accelerated relative to GDP compared to the past. Among the EEDS, China has been casting the longest shadow and having the utmost impact on the global economy. This is because of the sheer size of its economy and the extraordinary extent of its liberalization to trade and investment. In 2007, China accounted for 8.8 percent of total multilateral trade in goods, up from 4 percent in 2000 (Das, 2008c).

This will eventually imply a reduction in the dominance of the global economy by the advanced industrial economies. Also, the dynamic South will begin influencing the performance of the high-income industrial countries more than in the past. Brisk growth and a rapid increase in import demand from the dynamic South, as well as increasing investment by them, will benefit other sub-groups in the global economy by sustaining their growth. The benefiting group will include other developing economies, economies in transition and high-income industrial economies. As this economic scenario evolves further, global economic integration will begin to appear a win-win proposition. Together, these consequences may well initiate transformation in the global economic, financial and political architecture.

2.3 Was this Really Unprecedented?

The evolution of the dynamic South and the process of shifting global economic power are not extraordinary developments. Many of these economies have not come to the forefront for the first time. A historical perspective testifies to the fact that some of the member economies of the dynamic South, like China and India, were among the largest global economies in the 18th century, up until 1820 (Das, 2006).[6] However, these economies failed to participate in the Industrial Revolution, which remained confined for the most part to Western Europe. Also, they did not participate in the first phase of globalization, which ended in 1913 (Chapter 1). Consequently, they lagged behind. Given this history, their present rapid growth – and thus their acquisition of conspicuous status on the global economic stage – is tantamount to progressing towards restoration of the old economic order.

It is reasonable to inquire why only a small number of developing economies have advanced in their economic status during the current period and succeeded in moving towards achieving some serious convergence. There are two answers to this query and the first was given above in Section 1.1. The second reason is historical. Since the end of World War II, many members of the dynamic South had gradually accumulated modern manufacturing experience. Some also had some exposure to modern factory life during the pre-war period. This category included countries like China, India, Indonesia, Republic of Korea (hereinafter Korea), Malaysia, Taiwan and Thailand in Asia; Argentina, Brazil, Chile and Mexico in Latin America; and Turkey in the Middle East (Amsden, 2001). History reveals that these countries were not entirely neophytes to modern world industries and had acquired a reasonable amount of experience and expertise in manufacturing simple products (like cotton textiles, silk and foodstuff) and consumer goods for domestic markets. With the passage of time, they became ready to move into medium-technology products and subsequently into high-technology sectors. During the early years of this century, some of them, particularly the NIAEs and China and India, began to move into production of knowledge-intensive products. According to the nomenclature coined by Amsden (2001, p. 5), these economies were "the rest" and they improved their industrial base during the latter half of the 20th century and slowly advanced economically. She noted that this was the first instance of a group of developing economies industrializing "without proprietary innovations". They succeeded in moving into industries that required large amounts of technological capabilities without initially having advanced technological capabilities of their own. Their late industrialization was squarely based on learning from other advanced countries' commercialized technologies. This learning process was instrumental in their eventually establishing modern industries. This group of economies successfully moved from "a set of assets based on primary products, exploited by unskilled labor, to a set of assets based on knowledge, exploited by skilled labor".

3.   A NEW DIMENSION OF GLOBALIZATION

During the early postwar period, the developing economies were much too small in terms of the size of their GDP. Also, they did not interact much economically with each other. After West European economies had recovered from the war, the US and a small number of advanced industrial economies overwhelmingly dominated the global economy and trade and financial flows. The structural changes that took place in the global economy during the contemporary era of globalization include

dramatically increased South–South interaction through trade and investment channels. The significance of South–South trade in total multilateral
trade has been on the rise, and its share in total trade has increased, particularly in the post-1995 period.[7] One noticeable feature of South–South
trade is that the bulk of it occurs among economies of the same region.

3.1   Escalating South–South Trade in Goods

Although many developing economies were contracting parties (CPs) to
the General Agreement on Tariffs and Trade (GATT) during the early
postwar decades, they did not participate much in multilateral trade.[8]
There was hardly any South–South trade. They virtually ignored it. This
changed gradually and during the present phase of globalization, particularly during the decade of the 1990s, their trade picked up in terms of
momentum and quality. From \$82 billion in 1990, it reached \$2.0 trillion
in 2000. This testifies to the fact that the 1990s was a successful decade
for the developing economies; their trade increased 2.4 times. The rapid
growth continued and the value of their trade reached \$3.7 trillion in 2005
and \$4.5 trillion in 2006. South–South trade accounted for 37 percent of
the total in 2006. In 1985, the GATT league table of large exporters did
not include any developing economy, but in 1995 there were eight developing countries in the top 20 trading economies. In 2007, this number
increased to nine. The share of these countries in total merchandise trade
doubled from 13 percent in 1985 to 26 percent in 2006.

Intra-trade among the developing economies gathered pace during
the 1980s and since the mid-1990s it has expanded at an impressive pace.
Many large EEDS became regional locomotives of trade in their respective
regions. Between 1985 and 1995, intra-trade among the developing economies almost quadrupled, from \$14 billion to \$58 billion. Between 1995 and
2006, South–South trade more than tripled, increasing from \$577 billion
to over \$2 trillion. In 2006, it was 17 percent of world merchandise trade.
The volume of South–South trade accounted for 46 percent of the total
merchandise trade of the developing economies in 2006. It was 32 percent
in 1990 and 40 percent in 2000. Manufactured products accounted for half
of South–South trade. Trade in commodities, including fuels, were strong
drivers of South–South trade.

The increase in South–South trade was partly due to increasing
complementarities. While the so-called fundamentals are important in
determining what is produced in an economy and exported, they do not
completely determine what products a country will produce and trade.
By fundamentals, we mean physical and human capital, labor, natural
resources, location and institutional quality. Also, production of goods

is not alike in terms of its consequences for economic growth (Hausmann et al., 2007). What is produced by a developing economy – particularly for export – matters and this determines its level of integration with the global economy as well as its growth rate. That similar developing countries can develop dissimilar production and trade structures is explained by economic geography or spatial economic models (Fujita et al., 1999). As the economies of the South are at different stages of growth, they are diversified and different in their comparative advantage, and therefore in their specialization for trade. Their areas of high productivity and import demand patterns are diverse. This diversity creates opportunities for enhanced South–South trade. However, what is more important is that several EEDS were able to develop dynamic sectors of exportable goods and services. Private sector firms in the EEDS discover, or stumble upon, some products and services and endeavor to perfect their production, and subsequently their export. Many of them were products and services of high technological complexity. This changed the export baskets of the EEDS and rendered them more technology-intensive than those in the past. Many of these new exportables turned out to be high-growth products and services. This transformation in the export of goods and services made the exports of developing economies more dynamic. It favorably influenced both their exports in general as well as South–South trade.

UNCTAD (2007a) has identified the dynamic export products in emerging South–South trade. These product categories are concentrated in certain harmonized system (HS) categories:

(i)   ores and minerals (HS 25–7); actual products include iron, copper, nickel, cobalt and lead;
(ii) organic chemicals (HS 29);
(iii) iron and steel and other metal products (HS 71 and 72); actual products include ferrous waste, flat-rolled stainless steel, tubes and pipes, unwrought nickel;
(iv) plastic and articles (HS 39); actual products include acrylic polyamides, silicons in primary forms;
(v)   parts and components of mechanical appliances and electronics (HD 84 and 85), actual products include engines and motors, machine hand tools, electric storage batteries, transmission apparatus;
(vi) optical and precision articles (HS 90); actual products include optical fibers, liquid crystal devices, etc.[9]

These six categories of products can be plainly classified into three categories based on factor intensity, namely, (i) primary products like ores and minerals, (ii) low-skill and low-technology manufactures (like iron, steel and metal products) and (iii) high-skill and high-technology products like organic chemicals, plastic articles, appliances and precision tools.

The dynamic sectors and products of exportable goods and services, mentioned above, largely fell into the sectors listed above. This confirms that, in these dynamic sectors and products, the developing economies succeeded in creating supply capacities and specialized. The result was that they became significant exporters to the global marketplace. Also, in their exports in these sectors and products, their rate of market share increase was high. This applies more particularly to the group of high-skill and high-technology manufactures. Thus, the pace of specialization of the South in this group was more intense than for other groups of products. The dynamic products of exportable goods and services that are exported to the North from the EEDS demonstrated a concentration in some labor-intensive sectors as well. Two such important sectors are paper products (HS 48) and textiles and clothing (HS 56 and 61).

3.2 Escalating South-South Trade in Services

The importance of the services sector in the economy and its contribution to income generation has been on the rise. This applies to both developing and advanced industrial economies. This sector has also become an effective instrument of employment generation and a source of earning foreign exchange. As a proportion of GDP, this sector went on expanding. The share of services in GDP expanded from 65 percent to 73 percent over the 1990–2006 period in the advanced industrial economies and from 30 percent to 51 percent in the developing economies. Some EEDSs, like India, witnessed an unusually high growth rate in their services sector output after launching their economic liberalization and restructuring programs. Consequently, in India, the share of services in GDP has hovered around 60 percent and resembles that of a high-income industrial economy, although India's per capital income is still low.

This sector accounted for 72 percent of employment in the industrial economies and 35 percent in the developing economies. As an economic strategy, the EEDS have been focusing more on the services sector and trade in services. Multilateral trade in commercial services has been one of the fastest growing components of multilateral trade. It gathered further pace in the recent past, growing at a rate of 12 percent between 2000 and 2007. South–South trade in services accounts for over 10 percent of the total multilateral trade in services.[10] The exports of EEDS originating from the services sector rose from $155 billion in 1990 to $700 billion in

2006. Their place in the GATT/WTO league tables of trade in services has also improved. Mexico was the only developing economy to appear in the 1985 table. This number increased to four in 2005 and five in 2007. These five economies are China, India, Hong Kong SAR, Singapore and Korea. In the developing world, export of services has been highly concentrated. The top 15 services exporters account for close to 80 percent of the total exports from the South.[11]

Although transport and travel services are among the major traded commercial services for the South, many developing economies have acquired considerable niche markets in construction and other high-value-added services sectors, including finance and insurance, business services and computer and information services. Trade in ICT-enabled services grew at a faster pace compared to that for trade in services. Intra-South trade in ICT products recorded strong growth and is substantial. The latest comparable statistics available so far are for 2004, when South–South exports of ICT goods exceeded those from South to North. The value of South–South trade in ICT products was $410 billion, which was close to the value of North–North trade, $450 billion. The value of intra-South trade in ICT products was projected to surpass that of intra-North trade in 2006 (UNCTAD, 2008b). This confirms the fact that trade among developing economies is an important phenomenon and also indicates a shift in production of ICT equipment from the advanced industrial economies to those developing economies that have succeeded in raising the technology levels of their economies. It also demonstrates the growing importance of the developing economies as markets for ICT products. However, it goes counter to past trends when ICT trade took place essentially among the advanced industrial economies. A new trend is in the making, according to which South–South trade may well dominate trade in ICT products.

The share of developing countries in the export of ICT-enabled services was a measly 4 percent in 1995. It soared to 28 percent in 2005. ICT-enabled services include business process outsourcing (BPO) like communication services, insurance services, financial services, computer and information services, and the like. Hong Kong SAR was the only developing country among the top ten ICT-enabled services exporting countries in 2004. In 2005, India overtook Italy, Luxembourg and Hong Kong SAR, in that order, and became one of the top ten exporting economies. Its export value was $41 billion, with a market share of 3.8 percent. The average annual growth rate of exports of Indian ICT-enabled services between 2000 and 2005 was 37 percent, higher than the overall export growth for this category of exports. A developing country that was close on the heels of India was Hong Kong SAR, with total exports of $33 billion. Singapore, China and Korea, in that order, followed behind them and were attempting to catch up.[12]

The *State of the Industry Report 2008* from Oliver Wyman Group (2008) noted that firms from the EEDS had made great inroads into the global ICT market. Several compelling findings have emerged from this report, including the fact that these economies are home to both the largest ICT firms in the world, like China Mobil and Bharti Airtel, and that these firms are the driving force behind global revenue growth in many sectors, particularly mobile. In 2007, they captured around 60 percent of the world's market and earned $1.1 trillion in revenues.

3.3   Is Asia the Hub of South-South Trade?

As South–South trade grew, a hub-and-spoke pattern emerged, with Asia being the incontestable trade hub. Asia's exports to the South increased at a much faster rate than those to the rest of the world. In the realm of South–South trade, Asia is both a large exporter and large importer. The dynamic East and Southeast Asian economies and China were the most active in this respect. They have been influencing the established global trade pattern and creating a new trading paradigm. Besides, according to the 2006 statistics, approximately 86 percent of South–South trade was intra-Asia trade. Intra-trade only among the East, Southeast Asian economies and China was half of the total South–South trade. A noteworthy feature is the differing concentration of South–South trade in the three principal developing regions. In the case of developing Asia, over half (51 percent) of its exports went to the other developing economies. However, for Africa and Latin America, this proportion was much lower, at 30 percent and 27 percent, respectively. The pace of increase of South–South trade between 1995 and 2005 was discernibly brisker than that of North–South trade. While exports from the advanced industrial economies to the developing economies increased 140 percent over this period, South–South exports soared 200 percent (JETRO, 2008). To be sure, this could partly be attributed to the low base effect.

Although Asian economies have not until recently shown a strong proclivity towards institutionalized regionalization like economies in Europe, market-driven trade among the Asian economies has been expanding rapidly for several decades. Consequently, Asia has become a driving force as well as the focal point of South–South trade (Das, 2005d). Several Asian developing economies have emerged as the most successful trading economies. The four NIAEs and China fall into this category. Exports of manufactured products from Asia to other developing economies grew at a brisk pace. They were 45 percent of the total in 2005, up from 35 percent in 1995. Intra-Asian trade is particularly dominated by manufactured products of all factor intensities. In the recent past, there has been an increase in imports of Asian economies from other regions, particularly from Africa. This increase was driven by high demand for fuel and industrial raw materials by the Asian economies.

There are three apparent reasons that explain Asia's continuing dominance of South–South trade. First, it is larger in terms of the sheer size of GDP than the other two regions. Second, its openness to trade and, therefore, participation in multilateral trade are comparatively much greater. Its trade-to-GDP ratio was 35.1 percent in 2006, compared to 21.1 percent for Africa and 15.8 percent for Latin America (JETRO, 2008). Third, as indicated in the preceding paragraph, Asia's market-driven regional integration and proactive participation in regional production networks is much greater than those of the other two regions. China's role in this context cannot be disregarded. By being the center of integrated networked production, China has played a unique role in Asian trade. A significant amount of China's imports are intermediate goods, components and sub-assemblies to be processed by its export sector. Imports for final domestic consumption are much smaller.

3.4 Escalating South–South Foreign Direct Investment

Traditionally, FDI used to be mobilized from advanced industrial economies to developing economies. It was logical for capital to flow from capital-surplus to capital-scarce economies. This trend has been amended. The dynamic role played by the EEDS in the global economy is manifested by the recent drive in their capital exports. They have increasingly become a source of FDI to other economies in the South, and also in the North. Although trickles of outward FDI flows from the developing economies can be traced back to 1973, it increased during the 1985–9 period, gathering further momentum during 1991–7. Their FDI outflows increased from an average of $65 billion in the early 1990s to $193 billion in 2006, which was 16 percent of total FDI for that year. The stock of outward FDI from the developing economies was measured at $1.4 trillion in 2005, or 13 percent of the total global stock of FDI.

The number of EEDS investing in other economies has concurrently risen. In 1990, only six of them had FDI stocks of over $5 billion, while in 2005, this number leapt to 25.[13] Only a small number of EEDS are responsible for a major proportion of FDI outflows. FDI outflows are concentrated by both country of origin and industry. This could partly be due to the fact that this is still an emerging phenomenon. Hong Kong SAR is the largest developing country investor; it is the sixth largest in terms of the stock of global FDI.

A good number of TNCs from the developing economies have been expanding in other developing economies. International production from these TNCs can be expected to become an important part of ongoing global integration. In general, TNCs from the developing economies were technology followers. Many of these TNCs are fairly sophisticated in their operations and possess distinctive advantages over host country firms. Frequently, there are complementaries between the TNCs from the South and the North in the host country. For instance, TNCs from the four NIAEs in the electronics industries frequently resort to a division of labor, that is, TNCs from the advanced industrial economies retain R&D, product design, branding and marketing, while contract manufacturing is left to TNCs from the developing economies. Besides, the developing country TNCs stand to benefit from the home-country's locational factors, including access to natural resources and cheap capital.

Mergers and acquisitions (M&As) are an important mode of foreign entry for TNCs in general and TNCs from the developing world have started making frequent use of it. Since the late 1980s, they have been engaged in M&A activity, reaching an unprecedented level of $90 billion in 2005. Asian economies have been responsible for a large number of M&As. Their increasing financial strength encouraged them to engage in mega M&A deals, which went up from one in 1990 to 19 in 2005. Each one of these mega-mergers was worth $1 billion or more. Greenfield projects and expansions of current operations in other developing economies is another popular mode of FDI expansion for TNCs from the developing economies. ICT-related greenfield projects have recently been on the rise.

Asian economies have been the largest source of South–South FDI since the mid-1990s. Asia's share in total South–South FDI was 46 percent in 1990. This soared to 62 percent in 2005. The largest Asian investors are the four ANIEs, China and Malaysia. According to 2005 statistics, FDI from China reached $11 billion. Almost three-quarters of Chinese FDI goes to Hong Kong SAR, a part of which is attributed to round-tripping.

A novel development is rapidly growing FDI from the Russian Federation, which is a relatively new source country. Its stock of FDI soared from $20 billion in 2000 to $120 billion in 2005, when it became the third largest FDI exporter. The offshore financial center of the British Virgin Islands occupied the second position. Its principal destinations are the economies of Southeastern Europe and the Commonwealth of Independent States (CIS). A large proportion of Russian FDI went into the exploitation of natural resources.[14]

4. INNOVATIVE AND VALUABLE DESTINATIONS FOR GLOBAL INVESTORS

Growth, expansion and deepening of financial markets in the EEDS gave an impetus to financial globalization. Equity markets in several EEDS have developed rapidly and characteristically grown into markets that yield high returns. However, as these equity markets are considered markets in transition, they are not paragons of stability. Therefore, they are equity markets of interest for investors who are looking for high rates of returns on their portfolios and are not highly risk averse. Large institutional investors like investment banks, pension funds, mutual funds and hedge funds have increasingly taken a keen interest in these equity markets because they have proved to be lucrative destinations. Other than generating distinctively high rates of return, these markets offer rewarding opportunities for diversification, reducing portfolio risk. One of their functional attributes was their low correlation coefficient with stock markets in the advanced industrial economies.

Rapid growth of stock markets is regarded as a reflection of their increasing economic strength, rising financial vigor and creditworthiness. The realization has dawned on global investors that they are run with a certain degree of professional acumen. The performance indices of these equity markets were closely monitored. They have risen precipitously in the recent past. Equity markets in the EEDS have been instrumental in turning the global investment industry veritably global. In dollar terms, Morgan Stanley Capital International's (MSCI) emerging-market index soared more than fourfold between 2003 and 2007. The comparable performance of the S&P 500 was an increase of barely 70 percent. Since the early 1980s, these markets have become a standard part of the repertoire of portfolio and fund managers in the high-income industrial world, who treat them as markets with enormous growth potential. Equity markets in the EEDS have provided high returns to investors in the advanced industrial economies. They returned 34.9 percent in 2007 and a spectacular 37 percent per annum on average over the 2002–07 period (Hoguet, 2008). Until 2007, these markets proved to be resilient in the face of deteriorating conditions in global credit markets.

The significance of the EEDS in the global economy, and particularly for global financial markets, is denoted by intensive coverage of these economies by a large number of supranational and financial institutions. They provide up-to-date statistical, economic and financial environment data on the EEDS, for the purpose of "scenario analysis". The largest institutions include the International Monetary Fund (IMF), which in the past published quarterly *Emerging Market Financing* reports and at present publishes the *Global Financial Stability Report*; the Institute of International Finance (IIF) which focuses on financial and banking data; and the Economic Intelligence Unit, London, which constantly publishes detailed analytical studies and a plethora of statistics. Morgan Stanley Capital International (MSCI) publishes a widely followed index of the EEDS' equity markets. The MSCI is designed to measure equity market performance in these economies. To complete this coverage, J.P. Morgan publishes its well-known J.P. Morgan Emerging Market Bond Index Global or EMBI Global. It tracks the price of dollar-denominated emerging market debt. It publishes data on total returns for dollar-denominated debt instruments issued by emerging market sovereign and quasi-sovereign entities, like Brady bonds, bank loans and Eurobonds. This is the traditional gauge of the risk of emerging market debt.

The objective of such intensive coverage and monitoring of the EEDS was to size them up for portfolio investment. The majority of large foreign investment banks and institutions went on upgrading EEDS in their portfolios and increased their investment in them. These upgrades were based on current valuation and a range of other tactical indicators. The bull market was seen as intact in the EEDS until 2007. Based on this analysis, barring a global recession or stagnation scenario, these markets were judged highly attractive. Morgan Stanley strongly argued in favor of the economic decoupling thesis discussed below (Section 6). Against the background of sharply deteriorating conditions in the stock markets of the US and other industrial economies during 2008, foreign investors were convinced that the core EEDS assets class (Brazil, China, the Russian Federation and the Middle East) will come through relatively unscathed, with modest growth deceleration (DeRamos, 2008). Improved fundamentals in the EEDS, abundant reserves and strong GDP growth performance are likely to sustain capital flows into the equity markets in the EEDS. However, the EEDS in Europe do suffer from macroeconomic vulnerabilities, making them susceptible to deterioration in the external environment.

Conditions for the EEDS in the global capital markets have been growing benign and they have been increasingly successful in attracting finance at favorable rates. According to the EMBI Global, spreads on EEDS sovereign debt have been falling since 1999 in virtually all regions of the global economy. In 2007, they were at a historical low level. The EMBI Global yielded the "thinnest spread ever recorded over riskless US Treasury bonds" (Maier and Vasishtha, 2008, p. 2). There were two mutually related reasons behind thinning spreads. First, as discussed at length in Section 2.2, the EEDS undertook structural reforms and steadily improved their macroeconomic policy framework. They created a healthy macroeconomic climate in their respective domestic economies, promoted rapid growth and many of them reined in inflation. Improvements in fundamentals apparently reduced any risk of loan default, with the result that risk premia logically declined and spreads narrowed. Second, improvements in some of the individual macroeconomic variables had a positive effect on the spread. Factor analysis by Maier and Vasishtha (2008) revealed that reduction in long-term debt and inflation had the largest statistical impact on the contraction of spreads. They were followed by reduction in budget deficit and increase in export-to-GDP ratio. All these variables combined to improve macroeconomic fundamentals and reduced vulnerability to external shocks.[15]

4.1 Surging Assets in the Dynamic South

With a rising level of cross-border investment, the global economy is growing more financially integrated and interdependent than it was until the recent past. In 2006, the outstanding stock of cross-border investment reached $74.5 trillion in assets (Farrell et al., 2008). This included investment by TNCs, purchases of foreign debt and equities by investors around the globe, as well as foreign lending and borrowings. Notwithstanding the financial disruptions in the latter half of 2007, the available preliminary data indicated that this surge in cross-border investment continued in 2007. Importantly, the source and direction of cross-border capital flows discernibly shifted. As noted below (Section 5), due to windfall oil revenues, members of the GCC became major investors in the global financial markets. They joined the East Asian EEDS in 2006 to be among the largest net suppliers of capital in the world.

With the increase in their financial assets, the importance of EEDS in the global financial markets has been on the rise. Their financial assets rose by $5.3 trillion in 2006, reaching $23.6 trillion. The growth rate of financial assets in the EEDS between 1996 and 2006 was twice that of the advanced industrial economies. China alone accounted for a third of all financial assets of the EEDS and for almost one-half of their growth in 2006.

Bank deposits is the largest asset category for the EEDS. The reason is that, unlike the advanced industrial economies, financial markets are not highly sophisticated in these economies. Equity markets in these economies are growing as well as maturing. They are instrumental in and responsible for a large proportion of asset growth in the EEDS. Business corporations in the EEDS raised 35 percent of all capital raised globally through initial public offerings (IPOs) in 2006; in 2000, the corresponding proportion was a mere 10 percent (Farrell et al., 2008).

4.2 Credit Crunch and the Financial Markets in the Dynamic South

The credit crunch that erupted in the US economy in August 2007, and
spread to the European Union (EU), took several twists and worsened
the plight of the global financial markets in 2008. Although this severe
financial disorder affected the EEDS, the financial outlook in this group
of economies was still relatively better than in the industrial economies.
Bohme et al. (2008) noted that, even in the worst case scenario, financial
markets in the EEDS will record revenue growth in an absolute sense.
They may even record a dramatic increase in revenues in the short as well
as medium term. According to the projections of the McKinsey Global
Institute (2008), collective revenues from investment banking and capital
market activities in the EEDS are likely to match those in Canada and the
US by 2010.

Recovery from the turbulence of 2007 and 2008 in the global capital
markets will be directly influenced by three critical features: first, recovery
in the US economy and along with that, an upswing in the global economy;
second, the time lag in spreading of recovery to the credit markets; and,
third, reactions by investors and regulators during the recovery period.
Given this backdrop of financial turmoil in the advanced industrial
economies, financial markets in the EEDS stand to perform better. For
one thing, the benign macroeconomic policy framework discussed above
(Section 2.2) is sure to be an important contributory factor. Second, global
commodity and energy demand and the large infrastructure investment
outlays in the EEDS will continue to underpin their growth. Third, a new
group of TNCs from the large EEDS that have been successfully operating
globally have a need for sophisticated investment and banking services,
which only large multinational banks could provide in the past. These
TNCs will be an attractive fee pool for banks in the EEDS economies
at present. Capital markets in the EEDS will continue to evolve and be
an ever increasing source of capital in global financial markets. Besides,
industrial country-based global investment banks have been paying progressively more attention to the financial markets in the EEDS and redi-
recting their resources towards this group of economies because they are
being regarded as the new source of revenue. This applies to both human
and financial resources, which are being redirected towards financial
markets in the EEDS.

In the case of a benign scenario of early global economic recovery,
global capital markets are likely to start recovering in 2009. Bohme et
al. (2008) computed that, given this scenario, revenues from investment
banking activity in the EEDS by the large global investors are likely to
increase at a rate of 16 percent a year until 2010. At that point (that is, in

2010), the revenues will represent 28 percent of total revenue earnings. The EEDS from Asia will play a major role in this scenario.

4.3 Capital Outflows from the Dynamic South

Larger economies of the dynamic South have been growing assertive on the global financial stage as well, and with their large accumulations of foreign exchange reserves, they have become a noteworthy source of capital for the rest of the world (ROW). Trade expansion and the accumulation of foreign exchange reserves in Brazil, China, India and South Africa have led to incomplete liberalization of the capital account. Capital liberalization of financial inflows has been significant, while that for outflows has thus far been relatively limited. In Brazil and South Africa, capital account liberalization of outflows has been more than that in China and India. South Africa prioritized liberalization of financial outflows by all institutional investors, while Brazil and India liberalized outflows by corporations and individuals. Although initial liberalization in China was limited, it has recently implemented several policy measures to liberalize outward capital flows for institutions and individuals. All four economies have succeeded in accumulating considerable foreign assets, albeit in different forms. Brazilian assets are essentially in the form of FDI and those of South Africa in portfolio equity. In contrast, China and India have invested their international reserves abroad, much of them in US Treasury securities. This is partly attributed to their relatively limited capital account liberalization. These economies have been coming forward as "key outward investors" (Lane and Schmukler, 2007, p. 499).

Three of the economies began capital outflows during the 1990s. Beginning in 1991, Brazil was the first in this regard. It was followed by South Africa in 1995, India in 1997–8 and China since 2004. When these economies open their capital account further to financial outflows, it is likely that they will promote outflows of private capital, rather than official capital. In place of central banks and financial ministries, private sector business houses will make the decision regarding where, how and for how long to invest abroad. Portfolio allocation decisions made by domestic investors will play an important role. Gottschalk and Sodre (2008) show that since 2000, FDI from China and India went largely to other developing countries, while that from Brazil and South Africa did not. Portfolio investment from all four economies went to the mature industrial economies. There was a clear bias in FDI outflows; they were concentrated in neighboring regional economies in all four cases. Due to informational advantages, this trend of investing in neighboring economies is likely to persist.

5. SOVEREIGN-WEALTH FUNDS: TRANSFORMING THE WORLD OF GLOBAL FINANCE

Financial globalization has been accelerating. Over the last two decades the rate of increase in global cross-border investment was twice that of the rate of growth of multilateral trade in goods and services, which in turn exceeded the rate of global GDP growth (Lane and Milesi-Ferretti, 2006). The world of international finance has been in the process of transformation. It became *a fortiori* so in the post-2000 period. A new group of EEDS and members of the Gulf Cooperation Council (GCC)[16] have emerged as major exporters of capital. Sovereign Wealth Funds (SWFs) are the instruments by which these interact with global capital markets. Although they are an instrument of enhancing liquidity and financial resource allocation in the international capital market, they have become a source of controversy and threaten to escalate financial protectionism. SWFs are state-owned and managed and have started to play a decisive role in underpinning, sustaining, and expanding financial globalization. Total assets under the management of SWFs have been on the increase. However, their state ownership and lack of transparency have created considerable anxiety about their operations. The SWFs are being viewed as turning from creditors and investors to owners.

An age-old adage is that necessity is the mother of invention. It unquestionably applies to the birth of SWFs. No matter what the source, when countries have excess liquidity, it is neither desirable nor possible to channel it into present consumption by increasing the level of imports. Exploring the pragmatic possibilities for its intertemporal utilization is indeed the most prudent mode of utilization. This applies all the more if the sources of excess liquidity are exports of mineral wealth, precious stones, commodities or strategic raw materials like petroleum, because these natural resources are non-renewable and exhaustible. If not in the short term, there will come a day when they can no longer be exploited. Under these circumstances, SWFs can act as a pragmatic saving instrument for future generations. Second, utilizing present financial assets to generate future resources by prudently investing them is another objective of these financial entities. Third, even when the supply of mineral wealth or commodities is continuing, the economy can face price and supply volatility, leading to an unsteady revenue stream. In such cases, SWFs can help stabilize the revenue stream and eliminate volatility. Furthermore, an infrequent motive to create SWFs is to prepare domestic financial markets for the creation of an active international financial center. The governments of the Republic of Korea and Singapore had this motive when they created the Korean Investment

Corporation and the GIC, respectively. At present, the SWF industry has over 40 of these institutions in operation, run largely by Asian and Middle Eastern governments. Half a dozen more are in the planning stage.

To the extent that SWFs are an instrument for the accumulation of savings which cannot be invested domestically or spent on imports in the short term, they become lucrative sources of globally investible resources. In a globalizing world economy, owner governments either channel or recycle this surplus capital to advanced industrial economies where profitable investment opportunities in the real or financial sectors are available in abundance. Some advanced industrial countries, like the US, need capital to meet their current account deficits. These capital resources are also channeled to the EEDS and developing economies, where they go in search of lucrative investment opportunities, or are needed to meet the saving gap. These SWFs can take the form of stabilization funds, non-renewable resource funds, government-owned pension funds, investment companies and the like.

5.1   Rising Profile of the Sovereign-Wealth Funds

In spite of the large volume of their operations, the SWFs managed to remain by and large low-key and obscure for a long while. Only occasionally in the last three or four years, did they become the subject of heated debate, even sour controversy, when they tried to make a large and conspicuous acquisition in the industrial economies. The popular and financial media did not begin copious discussions regarding the operations of the SWF until the last quarter of 2007, when they acquired considerable eminence. The *Financial Times* and the *Wall Street Journal* have begun covering SWFs extensively and a new class of SWFs experts has emerged. Esteemed institutions like Deutsche Bank, Morgan Stanley and Standard Chartered began publishing well-researched pieces on the operations of SWFs. In rapidly globalizing financial markets, the growing role and activities of SWFs also began attracting a great deal of attention from central bankers and finance ministers in the industrial economies. In the Group-of-Seven (G-7) meeting, held in October 2007, leaders of the industrial economies expressed concern about the investments made by the SWFs, disapproving, in particular, of the lack of transparency in their operations.[17] The Senate Banking Committee in the US held lengthy and repeated hearings on the SWFs in October and November 2007.[18] In mid-November, the International Monetary Fund (IMF) convened its first annual roundtable on sovereign assets. For the first time, the US Treasury discussed SWF operations in its *Semi-Annual Report on International Economic and Exchange Rate Policies*, published in June 2007.

The sub-prime mortgage crisis, which started in mid-2007, resulted in daunting losses in the banking industry and a credit crunch ensued. The increase in seriously delinquent sub-prime mortgages, which amounted to an additional $34 billion of dubious loans, disrupted the $57 trillion US financial system (Dodd, 2007). Large US financial institutions sustained heavier losses than previously visualized. Paradoxically, this became a window of opportunity for the SWFs.[19] In an increasingly globalized economy, the SWFs played a notable salvaging role in the aftermath of the crisis. They rose to prominence during the credit crunch. It brought them to the public eye and they attracted a great deal of market and academic attention. Resourceful and enterprising SWFs took the initiative and became active even before the monetary authorities of industrialized countries stunned global financial markets with a dramatic joint plan to ease the liquidity squeeze. This synchronized central bank policy action was taken on December 12. The Federal Reserve Board, the European Central Bank (ECB), the Bank of Canada and the Swiss National Bank were its initiators, while the central banks of Japan and Sweden stood by to step in and act as necessary. In an ambiance of severe credit crunch, some of the largest financial institutions like Citicorp, Union Bank of Switzerland (UBS) and Merrill Lynch needed an infusion of fresh liquidity. The SWFs stepped in like chivalrous white knights and came to the rescue. The Abu Dhabi Investment Authority (ADIA) provided an emergency capital injection of $7.5 billion to Citigroup, Singapore's Government Investment Corporation (GIC) provided SFr 11 billion to UBS and Temasek Holdings of Singapore helped Merrill Lynch enhance its capital position by $6.2 billion. By January 2008, SWFs from Kuwait, Korea and Singapore had invested $21 billion in Citigroup and Merrill Lynch, two heavyweight financial institutions, because of serious losses in the credit crisis (the *Economist*, 2008g). High-profile participation in these leading investment activities helped SWFs to emerge as large investors of global significance. They contributed to the stability of international financial markets, presented a mature image and have begun to be regarded as a prominent segment of the global financial system. To an extent, this wave of sizeable investments by the SWFs was driven by the boom in petroleum prices.[20]

That said, the operations of the SWFs are unprecedented, even atypical, in several respects. First, they are huge, cash-rich funds, and are presently managing assets almost twice as large as the hedge funds segment of the international financial market. Second, a large majority of them are owned by developing economies, or to be more precise, the EEDSs. Third, states have conventionally invested their excess foreign exchange reserves in low-risk, high-grade, investment vehicles like US Treasury securities, but by investing through SWFs, states moved towards riskier assets like equities and corporate bonds, in the process significantly enhancing liquidity in the global financial markets. Fourth, SWFs changed the character and composition of investments made by states. For the first time, SWFs enabled states to diversify their portfolios. Like any prudent investors, taking advantage of increasing financial globalization, they began to diversify their holdings and look for higher risk-adjusted returns. Fifth, the foreign ownership of SWFs became a source of concern for host economies, particularly because they are owned by sovereign governments. This exposed them to accusations of their investments being motivated by strategic and political considerations, not by economic considerations or profit maximization. The reason for this indictment is that in the case of SWFs, it is the governments that are regarded as making decisions about their large investments and governments are not business entities. Therefore, it is believed that maximization of the risk-adjusted return on investment and shareholders' wealth may well take a lower priority for the SWFs. Sixth, as more SWFs buy into prestigious firms and business corporations in advanced industrial economies, an uncomfortable scenario of share croppers is conjured up, where foreign-owned firms employ the local high-skill workforce in the advanced industrial economies.

Large and diversified portfolio investments by SWFs entail few risks for the international financial market. Anxiety about them is exaggerated. Those who regard investments by SWFs as risky need to carefully assess the risks caused by them thus far. Restrictions on their activities by host economies would deprive the international financial markets of a cash-rich market player. The rise of financial protectionism would work as a barricade against expanding globalization. Participation of SWFs in the international financial system can be improved by policy initiatives at three levels, namely, the SWF level, the host economy level and by international institutions like the IMF, which needs to devise a set of best practices for the operation of SWFs. This chapter outlines various policy measures that are necessary at the present stage of operations of the SWFs. That said, in most industrial economies, legislation and regulatory barriers for keeping foreign investors out are already in existence. The specter of unwelcome and objectionable intrusion by cash-rich SWFs in a country's economic life is overly puffed up.

5.2   Market Size and Growth Dynamics

The SWFs have proliferated since 2000 and so has their global investment. The banking and financial sector has been one of their favored areas of interest. By January 2008, they invested close to $69 billion in recapitalizing some of the largest financial institutions in the high-income matured industrial economies (MIEs). As alluded to above, the majority of SWFs publish few operational details; the market has scant knowledge about them. Going by what is available, Deutsche Bank Research (DBR, 2007) has compiled basic statistical data on SWFs. According to this compilation, the ADIA of Abu Dhabi is the largest SWF, with $875 billion of assets under management (AuM) and the GIC of Singapore the second largest, with $330 billion worth of AuM. Although Norway does not come under the EEDS or GCC categories, its Government Pension Fund-Global (GPFG) comes next with $322 billion of AuM. The fourth on this reckoning is the SWFs of Saudi Arabia, with $300 billion of AuM. KIA, the first SWF to be launched, comes fifth, with $250 billion in AuM and China's recently established CIC is the sixth largest, with $200 billion in AuM. Hong Kong Monetary Authority Investment Portfolio manages assets worth $140 billion and is the seventh largest, followed by the Stabilization Fund of the Russian Federation (SFRF), with $127 billion in AuM. The ninth position is held by Temasek Holdings of Singapore, with $108 billion in AuM and the tenth by the Central Hujin Investment Corporation of China, with $100 billion in AuM.

Although their global operations are larger than those of hedge funds ($1.4 trillion), SWFs account for less than one-eighth of the global investment fund industry, which has $21 trillion worth of AuM. Another revealing comparison can be made with the assets held by the global banking sector ($63.5 trillion). The SWFs hold only 5 percent of the total assets held by the global banking sector (DBR, 2007).[21] Thus, at present, SWFs are much smaller in size when compared to other large institutional investors. However, their importance and weight in the global financial market will continue to grow steadily. According to the projections made by the IMF (2007a), the SWFs will continue to accumulate global assets at a rate of $800 billion to $900 billion annually. This rate of expansion could bring the aggregate foreign assets under SWFs' management to approximately $12 trillion by 2012. Growth in international reserves in the EMEs would be the principal factor buttressing this growth dynamic (Das, 2008a).

Towards the end of 2007, due to large losses from the US sub-prime mortgage crises, many major financial institutions were in desperate need of additional capital. Large SWFs, like Temasek and the ADIA, frequently came to the rescue of these institutions. After November 2007, several high-profile operations of the SWFs attracted attention in the global financial markets. The large capital injections by SWFs augmented the capital buffers of the borrowing financial institutions and were helpful in reducing their risk premium. Given their long-term investment horizon and limited need for liquidity, the SWFs played a shock-absorbing role, successfully abating short-term volatility in the financial markets (IMF, 2008a).

6. CHANGING DYNAMICS OF GLOBAL GROWTH: DECOUPLING OR REVERSE COUPLING

Since 2000, it has been observed that the EEDS characteristically began to develop independently of the influence, or pull factor, of the advanced industrial economies. Business cycle swings in the advanced industrial economies affected the EEDS much less than before. The business cycles in the two country groups are increasingly becoming desynchronized. A sizeable economic literature developed around this so-called decoupling theme.

Rapid and sustained growth in the EEDS altered global growth dynamics. Between 2005 and 2007, growth in the global economy was dominated by the EEDS (IMF, 2008b).[22] China alone accounted for about a quarter of global growth during these three years. The four largest members of this group, namely, Brazil, China, India and the Russian Federation, together accounted for close to one-half of global growth during this period. All the EEDS combined accounted for about two-thirds of global growth. As growth in these economies was largely resource-intensive, they caused an increase in demand for key commodities, minerals and raw materials, such as oil, metals and foodstuffs. Since 2002, the EEDS accounted for 90 percent of the increase in the consumption of oil and 80 percent of the increase in the consumption of food grains. This sustained demand pull led to the firming of prices of key commodities, particularly oil and food grains. The commodity-exporting economies of Africa and Latin America and the members of the GCC were the direct beneficiaries of this trend, which was reflected in their strong economic performance.

6.1 Key Rationale behind Decoupling

As alluded to earlier (in Section 2.2), confluence of macroeconomic reforms and restructuring and the adoption of resilient domestic policy frameworks contributed to strong domestic economic performance in the EEDS. They upgraded their productive capacities and structurally diversified their economies, which made their economies more resilient than ever in the past. Second, technological advances facilitated an unbundling of production processes. It facilitated the global harnessing of underutilized labor resources in many economies of the dynamic South. This happened notably in China, India, the Russian Federation,

Southeast Asia and Eastern Europe. This process buttressed the rapid increase in TFP in the EEDS and contributed to their economic stability. These important factors were responsible for the divergence in GDP growth performance between the dynamic South and the high-income industrial economies.

GDP growth in the EEDS has been holding up, by and large despite a marked slowdown in the US economy and the EU. In mid-2008, some of the EEDS experienced slowdowns or decelerations, but they were slowing down from very high growth rates, which had been overheating these economies. What is remarkable is that the financial markets in the US and industrial economies were roiled by the turmoil that started in August 2007, yet the financial markets in the EEDS that were not regarded as paragons of stability, proved to be fairly resilient. Until mid-2008, disruptions in the US and other advanced industrial economies had a partial impact on money markets and financial indicators in the EEDS. In addition, while there were portfolio outflows during periods of market nervousness, most EEDS stock markets "significantly outperformed those in advanced economies" (IMF, 2008c, p. 22). However, an amber signal is necessary here, that is, in mid-2008, spreads on sovereign and corporate debt of the EEDS widened and equity prices retreated. These developments justify the question whether the global economy is in reality experiencing a decoupling or divergence in economic and financial performance of the advanced industrial economies and the EEDS. Is decoupling merely a myth?

6.2 Probability of Reverse Coupling

Despite tepid growth in the US in 2007, the EEDS were able to turn in a strong GDP growth performance. The post-August 2007 growth momentum in the EEDS came largely from the strong productivity gains noted above (Section 2). Several of them also recorded terms-of-trade improvements in their commodity trade, which included oil and raw materials exports, whose international market prices trended up. Their improved macroeconomic policy frameworks also benefited them. It appears absolutely logical to see a reverse coupling here, that is, advanced industrial economies becoming dependent on demand from the fast-growing emerging markets of the dynamic South.

Global GDP growth was an impressive 5 percent in 2006 and 4.9 percent in 2007, but according to the projections of the IMF (2008b), it is expected to fall to 4.1 percent in 2008 and 3.9 percent in 2009. Projected GDP growth for the advanced industrial economies was 1.7 percent for 2008 and 1.4 percent for 2009. In tandem, growth rates in the EEDS are expected to decelerate somewhat, which will be a reflection of efforts to prevent overheating, some spillover effect from the advanced industrial economies and some moderation in commodity prices. Nevertheless, their growth rate was projected to be 6.3 percent for 2008 and 7.3 for 2009 (IMF, 2008c). These projections tend to suggest that some decoupling of the dynamic economies of the South from the advanced industrial economies has occurred. However, a closer look at this scenario points to a reverse coupling. That is, the continued buoyant performance of the EEDS is fostering and underpinning the advanced industrial economies. In 2007 and 2008, the advanced industrial economies recorded high export growth. For the most part, demand for these increased exports originated in the EEDS. Quarterly trade statistics for this period revealed that the Eurozone economies increased their exports to Eastern Europe, while Japan and the US exported more to China. The fall-off in US demand was by and large offset by the EEDS' import increases (EIU, 2008b).

6.3   US Financial Crisis and Evidence of Decoupling

The festering sub-prime crisis took a turn for the worse in mid-September 2008 and grew into a veritable financial maelstrom. It was reminiscent of the Great Depression. The financial carnage had an air of the surreal, although the losses were all too real. In a CNN interview, Alan Greenspan called it a "one in a century event".[23] The magnitude of this catastrophe was so dizzying that it put paid to the decoupling theory right away.

J.P. Morgan's emerging-market bond index fell by 5 percent in the week to September 16, in the process wiping out all the gains for 2008. Contagion spread to the Asian and European stock markets, which suffered precipitous falls. Financial markets in the large EMEs were seriously affected and foreign institutional investors changed their minds about them. Russia's main bourses suspended trading in stocks and bonds for three days. The MSCI emerging-market index plunged and the EMEs stopped being treated as a desirable alternative to markets in the high-income industrial economies. With the changing mindset about the EMEs, in mid-September 2008, fund managers had smaller positions in emerging-market equities than at any time since 2001.

6.4   Growing Diversification in Trade and Investment

Another equally important structural change that has taken place in the recent past is that the EEDS and other developing economies progressively became important traders. In the past, the majority of these economies were small or marginal traders. China was close to an autarky until 1978 and India avidly followed an inward-oriented economic strategy until 1991. This status has changed. Many of the EEDS are now a significant part of the multilateral trade structure and China is the second largest trading economy in the world. Together, the EEDS account for more than a third of total multilateral trade. Since 2000, this group accounted for a half of the total increase in import volumes. In addition, the pattern of world trade has been transformed. The EEDS and other developing economies have diversified their trade destinations significantly. Their export bases have become much wider than they were in the past and their trade has become geographically diversified. Almost half of total exports from the EEDS and other developing economies presently goes to other members of the same country groups. That is, as set out above (Section 3), so-called South–South trade increased at a rapid pace. In particular, intra-EEDS trade recorded a hefty increase. These economies also paid a lot of attention to increasing exports of higher-value added manufactured products; while success was far from uniform, many of them succeeded.

Due to escalating geographical diversification of trade as well as intra-EESD and South–South trade, when exports from the EEDS to the US stumbled after mid-2007, those to other EEDS and developing economies surged. China's experience in this regard is illuminating. Its exports to the US declined by 5 percent in dollar terms during 2007, while those to Brazil, India and the Russian Federation soared by 60 percent and those to the GCC by 45 percent. The East Asian EEDS and many large developing economies followed this trend. Another factor that insulated the EEDS from the slowdown in the US and the EU was domestic consumption and investment, which picked up in 2007 and continued to do so in 2008. The EEDS consumer spending increased at three times the rate in the advanced industrial countries (the *Economist*, 2008f). Many of the EEDS are in an infrastructure-building cycle. They have launched multi-year construction projects to build power plants, highway systems, railways and airports. However, believing that a recession in the US would not affect the EEDS is not realistic. That said, its effect will surely be much less pronounced than in previous downturns.

Past recessions in the US and the other advanced industrial economies caused softening of commodities, raw materials and energy prices. This is not happening this time. Strong demand from the large EEDS, particularly China and India, have propped up world market prices. If anything, Brazil, the Russian Federation and the GCC economies are benefiting from a price-induced economic boom. Firm commodity and raw material prices will in turn boost exports from China and other manufacturing goods-producing economies. It is plausible that a slowdown in the Chinese economy would hurt the EEDS more than a recession in the US economy.

6.5 Desynchronization in the Business Cycles

These new trends and recent developments affected the structural dynamics of the global economy. Consequently, the business cycle in the advanced industrial economy began to play a less dominant role in driving swings in economic activity in the EEDS, notwithstanding the fact that they have liberalized their economies to increased trade and financial flows, as well as integrating with the global economy. However, the impact of advanced industrial economies on other groups of economies has not been completely eliminated. Akin and Kose (2007) have estimated that growth spillover from advanced industrial economies to the EEDS has declined markedly since the mid-1980s, but this was not reduced to zero. The pass-through for the EEDS was found to be 35 percent, while for the commodity-reliant developing economies it was 45 percent. Thus, decoupling is not complete. For the highly open EEDS, the pass-through was still non-trivial.

Using data for 106 countries for the 1960–2005 period, Kose et al., (2008a, p. 7) concluded that there was moderate convergence in the business cycle among advanced industrial economies and separately among the EEDS. This implies that "group specific factors have become more important than global factors in driving cyclical fluctuations in these two groups of economies". These data confirmed that the group-specific business cycle is a robust feature. This demonstrates that as globalization has progressed, group-specific factors have become relatively more important, while global factors have become less so. More importantly, there was a concomitant divergence, or decoupling, of business cycles between the advanced industrial economies on the one hand and the EEDS on the other. To put it succinctly, the data provide evidence of business cycle convergence *within* each of the two country groups, and at the same time, of divergence or decoupling *between* them. Thus, the influence of the advanced industrial economies on the growth rate of the EEDS has declined sharply. This demonstrates the fact that, with ongoing structural transformations in the global economy, global economic integration and decoupling can occur concurrently.

7. INSTITUTIONS OF GLOBAL ECONOMIC GOVERNANCE AND THE EEDS

In view of the increasing prominence of the EEDS, particularly of the Asian economies, the principal institutions of global economic governance need to adapt, update and adjust their structure, focus and pursuits.

Two of the most important institutions, the Bretton Woods duo, have begun to look like outmoded institutions, created for a different time period to resolve global economic issues that are somewhat different from the current ones. They were created in the mid-1940s, when memories of the two wars and the Great Depression were still fresh in the minds of the architects of these two institutions. The contemporary phase of globalization has ushered in a sea change in the global economy. It has undergone a significant structural transformation. Given the evolving novel global economic structure, these institutions are ripe for fundamental reform and reorganization in line with the new contours of the global economy.

Not only do the reform and updating of these institutions need to take into account the new global economic structure but also the coming into their own of the EEDS. Besides, every now and then there are reminders of the probability that the 21st century will be the Pacific Century. It would be pragmatic and clairvoyant for these institutions to adjust and fine-tune their activities in light of such a transformation of the global economy. The other prominent institutions that were created to assist in the management of the global economy include: (i) the Organization for Economic Cooperation and Development (OECD), a high-profile think-tank set up by the advanced industrial economies in 1961; (ii) the Bank for International Settlements (BIS), the central bankers' bank, which commenced its activities in 1930, making it the oldest international financial institution in the world; and (iii) the WTO, created on the erstwhile foundation of the GATT in 1995, which in turn was set up in 1948.

The Bretton Woods duo has been traditionally steered by its large industrial country members because they are the largest shareholders and wield most voting power. Few changes have been initiated in these age-old practices. The Bretton Woods twins, and most of all the WTO, have attempted to adapt and adjust in fits and starts. While they have not been conducted in accordance with a well-laid-out plan, some of the recent adaptation measures include the following. Voting and financial contributions in the IMF were restructured in March 2008, when China, Korea, Mexico and Turkey were given greater voting power. The adjustment exercise was essentially based on the size of a member country's foreign-exchange reserves, its GDP and some other indicators. China's voting power in the IMF increased to a much higher level than in the past, 3.81 percent. However, the new voting power was still not in keeping with its economic weight in the global economy. The Executive Board also decided that realignment of voting power would take place every five years.

As the lender of the last resort for the global economy, the IMF has been busy in the past lending cash to many member countries when they needed it. However, many economies that were borrowers in the past are now awash with their own funds. Therefore, this one task has been significantly reduced, if not eliminated from the IMF's agenda. To be relevant in the evolving global economic milieu, the Executive Board of the IMF voted to reduce its personnel in early 2008. To cover the funding shortfall, the Executive Board voted to sell part of the 400 tonnes of gold reserves of the IMF. Its future is being seen as a macroeconomic and financial adviser to the 185 member economies. Also, new sources of capital have emerged, namely, SWFs, hedge funds, large investment banks and global financial markets in general. A new role for the IMF could be to devise best practices for such global capital flows, monitor them and set basic rules for them.

As a lender for economic growth and development, the World Bank's role is sure to continue as long as there are economies at a low level of income and economic growth. However, it is facing competition from both global capital markets and bilateral donors like China and India, who have been lending to low-income developing countries for their infrastructure projects. Also, many of the previous borrowers have benefited from the upswing in world market prices of commodities, food grains and minerals in the recent past. The World Bank's future role could entail being an expert mentor on developmental issues and financer of unfashionable projects in the areas of agriculture, energy, infrastructure and the environment. The last-named area is a global public good.

Changes in multilateral trading rules and "modalities" are made in the apex body of the WTO, the Ministerial Conference, which meets every two years.[24] Although all the members of the WTO participate in any such exercises, they operate through negotiations between country groups, which tend to be complex and long drawn out. These groups of trading countries, represented by their trade/commerce ministers, are taken to represent the interests of all members. Although all the 153 member countries have a vote, and some large developing economies (like Brazil, China and India) have begun playing a well-defined and meaningful role in negotiations, it has not proved to be beneficial in laying down fair-minded trade regulations. A distressing reminder is the way the Doha Development Round became bogged down due to serious disagreements between the developing and advanced industrial economies on two principal issues, namely, farm subsidies and non-agricultural market access (NAMA). The prospect of agreement in other important areas, like trade in commercial services, looked dim (Das, 2007d). Despite the indefatigable endeavors of Pascal Lamy, the Director General of the WTO, the July 2008 meeting in Geneva failed to settle the so-called range questions and broke down in an acrimonious manner. Considered relatively, the WTO has been adjusting better to the changing global economic milieu and bringing in swifter

changes than the Bretton Woods duo. Its previous Director General was
from Thailand.

8.   CONCLUSIONS AND SUMMARY

As the contemporary phase of globalization picked up momentum and
widened its scope during the 21st century, it *inter alia* succeeded in benefiting a group of developing and transition economies more than others.
GDP growth in this subset of economies has been much faster than in
other developing and advanced industrial economies. This country group
played, and is continuing to play, a crucial role in the evolution of a novel
global economic geography. The emergence of the so-called dynamic
South is leading to startlingly rapid changes in the geographical locus of
global economic activity. This transformation of the global economy was
regarded as an economic revolution. This chapter examines how a steady
rise in the economic prominence of these EEDS contributed to the changing *mise-en-scene* of the global economy. There are several classifications
and definitions of the EEDS; therefore, their total number and country
groupings differ marginally. Principal economic indicators reveal that,
for the most part, the majority of the EEDS are on a sound economic
footing.

As the EEDS carried out their market-oriented reforms and adopted an
outer-oriented economic strategy, their net exports continued to increase
and contributed sizeably to aggregate demand and economic growth. In
the post-1990 period, the EEDS economies have emerged as large holders
of foreign-exchange reserves. Many of them run large current account surpluses, which became their principal sources of foreign currency earnings.
With one exception, their budget deficits were either manageable or enviably small. For the most part, inflation was contained, although there was
a small number of problem cases. It can be inferred that their economies
were by and large on a sound footing.

Some of the idiosyncratic features of the EEDS include their movement
towards an open market economy and transparency and efficiency in the
capital market. They endeavored to reform their exchange rate regimes,
which is an indispensable condition for attracting foreign direct and
portfolio investments. They were able to attract both direct and portfolio
capital from global financial markets. Inflows for external capital denote,
first, that the economy has come into its own and that the global investing
community feels confident in investing in it. Second, these capital inflows
serve to enhance the volume of domestic equity markets in the EEDS.
Third, they also increase investment in the long-term infrastructure of an

economy, resulting in steady gains in TFP. Another essential characteristic of the EEDS is their proactive and conscious global economic integration, which has lent a helpful hand to this group of the developing economies. Many of them have emerged as large trading economies in both goods and services.

With the rapid growth in the EEDS, South–South economic integration steadily increased. The structural changes that have taken place in the global economy during the contemporary era of globalization include dramatically increased South–South interaction through trade and investment channels. The significance of South–South trade in total multilateral trade has been on the rise, and its share in total trade has increased, particularly in the post-1995 period. One noticeable feature of the South–South trade is that the bulk of it occurs among economies in the same region.

This sub-group of economies has also given an impetus to financial globalization. Equity markets in several EEDS have developed rapidly and have typically grown into markets that yield high return. Large institutional investors, such as investment banks, pension funds, mutual funds and hedge funds, have increasingly taken a keen interest in these equity markets because they have proved to be lucrative destinations. Returns on investments in these markets rose precipitously in the recent past. Equity markets in the EEDS have helped to turn the global investment industry veritably global.

Another transformation in the world of global finance led by the EEDS occurred through Sovereign Wealth Funds (SWFs). A new group of EEDS and members of the GCC emerged as major exporters of capital; SWFs were their instruments of interacting with global capital markets. Although they are an instrument for enhancing liquidity and financial resource allocation in the international capital market, they have also become a source of controversy and threaten an escalation in financial protectionism.

Since 2000, it has been observed that the EEDS characteristically began to develop independently of the influence – or the pull factor – of the advanced industrial economies. Business cycle swings in the advanced industrial economies affected them much less than before. The confluence of macroeconomic reforms and restructuring and the adoption of resilient domestic policy frameworks contributed to strong domestic economic performance in the EEDS. They upgraded their productive capacities and structurally diversified their economies. Also, technological advances facilitated an unbundling of production processes. It facilitated the global harnessing of underutilized labor resources in many economies in the dynamic South. This happened notably in China, India, the Russian Federation, Southeast Asia and Eastern Europe. This process buttressed a rapid increase in TFP in the EEDS and promoted economic stability. This was an important factor responsible for the divergence in GDP growth performance between the dynamic South and the high-income industrial economies.

The emergence of this new group of EEDS calls for the adapting, updating and adjusting of the structure of the institutions of global governance. Two of the most important institutions, the Bretton Woods twins, have begun to look like outmoded institutions, created for a different time period to resolve global economic issues that are rather different from the current ones. Efforts to adapt and update these institutions have been made on an ad hoc basis.

NOTES

1. Comprising Hong Kong SAR, Korea, Singapore and Taiwan.
2. The trail-blazer of this economic path was postwar Japan.
3. Not all the members of the OECD are rich. Present OECD membership includes countries like Mexico and Poland, neither of which is a high-income country. The per capita income of Mexico in 2007 was $8340 and of Poland $9840. Ironically, it excludes high per capita GDP countries like Hong Kong SAR, Singapore and the United Arab Emirates (UAE), whose per capita income is over $31 000.
4. The source of this ranking is WTO (2008), appendix tables 3 and 5.
5. See IMF (2008b), chapter 1, for the contribution to global GDP growth from the rapidly growing developing economies.
6. Various writings of Angus Maddison prove this point beyond doubt. See, for instance, Maddison (2007 and 2003).
7. This section draws on UNCTAD (2008a).
8. Half of the 23 founding contracting parties of the GATT were developing economies, which included China and India. The former withdrew from the GATT in 1953.
9. The source of this categorization is UNCTAD (2007a), p. 6.
10. Statistical data used here come from UNCTAD (2008b).
11. Statistical data used here come from UNCTAD (2008b) and WTO (2008).
12. Statistical data used here come from UNCTAD (2007b), table 2.14, pp. 146–7.
13. The sources of these statistical data are UNCTAD (2008b) and UNCTAD (2006).
14. Ibid.
15. Fostel and Kaminsky (2007) also found similar results.
16. The Gulf Cooperation Council (GCC) was established in 1981. Its members are Bahrain, Kuwait, Oman, Qatar, Saudi Arabia and the United Arab Emirates (UAE).
17. This G-7 meeting was hosted by the US Treasury Secretary Henry Paulson and Federal Reserve Chairman Ben S. Bernanke in Washington, DC, on October 22. Apart from the US, members of the G7 include Japan, Germany, France, Britain, Italy and Canada.
18. Several noted scholars, including Kenneth Rogoff, Patrick Mulloy and Edwin Truman, participated in these hearings. Christopher Cox, the Chairman of Securities and Exchange Commission, expressed his concern regarding the operations of the SWFs in a speech at Harvard University on October 24, 2007.
19. The sub-prime mortgage financial crisis of 2007 entailed a precipitous increase in home foreclosures. Although it started in an inchoate manner in the US during the fall of 2006, it began affecting the global economy in mid-2007, a gloomy year for some of the largest financial institutions in the world. The bursting of the US housing bubble and

large defaults on sub-prime loans were the principal cause of this crisis. The term sub-prime lending implies lending to those borrowers whose creditworthiness is low. Such borrowers did not qualify for loans at market interest rates. A large number of them began defaulting. By May 2008, the rate of default exceeded 25 percent.

20. During 2007, the supply-demand fundamentals for crude oil were in clear deficit. Towards the end of September 2007, the average petroleum spot price (APSP) of benchmark West Texas Intermediate (WTI) shot up to $83.90 per barrel and in early November it topped $99. This was a 65 percent increase in petroleum prices in one year. The global consumption of oil has been growing at an average annual rate of 1.9 percent; 2007 was the sixth consecutive year of oil price increases. The APSP continued its climb and touched $145 per barrel on July 3, 2008. Global supply uncertainties, combined with significant demand growth in the EEDS, particularly in China, India, the Middle East, and Latin America, are expected to continue to put pressure on oil markets.

21. See DBR (2007), table 4.

22. See also IMF (2008a), table 1.1, p. 2.

23. This interview of Alan Greenspan was televised on the morning of September 17 by CNN.

24. In GATT/WTO parlance, the term modality means the method of doing something. Members have to agree to slash subsidies or tariffs, but before doing that they first need to agree on how to go about doing so. Once the modalities are agreed, members apply those formulas to their subsidies and tariffs.

Bibliography

Abdelal, R. and A. Segal (2007), "Has globalization passed its peak?" *Foreign Affairs*, **86** (1), 103–14.

Abu-Lughod, J. (1989), *Before European Hegemony: The World System A.D. 1250–1350*, New York: Oxford University Press.

Agenor, P.R. (2004), "Does globalization hurt the poor?" *International Economics and Economic Policy*, **1** (1), 21–51.

Ajaga, E. and P. Nunnenkamp (2008), "Inward FDI, value added and employment in US states: a panel co-integration approach", Kiel Institute for the World Economy working paper no. 1420, May, Kiel, Germany.

Akamatsu, K. (1961), "A theory of unbalanced growth in the world economy", *Weltwirtschaftliches Archiv*, **86** (2), 196–215.

Akin, Ç. and M. Ayhan Kose (2007), "Changing nature of North-South linkages: stylized facts and explanations", International Monetary Fund working paper WP/07/280, Washington, DC.

Aldonas, G.D., R.Z. Lawrence and M.J. Slaughter (2007), "Succeeding in the global economy", The Financial Services Forum, policy research paper, June, New York.

Alexander, C.H. and K. Warwick (2007), "Government, exports and growth: responding to the challenges and opportunities of globalization", *The World Economy*, **30** (1), 177–94.

Amiti, M. and J. Koning (2005), "Trade liberalization, intermediate inputs, and productivity: evidence from Indonesia", International Monetary Fund working paper WP/05/146, Washington, DC.

Amiti, M. and S.J. Wei (2005a), "Service offshoring, productivity and employment: evidence from the United States", International Monetary Fund working paper WP/05/238, Washington, DC.

Amiti, M. and S.J. Wei (2005b), "Fear of service outsourcing: is it justified?" *Economic Policy*, **20** (42), 308–47.

Amsden, A.H. (2001), *The Rise of the Rest*, New York: Oxford University Press.

Anderson, K., W. Martin and D. van der Mensbrugghe (2006), "Doha Merchandise Trade Reform: What's at Stake for Developing Countries", The World Bank policy research working paper no. 3848, February, Washington, DC.

Arnold, J.M., B.S. Javorcik and A. Mattoo (2007), "Does services liberalization benefit manufacturing firms?" World Bank Policy Research working paper no. 4190, January, Washington, DC.

Aslund, A. (2007), *Russia's Capitalist Revolution*, Washington, DC: Peterson Institute for International Economics.

Atkinson, A. (2000), "Increased income inequality in the OECD countries and the redistributive impact of the government budget", World Institute for Development Economic Research United Nations University working paper 202, Helsinki.

Atkinson, A. and T. Piketty (2006), *Top Incomes over the Twentieth Century*, Oxford: Oxford University Press.

Autor, D.H., L.F. Katz and M.S. Kearney (2006), "The polarization of the US labor market", *American Economic Review: Papers and Proceedings*, **96** (2), 189–94.

Bairoch, P. and R. Kozul-Wright (1996), "Globalization myths: some historical reflections on integration, industrialization, and growth in the world economy", UNCTAD discussion paper no. 113. March, New York and Geneva.

Bairoch, P. (1999), *Economics and World History: Myths and Paradoxes*, Chicago: University of Chicago Press.

Barquet, N. and P.Domingo (1997), "Smallpox: the triumph over the most terrible of the ministers of death", *Annals of Internal Medicines,* October 15, pp. 636–8.

Bartiromo, M. (2008), "Food emergency: on the front lines with the UN's Josette Sheeran", *Business Week*, May 1, pp. 21–2.

Baten, J. and U. Fraunholz (2004), "Did partial globalization increase inequality? The case of the Latin American periphery, 1850–2000", *CESifo Economic Studies*, **50** (1), 45–84.

Becker, T.I. and P. Mauro (2006), "Output drops and the shocks that matter", International Monetary Fund working paper WP/06/172, Washington, DC.

Berg, A. and A.O. Krueger (2003), "Trade, growth and poverty: a selective survey", International Monetary Fund working paper WP/03/30, Washington, DC.

Bernanke, B.S. (2007), "The level and distribution of economic wellbeing", address before the Greater Omaha Chamber of Commerce, February 6, Omaha, NE.

Bernanke, B.S. (2006), "Global economic integration: what's new and what's not?" in *The New Economic Geography: Effects and Policy Implications,* Kansas City, MO: The Federal Reserve Bank of Kansas City, pp. 1–14.

Bhagwati, J.N. (2004), *In Defense of Globalization*, New York: Oxford University Press.

Bivens, L.J. (2007a), "Globalization, American wages and inequality", Economic Policy Institute working paper 279, Washington, DC.

Bivens, L.J. (2007a), "The gains from trade: how big and who gets them?", Economic Policy Institute working paper, December 17, Washington, DC.

Blanchflower, D.G. (2000), "Globalization and the labor market", Dartmouth College Department of Economics, Hanover, NH, at http://govinfo.library.unt.edu/tdrc/research/fedtc4thdraft.pdf.

Blinder, A. (2007), "Offshoring – big deal or business as usual?" Princeton University CEPS working paper no. 149, Princeton, NJ.

Blinder, A.S. (2006), "Offshoring: the next Industrial Revolution?" *Foreign Affairs*, **85** (2), March/April, 113–28.

Bohme, M., D. Chiarella and M. Lemerle (2008), "The growing opportunities for investment banks in emerging markets", *The McKinsey Quarterly*, August, accessed at www.mckinseyquarterly.com/article_print.aspx?L2=10&L3=51&ar=2183.

Borjas, G.J., R.B. Freeman and L.F. Katz (1997), "How much do immigration and trade affect labor market outcomes?", *Brookings Papers on Economic Activity*, (1), 1–90.

Boston Consulting Group (BCG) (2007), "The 2008 BCG 100: new global challengers", December, Boston.

Boston Consulting Group (BCG) (2006), "The new global challengers", May, Boston.

Bosworth, B.S. and S.M. Collins (2003), "The empirics of growth: an update", *Brookings Papers on Economic Activity*, (1), 113–79.

Bourguignon, F., D. Coyle, R. Fernández, F. Giavazzi, D. Marin, K. O'Rourke, R. Portes, P. Seabright, A. Venables, T. Verdier, and L.A. Winters (2002), "Making sense of globalization", policy paper no. 8, Centre for Economic Policy Research London.

Bourguignon, F. and C. Morrisson (2002), "Inequality among world citizens: 1820–1992", *American Economic Review*, **92** (4), 727–44.

Bradford, S.C., P.L.E. Grieco and G.C. Hufbauer (2006), "The payoff to America from globalization", *The World Economy*, **29** (7), 893–916.

Braeuninger, D. (2008), "Has globalization deepened inequality?" in *Yale Global*, February 6, New Haven, CT: Yale University.

Buira, A. and M. Abeles (2006), "The IMF and the adjustment of global imbalances", paper submitted to the G-24 Technical Group Meeting, March 16–17, Geneva.

Bumiaux, J.M., F. Padrini and N. Brandt (2006), "Labor market performance, income inequality and poverty in OECD economies", Organisation for Economic Co-operation and Development Economics Department working paper no. 500, Paris.

Bussolo, M., E.D. Rafael, D. Medvedev and D. van der Mensbrugghe (2008), "Global growth and distribution: are China and India reshaping the world?", The World Bank policy research working paper 4392, Washington, DC.

Carter, J.K. (2007), "After the fall: globalizing the remnants of the Communist Bloc", *Federal Reserve Bank of Dallas Economic Letter*, **2** (2), 1–8.

Cashin, P. and A. Scott (2002), "Booms and slumps in world commodity prices", *Journal of Developing Economies*, **69** (4), 277–96.

Chen, S. and M. Ravallion (2007), "Absolute poverty measures for the developing world, 1981–2004", The World Bank policy research working paper no. 4211, April, Washington, DC.

Chen, S. and M. Ravallion (2004), "How have the world's poorest fared since the early 1980s?", *World Bank Research Observer*, **19** (2), 141–70.

Commission of the European Communities (CEC) (2005), *The EU Economy: 2005 Review*, November, Brussels: Directorate General of Economics.

Chow, G.C. (2006), "Globalization and China's economic development", *Pacific Economic Review*, **11** (3), 271–85.

Clark, W.C. (2001), "Environmental globalization", in R.O. Keohane and J.S. Nye (eds), *Governance in a Globalizing World,* Washington, DC: Brookings Institution Press, pp. 68–108.

Cline, W.R. (1999), "Trade and income distribution: the debate and new evidence", Institute for International Economics policy brief 99–7, Washington, DC.

Coe, D.T. (2008), "Jobs on another shore", *Finance and Development*, **45** (1), 48–52.

Collier, P. (2007), *The Bottom Billion*, Oxford: Oxford University Press.

Cooper, R.N. (2004), "A false alarm: overriding globalization's discontents", *Foreign Affairs*, (January/February), 44–8.

Cordon, W.M. (2007), "Those current account imbalances: a skeptical view", *The World Economy*, **30** (3), March, 363–82.

Council for Economic Planning and Development (CEPD) (2008), *Taiwan Economic Statistics 2008*, vol. 6, no. 5, May, Taipei: CEPD.

Das, Dilip K. (2008a), "Sovereign-wealth funds: a new role for the emerging market economies in the world of global finance", *International Journal of Development Issues*, **7** (2), (December), 80–96.

Das, Dilip K. (2008b), "Repositioning the Chinese economy on the global economic stage", *International Review of Economics*, **55** (4), (December), 130–52.

Das, Dilip K. (2008c), *The Chinese Economic Renaissance: Apocalypse or Cornucopia*, Houndmills: Palgrave Macmillan Ltd.

Das, Dilip K. (2008d), "Suspension of the Doha Round of multilateral trade negotiations and the need for its resuscitation", *The Estey Journal of International Law and Trade Policy*, **9**.(1), (April), 51–73.

Das, Dilip K. (2007a), "The East is rich: China's inexorable climb to economic domination", Sydney: Macquarie University Center for Japanese Economic Studies research paper no. 2007-04, December.

Das, Dilip K. (2007b), "Shifting paradigms of regional integration in Asia", University of Warwick Centre for the Study of Globalization and Regionalization, working paper no. 230/07, June, accessed at www2.warwick.ac.uk/fac/soc/csgr/research/workingpapers/230/wp23007/pdf.

Das, Dilip K. (2007c), "Integration of South Asian economies: an exercise in frustration?", *Asian-Pacific Economic Literature*, **21** (1), 55–68.

Das, Dilip K. (2007d), *The Evolving Global Trade Architecture*, Cheltenham, UK and Northampton, MA, USA: Edward Elgar.

Das, Dilip K. (2006), *China and India: A Tale of Two Economies*, London and New York: Routledge.

Das, Dilip K. (2005a), *The Doha Round of Multilateral Trade Negotiations: Arduous Issues and Strategic Responses*, Houndmills Palgrave Macmillan Ltd.

Das, Dilip K. (2005b), "The anatomy of a crisis: Asia as ground zero", Sydney, Macquarie University Center for Japanese Economic Studies research paper no. 2005-4, October.

Das, Dilip K. (2005c), *Asian Economy and Finance: A Post-crisis Perspective*, Cambridge, UK and New York: Springer Publications.

Das, Dilip K. (2005d), "Market-driven regionalization in Asia", *Global Economy Journal*, **5** (3) (September), article 2, The Berkeley Electronic Press, CA, accessed at www.bepress.com/cgi/viewcontent.cgi?article=1082&context=gej.

Das, Dilip K. (2004a), *Financial Globalization and the Emerging Market Economies*, London and New York: Routledge.

Das, Dilip K. (2004b), *The Economic Dimensions of Globalization*, Houndmills: Palgrave Macmillan Ltd., Hampshire, UK.

Das, Dilip K. (2003), "The Doha Round of multilateral trade negotiations: causal issues behind failure in Cancún", Harvard University Center for International Development, Cambridge, MA, October, accessed at www.cid.harvard.edu/cidtrade/site/new.html.

Das, Dilip K. (1999), "Asian economic and financial crisis: the morning after the night before", *The Asia Pacific Journal of Economics and Business*, **3** (1), (June), 43–65.

DeLong, J.B. (1998), "Estimating world GDP, one million B.C. to present", University of California, Department of Economics Berkeley,

CA, accessed at http://econ161.berkeley.edu/TCEH/1998_Draft/World_ GDP/Estimating_World_GDP.html.

DeLong, J.B. (2007), "Buying up the US, Chinese-style", *Taipei Times*, June 4, p. 6.

de la Dehesa, G. (2006), *Winners and Losers of Globalization*, Oxford: Blackwell.

DeRamos, R.R. (2008), "Morgan Stanley upgrades emerging markets", *Business Week*, July 25, p. 65.

Deutsche Bank Research (DBR) (2007), "Sovereign wealth funds: state investment on the rise", DBR economics research paper no. 12, 10 September, Frankfurt.

Deutsche Bank Research (DBR) (2004), "Digital economy and structural change", economics research paper no. 45, September 27, Frankfurt.

Dew-Becker, I. and R.J. Gordon (2005), "Where did the productivity growth go?", Center for Economic Policy Research discussion paper DP (5419), London.

Dicken, P. (2007), *Global Shift: Mapping the Changing Contours of the World Economy*, 5th edn. New York: Guilford Press.

DiGiovanni, J. and A. Levchenko (2006), "Trade openness and volatility", International Monetary Fund, unpublished, Washington, DC.

Dodd, R. (2007), "Subprime: tentacles of a crisis", *Finance and Development*, **44** (4), 15–19.

Dollar, D.R. (2007), "Asian century or multi-polar century?" The World Bank policy research working paper (4174), March, Washington, DC.

du Preez, M.L. (2007), "Is three a crowd or a coalition? India, Brazil and South Africa in the WTO", unpublished dissertation at the University of Stellenbosch.

The Economist (2008a), "A bigger world", September 20, a special report after p. 52.

The Economist (2008b), "In praise of stateless multinationals", September 20, p. 20.

The Economist (2008c), "The came, they jawed, they failed to conquer", July 12, pp. 68–69.

The Economist, (2008d), "In the nick of time: a special report on EU enlargement", pp. 52–54.

The Economist (2008e), "Asia's other miracle", April 26, p. 16.

The Economist (2008f), "The decoupling debate", March 8, pp. 79–81.

The Economist (2008g), "The invasion of the sovereign-wealth funds", January 19, p. 11.

The Economist (2008h), "The challengers", January 12, pp. 62–4.

The Economist (2007a); "You've never had it so good", February 3, p. 12.

The Economist (2007b), "Rich man, poor man", January 20, pp. 15–16.

The Economist (2007c), "Dizzy in boomtown", November 15, pp. 11–12.

The Economist (2006), "The new titans: a survey of the world economy", September 16, pp. 13–15.

Economic Intelligence Unit (EIU) (2008a), World economy: FDI in 2008 – how resilient?, July 4, London, accessed at www.animaweb.org/en/actu-detail.php?actu= (4012).

Economic Intelligence Unit (EIU) (2008b), "Emerging market: too hot for comfort", June 6, London, accessed at www.viewswire.com/index.asp?layout=VWArticleVW3&article_id=1423425527&rf=0.

Economic Intelligence Unit (EIU) (2007), "China: telecoms and technology forecast", London, February 7.

Economic Intelligence Unit (EIU) and Columbian Program on International Investment (CPII) (2007), *World Investment Prospects to* 2011. London and New York: Economist Intelligence Unit in co-operation with the Columbia Program on International Investment.

Engman, M., O. Onodera and E. Pinali (2007), "Export promotion zones: past and future roles", Organisation for Economic Co-operation and Development trade policy working paper no. 53, May 22, Paris.

Europe in a Globalized World, European Economic Advisory Group (2008), February, Munich. EEAG, CESifo.

Farrell, D. (2004), "The case for globalization", *The International Economy*, (Winter), 52–6.

Farrell, D., C.S. Folster and S. Lund (2008), "Long-term trends in the global capital markets", *The McKinsey Quarterly*, February, accessed at www.mckinseyquarterly.com/article_print.aspx?L2=10&L3=51&ar= (2100).

Farrell, D. and S. Lund (2008), "The new role of oil wealth in the world economy", *The McKinsey Quarterly*, January, accessed at www.mckinseyquarterly.com/article_print.aspx?L2=5&L3=2&ar= (2093).

Faruqee, H. (2008), "IMF sees global imbalances narrowing", *IMF Survey*, February 19, 12–14.

Findlay, R. and K.H. O'Rourke (2007), *Power and Plenty*, Princeton, NJ: Princeton University Press.

Findlay, R. and K.H. O'Rourke (2002), "Commodity market integration", Center for Economic Policy Research discussion paper no. (3125), January, London.

Fischer, S. (2006), "The new global economic geography", in *The New Economic Geography: Effects and Policy Implementations*. Kansas City, MD: The Federal Reserve Bank of Kansas City, pp. 177–94.

Forrester, J.W. (1958), "Industrial Dynamics: A Major Breakthrough for Decision Makers". *Harvard Business Review*, **38** (3), 37–66.

Fostel, A. and G. Kaminsky (2007), "Latin America's access to international capital markets", Central Bank of Chile working paper no. 442, August, Santiago.

Frank, A.G. (1998), *ReOrient: Global Economy in the Asian Age*, Berkeley, CA: University of California Press.

Frankel, J. (2000), "Globalization of the economy", in J.S. Nye and J.D. Donahue (eds), *Governance in a Globalizing World*. Washington, DC: The Brookings Institution Press.

Frankel, J. (2006), "What do economists mean by globalization?", paper presented at the Academic Consultants Meeting organized by the Board of Governors of the Federal Reserve System, September 28, Washington, DC.

Friedman, T.L. (1999), *The Lexus and the Olive Tree*, New York: Farrar, Straus and Giroux.

Friedman, T.L. (2000), "Dueling globalization: a debate between thomas friedman and ignacio ramonet", *Foreign Policy*, (Fall), 110–19.

Fujita, M., P. Krugman and A.J. Venable (1999), *The Spatial Economy: Cities, Regions and International Trade*, Cambridge, MA and London: The MIT Press.

Gaulier, G., F. Lemoine and D. Unal-Kesenci (2007), "China's integration in East Asia: production sharing, FDI and high-tech trade", *Economic Change and Restructuring*, **40** (1–2), 27–63.

Goldin, C. and L.F. Katz (2007), "Long-run changes in the U.S. wage structure: narrowing, widening, polarizing", National Bureau of Economic Research working paper no. 13,568, Cambridge, MA.

Goldman Sachs (2008), "Africa rising", global economics paper no. 170, September, New York.

Goldman Sachs (2005), "How solid are the BRICs?", Global Economics paper no. 134, December, New York.

Goldman Sachs (2003), "Dreaming with BRICs: the path to 2050", Global economics paper no. 99, October, New York.

Goodman, D. and X. Zang (2008), "The new rich in China: the consequences of social change", in D. Goodman (ed.) *The New Rich in China*, London and New York: Routledge, pp. 3–22.

Gottschalk, R. and C.A. Sodre (2008), "The liberalization of capital outflows in CIBS", United Nations University-World Institute for Development Economics Research research paper no. 2008/68, August, Helsinki.

Gourinchas, P.O. and O. Jeanne (2006), "The elusive gains from international financial integration", *Review of Economic Studies*, **73** (3), 715–41.

Greider, W. (1997), *One World Ready or Not: The Manic Logic of Global Capitalism*, New York: Simen and Schuster.

Grossman, G.M. and E. Rossi-Hansberg (2006a), "Trading tasks: a simple theory of offshoring", National Bureau of Economic Research working paper no. W12721, December, Cambridge, MA.

Grossman, G.M. and E. Rossi-Hansberg (2006b), "The rise of offshoring" in *The New Economic Geography: Effects and Policy Implications*, Kansas City, MD: The Federal Reserve Bank of Kansas City, pp. 59–102.

Gunasekaran, A. and E. Ngai (2005), "Build-to-order supply chain management: a literature review", *Journal of Operations Management*, **23**, (2), 423–51.

Guscina, A. (2007), "Effects of globalization on labor's share in national income", International Monetary Fund working paper no. WP/07/294, January, Washington, DC.

Gustafsson, B. and W. Zhong (2000), "How and why has poverty in China changed?", *China Quarterly*, (164), 983—1006.

Hallaert, J.J. (2006), "A history of empirical literature on the relationship between trade and growth", *Mondes en developpement*, **34** (1), 63–77.

Hamashita, T., M. Selden and L. Grove (2008), *China, East Asia and the Global Economy*, London and New York: Routledge.

Hamilton, D.S. and J.P. Quinlan (2008), *Globalization and Europe: Prospering in the New Whirled Order*, Washington, DC: Center for Transatlantic Relations, The Johns Hopkins University.

Harrison, A. (2006), *Globalization and Poverty*. Cambridge, MA: National Bureau of Economic Research.

Hausmann, R., J. Hwand and D. Rodrik (2007), "What you export matters", *Journal of Economic Growth*, **12** (1), 1–25.

Hawksworth, J. (2006), *The World in 2050: How Big Will the Major Emerging Market Economies Get?* March, London: PriceWaterhouseCooper.

Helleiner, G.K. (2000), "Markets, politics and globalization: can the global economy be civilized?", the Tenth Raul Prebisch Lecture, December 11, UNCTAD, Geneva.

Helliwell, G.K. (1998), *Trade Policy and Internationalization in Turbulent Times*, London and New York: Routledge.

Henry, P.B. and D.L. Sasson (2008), "Capital account liberalization, real wages, and productivity", National Bureau of Economic Research working paper no. 13880, Cambridge, MA.

Heshmati, A. (2007), "The relationship between income inequality, poverty and globalization", in M. Nissanke and E. Thorbecke (eds), *The Impact of Globalization on the World's Poor*, Houndsmills Palgrave Macmillan Ltd., pp. 59–93.

Hijzen, A., P. Mauro, R. Upward and P. Wright (2007), "Employment,

job turn over and trade in producer services: firm-level evidence",
University of Nottingham GEP working paper no. 2007/37, August,
Nottingham.

Hitchner, B. (2003), "Roman Empire", in J. Mokyr (ed.), *The Oxford
Encyclopedia of Economic History*, Oxford: Oxford University Press,
volume 4, 397–400.

Hoekman, B.M., M. Olarreaga and E. Zedillo (2007), *Global Trade and
Poor Nations*, Washington, DC: Brookings Institution Press.

Hoguet, G.R. (2008), "Outlook for emerging market economies", State
Street Global Advisor, January 8, New York, accessed at www.ssga.
com/library/mkcm/georgehoguetoutlookforemergingmarketeconomies
20080103/page.html.

Holms, S. (2008), "Free marketeering", *London Review of Books*, **30** (10)
(May 8), 12–19.

Huang, J., Q. Zhang and S. Rozelle (2008), "Economic growth, the nature
of growth and poverty reduction in China", *China Economic Journal*, 1
(1), 107–122.

Hufbauer, G.C. (2008), "Answering the critics: why large American gains
from globalization are plausible", Peterson Institute for International
Economics, Washington, DC, accessed at www.iie.com/publications/
papers/print.cfm?doc=pub&ResearchID-929.

Hummels, D. (2007), "Transportation costs and international trade in
the second era of globalization", *Journal of Political Economy*, 2 (3)
(Summer), 131–54.

The International Monetary Fund (IMF) (2008a), *Global Financial
Stability Report*, April, Washington, DC.

The International Monetary Fund (IMF) (2008b), *World Economic
Outlook*, April, Washington, DC.

The International Monetary Fund (IMF) (2008c), *World Economic
Outlook: Update*, April, Washington, DC.

The International Monetary Fund (IMF) (2008d), *Regional Economic
Outlook: Sub-Saharan Africa*, April, Washington, DC.

The International Monetary Fund (IMF) (2007a), *Global Financial
Stability Report*, September, Washington, DC.

The International Monetary Fund (IMF) (2007b), *World Economic
Outlook*, October, Washington, DC.

The International Monetary Fund (IMF) (2007c), *World Economic
Outlook, April,* Washington, DC.

The International Monetary Fund (IMF) (2007d), *Asia and Pacific:
Regional Economic Outlook*, October, Washington, DC.

The International Monetary Fund (IMF) (2002), *World Economic Outlook*,
April, Washington, DC.

The International Monetary Fund (IMF) (2001), *Globalization: Threat or Opportunity?*, Washington, DC.

Irwin, D.A. (1996), *Against the Tide: An Intellectual History of Free Trade*, Princeton NJ: Princeton University Press.

Japan External Trade Organization (JETRO) (2008), *South-South Trade in Asia*, Tokyo: Japan.

Jaumotte, F. (2007), "Technology widens rich-poor gap", *IMF Survey*, October 10, accessed at www.imf.org/external/pubs/ft/survey/so/2007/RES1010A.htm.

Jenkins, R. (2007), "Globalization, production and poverty", in M. Nissanke and E. Thorbecke (eds), *The Impact of Globalization on the World's Poor*, Houndsmills: Palgrave Macmillan Ltd.,. pp. 163–90.

Johnson, S. (2008), "Straight talk: emerging markets emerge", *Finance and Development*, **45** (3), 54–6.

Kalwij, A. and A. Verschoor (2007), "Globalization and poverty trends across regions", in M. Nissanke and E. Thorbecke (eds), *The Impact of Globalization on the World's Poor*, Houndsmills: Palgrave Macmillan Ltd., pp. 94–113.

Keohane, R.O. and J.S. Nye (2001), "Introduction" in R.O. Keohane and J.S. Nye (eds), *Governance in a Globalizing World*, Washington, DC: Brookings Institution Press, pp. 1–41.

Keohane, R.O. and J.S. Nye (1977), *Power and Independence: World Politics in Transition*, Boston. MA: Little Brown.

Keynes, J.M. (1919), *The Economic Consequences of the Peace*, London: The Macmillan Press Ltd.

Klein, L.R. (2005), "South and Southeast Asia: leading the world economy", the Thirteenth Raul Prebisch Lecture delivered at the UNCTAD, November 2, Geneva.

Klein, Naomi (2000), *No Logo*, London: Flamingo.

Klein, Naomi (2002), *Fences and Windows*, London: Flamingo.

Kohler, H. (2002), "Strengthening the framework for the global economy", address given on the occasion of the Award Ceremony of the Konrad Adenauer Foundation, November 15, 2002, Berlin, accessed at www.imf.org/external/np/speeches/2002/111502.htm.

Kohn, D.L. (2008), "Global economic integration and decoupling", speech given at the International Research Forum on Monetary Policy, June 26, Frankfurt, Germany.

Kose, A.M., C. Otrok and E.S. Prasad (2008a), "Global business cycles: convergence or decoupling?", International Monetary Fund working paper no. WP/08/143, June, Washington, DC.

Kose, A.M., C. Otrok and E.S. Prasad (2008b), "How much decoupling? How much converging?", *Finance and Development*, **45** (2) June, 36–40.

Kose, M.A., E.S. Prasad and M.E. Terrones (2007), "How does financial globalization affect risk sharing?", International Monetary Fund working paper WP/07/238, September, Washington, DC.

Kose, M.A., E.S. Prasad, K. Rogoff and S.J. Wei (2006), "Financial globalization: a reappraisal", International Monetary Fund working paper WP/06/189, August, Washington, DC.

Kose, M.A., E.S. Prasad and M.E. Terrones (2005), "Financial integration and macroeconomic volatility", *IMF Staff Papers*, **50** (Special Issue), 119–42.

Krueger, A.O. (2008), "Trade liberalization and growth in developing countries", paper presented at the American Economic Association meeting, January 4–6. New Orleans, LA.

Krueger, A.O. (2007), "An enduring need: multilateralism in the twenty-first century", *Oxford Review of Economic Policy*, **23** (3), 335–46.

Krueger, A.O. (2006), "The world economy at the start of the 21st century", The Gilbert Lecture given April 6 at the Rochester University, New York.

Krueger, A.O. (2003), "On globalization", Address given at the Seventh St Petersburg International Forum, June 18, St. Petersburg, Russia.

Krueger, A.O. (2000), "Trading phobias: governments, NGOs and the multilateral systems", The Seventh Annual John Bonython Lecture, delivered October 10 in Melbourne, Australia.

Krueger, A.O. (1995), "The role of trade in growth and development", in R.G. Enzo Grilli and J. Riedel (eds), *Sustaining Export-oriented Development: Ideas from East Asia*, New York: Cambridge University Press, pp. 1–30.

Krugman, P. (2008a), "The great illusion", *The New York Times*, August 15, p. 14.

Krugman, P. (2008b),"Trade and wages, reconsidered", *Brookings Paper on Economic Activity*, (1).

Krugman, P. (2007a), "Trade and inequality, revisited", June 15, accessed at www.voxeu.org/index.php?=node/261.

Krugman, P. (2007b), *The Conscience of a Liberal*, New York: W.W. Norton & Company, Inc.

Krugman, P. (2006), "The great wealth transfer", September 18, accessed at www.rollingstone.com/politics/story/12699486/paul_krugman_on_the_great_wealth_transfer/print.

Krugman, P. (1995), "Growing world trade: causes and consequences", *Brookings Paper on Economic Activity*, (1), 327–62.

Krugman, P.R. and M. Obstfeld (forthcoming), *International Economics: Theory and Policy*, 8th edn, Boston: Pearson Addison Wesley.

Kuznets, S. (1955), "Economic growth and income inequality", *American Economic Review*, **45** (1), 1–28.

Lane, P.R. and G.M. Milesi-Ferretti (2006), "The external wealth of nations mark II", Center for Economic Policy Research discussion paper no. 5644, London.

Lane, R.L. and S.L. Schmukler (2007), "The evolving role of China and India in the global financial system", *Open Economy Review*, **18** (4), 499–520.

Lawrence, R.Z. (2008), *Blue Collar Blues: Is Trade to Blame for Rising US Income Inequality?*, Washington, DC: Peterson Institute for International Economics, January.

Leamer, E. (2007), "A flat world, a level playing field, a small world after all, or none of the above", *Journal of Economic Literature*, **45** (2) (March), 83–126.

Levitt, T. (1983), "The globalization of markets", *Harvard Business Review*, **61** (3), 92–102.

Levy, F.S. and P. Temin (2007), "Inequality and institutions in 20th century America", MIT Department of Economics working paper 07-17, June 27, Cambridge, MA.

Lipsky, J. (2007), paper presented on "Understanding China" at the conference on Global Implications of China's Trade, Investment and Growth, April 6, International Monetary Fund, Washington, DC.

Lindert, P.H. and J.G. Williamson (2005), "Does globalization make the world more unequal?", in M.D. Bordo, A.M. Taylor and J.G. Williamson (eds), *Globalization in Historical Perspective*, Conference report, Cambridge, MA. National Bureau of Economic Research, pp. 227–71.

Ljungwall, C. and O. Sjoberg (2007), "The economic impact of globalization in Asia-Pacific: the case of flying geese", China Center for Economic Research, Peking University, research paper no. E2005007, November, Beijing.

Lucas, R.E. (2000), "Some macroeconomics for the 21st century", *Journal of Economic Perspectives*, **14** (1), 159–68.

Maddison, A. (2007), *Contours of the World Economy*, Oxford: Oxford University Press.

Maddison, A. (2005), "Evidence submitted to the Select Committee on Economic Affairs, House of Lords, London, UK, for the inquiry into Aspects of the Economics of Climate Change", February 2005, accessed at www.ggdc.net/maddison.

Maddison, A. (2003), *The World Economy: Historical Statistics*, Paris: Development Center, Organization for Economic Co-operation and Development.

Maddison, A. (2001), *The World Economy: A Millennium Perspective*, Paris: Development Center, The Organisation for Economic Co-operation and Development.

Maier, P. and G. Vasishtha (2008), "Good policies or good fortune: what drives the compression in emerging market spreads?", Bank of Canada working paper no. 2008-25, August, Ottawa, ON.

Mallaby, S. (2007), "The next globalization backlash", *Washington Post*, June 25, p. 17.

Mankiw, N.G. and P. Swagel (2006), "The politics and economics of off-shore outsourcing", National Bureau of Economic Research working paper no. W12398, July, Cambridge, MA.

Martin, W., K. Anderson and C.S. Pham (2007), "Effects of GATT/WTO on Asia's trade performance", paper presented at the Pacific Trade and Development (PAFTAD) Forum Conference, December 17–19, Hanoi.

Mayer, J. (2003), "Dynamic products in world exports", *Review of World Economics*, **139** (4), 762–95.

McKinsey Global Institute (MGI) (2008), "Mapping Global Capital Markets: Fourth Annual Report", San Francisco: MGI.

McKinsey Global Institute (MGI) (2007), "The coming global labor market", February, accessed at www.mckinseyquarterly.com/newsletters/chartfocus/2007_02.htm.

Milanovic, B., P.H. Lindert and J.G. Williamson (2007), "Pre-industrial inequality: an early conjectural map", Harvard University, Department of Economics, August 23, Cambridge, MA, accessed at www.economics.harvard.edu/faculty/williamson/jwilliamsonworkingpapers.

Milanovic, B. (2006), "Global income inequality: a review", *World Economics*, **7** (1), 131–57.

Milanovic, B. (2003), "The two faces of globalization: against globalization as we know it", *World Development*, **31** (4), 667–83.

Milanovic, B. (2002), "Can we discern the effects of globalization on income distribution?", The World Bank, policy research working paper no. 2876, April, Washington, DC.

Mishkin, F.S. (2006), *The Next Great Globalization*, Princeton, NJ: Princeton University Press.

Mittelman, J.H. (2002), "Globalization: an ascendant paradigm", *International Studies Perspective*, **3** (1), 1–14.

Moore, M. (2000), 'Back on the track of trade and development', *Social Development Review*, **3** (4), 88–106.

Mundell, R.A. (2002), "Does Asia need a common currency market?", *Pacific Economic Review*, **7** (1), 3–12.

Mundell, R.A. (2000), "Global policy issues: new challenges for development", paper presented at the World Bank's Annual Conference on Development Economics in Europe, June 28, Paris.

Nayyar, D. (2008), "China, India, Brazil and South Africa in the world economy", United Nations University – World Institute of Development Economics Research, discussion paper no. 2008/05, June, Helsinki.

Nayar, B.R. (2007), *India's Globalization: Evaluating the Economic Impact*, New Delhi: Sage.

Nissanke M. and E. Thorbecke (2007a), "Channels and policy debate in the globalization-inequality-poverty-nexus", in M. Nissanke and E. Thorbecke (eds), *The Impact of Globalization on the World's Poor*, Houndsmills: Palgrave Macmillan Ltd., pp. 22–58.

Nissanke, M. and E. Thorbecke (2007b), "Overview" in Nissanke, M. and E. Thorbecke (eds), *The Impact of Globalization on the World's Poor*, New York: Palgrave Macmillan Ltd., pp. 1–18.

Nissanke, M. and E. Thorbecke (2007c), "Globalization, growth, and poverty in Africa", *WIDER Angle*, **8** (2), pp. 6–10.

Norris, P. (2001), "Global governance and cosmopolitan citizens", in R.O. Keohane and J.S. Nye (eds), *Governance in a Globalizing World*, Washington, DC: Brookings Institution Press, pp. 155–77.

Oliver Wyman Group (2008), *State of the Industry Report (2008)*, New York: Oliver Wyman Group.

O'Neill, J. (2008), "Boom time for the global bourgeoisie", *The Financial Times*, July 15, p. 16.

Organisation for Economic Co-operation and Development (OECD), (2007a), *Offshoring and Employment: Trends and Impacts*, November, Paris.

Organisation for Economic Co-operation and Development (OECD) (2007b), *OECD Economic Outlook*, No. 81, May, Paris: OECD.

Organisation for Economic Co-operation and Development (OECD) (2006), *Information and Technology Outlook (2006)*, Paris: OECD.

Organisation for Economic Co-operation and Development (OECD) (2005a), "China overtakes the US as world's leading exporter of information technology goods", December 12, Paris, accessed at www.oecd.org/document/60/0,2340,en_2649_201185_35834236_1_1_1_1,00.html.

Organisation for Economic Co-operation and Development (OECD) (2005b), *OECD Economic Survey: China*, Vol. 2005/13, September, Paris: OECD.

Organisation for Economic Co-operation and Development (OECD) (1997), *Economic Globalization and the Environment*, September, Paris: OECD.

Ozawa, T. (2006), "Asia's labor-driven economic development, flying geese style", WIDER research paper 2006/59, June, Helsinki.

The People's Bank of China (PBC) (2008), "China's foreign exchange reserves soar", July 17, Beijing, accessed at afp.google.com/article/ALeqM5jV-Vqd3eFprUamekQ_ctIU89Txyw.

Pierce, B. (2001), "Compensation inequality", *Quarterly Journal of Economics*, **116** (4), 1493–525.

Piketty, T. and E. Saez (2006), "The evolution of top incomes: a historical and international perspective", National Bureau of Economic Research working paper 11955, January, Cambridge, MA.

Prasad, E.S., R.G. Rajan and A. Subramanian (2007), "Foreign capital and economic growth", *Brookings Papers on Economic Activity*, (1), 153–230.

Rachman, G. (2008), "The political threats to globalization", *The Financial Times*, April 7, p. 11.

Ravallion, M., S. Chen and P. Sangrauls (2008), "Dollar a day revisited", The World Bank policy research working paper 4620, Washington, DC.

Ravallion, M. (2007), "Looking beyond averages in the trade and poverty debate", in M. Nissanke and E. Thorbecke (eds), *The Impact of Globalization on the World's Poor*, Houndsmills: Palgrave Macmillan Ltd., pp. 118–44.

Ravallion, M. (2004), "Competing concepts of inequality in the globalization debate", paper presented at the Brookings Trade Forum on Globalization, Poverty and Inequality Debate, May 13–14, Washington, DC.

Reddy, Y.V. (2007), "Converting a tiger", *Finance and Development*, **44** (1), 40–48.

Reiser, O.L. and B. Davies (1944), *Planetary Democracy: An Introduction to Scientific Humanism*, New York: Creative Age Press.

Reynolds, A. (2007), "Has US income equality really increased?", Cato Institute policy analysis paper no. 568, January, Washington, DC.

Ricardo, David (1817), *On the Principles of Political Economy and Taxation*, London: John Murray.

Roach, S.S. (2006), "From globalization to localization", *Global Economic Forum*, accessed at www.morganstanley.com./views/gef/archieve/2006/20061214-Thu.html.

Rodrik, D. (2007a), *One Economics, Many Recipes*, Princeton. NJ: Princeton University Press.

Rodrik, D. (2007b), "The globalization number game", Dani Rodrik Weblog, accessed at http://rodrik.yypepad.com.

Rodrik, D. (2007c), "How to save globalization from its cheerleaders?",

July, accessed at http://ksghome.harvard.edu/~drodrik/Saving%20glo-
balization.pdf.
Rose, S. (2007), *Does Productivity Growth Still Benefit Working Americans?*
June, Washington, DC: The Information Technology and Information
Foundation.
Rose, A. (2004), "Do we really know that the WTO really increases
trade?", *American Economic Review*, **94** (1), 80–114.
Rosenau, J.N. (1980), *The Study of Global Interdependence: Essays
on Transnationalization of World Affairs*, London: Pinter Publications.
Saito, M. and I. Tokutsu (2006), "Impact of trade on wages", International
Monetary Fund working paper WP/06/155, Washington, DC.
Sala-i-Martin, X. (2006), "The world distribution of income: falling
poverty and ... convergence, period", *Quarterly Journal of Economics*,
121 (2), 351–97.
Scholte, J.A. (2005), "The sources of neoliberal globalization", United
Nations Research Institute for Social Development program paper no.
8, October, Geneva.
Scholte, J.A. (2002), "What is globalization? The definition issue",
University of Warwick Center for the Study of Globalization and
Regionalization working paper no. 109/02, Coventry.
Schwab, S.C. (2007), "US trade update and agenda", presentation of the
United States Trade Representative to the Senate Finance Committee,
February 15, Washington, DC.
Segerstrom, P. (2005), "Naomi Klein and Anti-globalization Movement",
Center for Economic Policy Research discussion paper no. 4141,
December, London.
Serra, N. and J.E.Stiglitz (2008), *The Washington Consensus Reconsidered*,
New York: Oxford University Press.
Sindzingre, A. (2005), "Explaining threshold effects of globalization on
poverty", WIDER research paper 2006/53, August, Helsinki.
Sirkin, H.L., J.W. Hemerling and A.K. Bhattacharya (2008), *Globality:
Competing with Everyone*, New York: Grand Central Publishing.
Slaughter, M.J. (2000), "What are the results of product-price studies?"
in R.C. Feenstra (ed.) *The Impact of International Trade on Wages*,
Chicago: University Press, pp. 143–87.
Soros, G. (2005), *George Soros on Globalization*, New York: Perseus
Books Group.
Srholec, M. (2007), "High-tech exports from developing countries",
Review of World Economics, **143** (2), 227–55.
Srinivasan, T.N. (2002), "Globalization: is it good or bad?", Stanford
Institute for Economic Policy Research economic policy brief, December
23, Stanford. CA.

Standage, T. (1998), *The Victorian Internet*, New York: Walker Publishing Company.

Stiglitz, J.E. (2006), *Making Globalization Work*, New York: W.W. Norton & Company.

Stiglitz, J.E. (2005), "The overselling of globalization", in M.M. Weinstein (ed.), *Globalization: What's New*, New York: Columbia University Press, pp. 228–61.

Stiglitz, J.E. (2003a), *Globalization and its Discontents*, New York and London: W.W. Norton.

Stiglitz, J.E. (2003b), "We have to make globalization work for all", Yale Center for the Study of Globalization, Yale University, *Yale Global*, No. 17, October, New Haven, CT.

Stiglitz, J.E. (1997), "Some lessons from the East Asian Miracle", *The World Bank Research Observer*, **11** (2), 151–77.

Stolper, W. and P.A. Samuelson (1941), "Protection and real wages", *Review of Economic Studies*, **9** (1), 58–73.

Subramanian, A. and S.J. Wei. (2007), "The WTO promotes trade, strongly but unevenly", *Journal of International Economics*, **72** (1), 151–75.

Tassell, T. and J. Chung (2007), "The $2,500bn question", *The Financial Times*, May 25, p. 12.

Teixeira, R. (2007), "What the public really wants on globalization and trade", The Center for American Progress, January 18, Washington, DC, accessed at http://www.tcf.org and at http://www.americanprogress.org, February 18.

Temin, P. (2006), "The Economy of the Early Roman Empire", *Journal of Economic Perspective*, **20** (1), 133–51.

Thirlwell, M. (2007a), "Globalization was good then, not now", *Yale Global*, Yale University. September, New Haven, CT, accessed at http://yaleglobal.yale.edu/article.print?id=9677.

Thirlwell, M.P. (2007b), "Second thoughts on globalization", Lowy Institute for International Policy institute paper no. 18, Sydney.

Tomz, M., J. Goldstein and D. Rivers (2007), "Do we really know that the WTO really increases trade? Comment", *American Economic Review*, **97** (8), 2005–18.

Topalova, P. (2004), "Trade liberalization and firm productivity: the case of India", International Monetary Fund working paper WP/04/28, Washington, DC.

United Nations Conference on Trade and Development (UNCTAD) (2008a), "Emergence of a new South", TD/425, February 11, Geneva and New York.

United Nations Conference on Trade and Development (UNCTAD)

(2008b), *Handbook of Statistics (2007)*, Geneva and New York: UNCTAD.

United Nations Conference on Trade and Development (UNCTAD) (2008c), *Globalization for Development*, Geneva and New York: UNCTAD.

United Nations Conference on Trade and Development (UNCTAD) (2008d), *Trade and Development Report (2008)*, Geneva and New York: UNCTAD.

United Nations Conference on Trade and Development (UNCTAD) (2007a), "New and dynamic sectors of trade: the South-South dimension", TD/B/COM.1/EM.24/2, August 10, Geneva and New York.

United Nations Conference on Trade and Development (UNCTAD) (2007b), *Information Economy Report 2007–2008*, Geneva and New York: UNCTAD.

United Nations Conference on Trade and Development (UNCTAD) (2006), July, *World Investment Report 2006*, Geneva and New York: United Nations Conference on Trade and Development.

United Nations Development Program (UNDP) (2008), *Human Development Report 2008*, New York: United Nations Development Program.

US Department of Treasury (2007), *Semi-annual report on international and exchange rate policies*, June, Washington, DC.

Venables, A.J. (2006), "Shift in economic geography and their causes", in *New Economic Geography: Effects and Policy Implications*, Kansas City, MO. The Federal Reserve Bank of Kansas City, pp. 15–40.

Wade, N. (2006), *Before the Dawn: Recovering Lost History of Our Ancestors*, New York: Penguin.

Wan, G. (2008), "Poverty and inequality in China", *Review of Development Economics*, **12** (2), 416–18.

Wilson, D. (2007), "Changes in income inequality across the US", *Federal Reserve Bank of San Francisco Economic Letter*, November 28, San Francisco.

Wilson, D. and R. Dragusanu (2008), *The Expanding Middle: The Exploding World Middle Class*, July, New York. Goldman Sachs.

Williamson, J.G. (2002), "Winners and losers over two centuries of globalization", National Bureau of Economic Research working paper 9161, September, Cambridge, MA.

Winters, L.A., N. McCulloch and A. McKay (2004), "Trade liberalization and poverty: the evidence so far", *Journal of Economic Literature*, **42** (1), pp. 72–115.

Winters, L.A. and S. Yusuf (2007), "Introduction", in L.A. Winters and S. Yusuf (eds), *Dancing with Giants*, Washington, DC: The World Bank.

Wolf, M. (2005a), "Will globalization survive", Third Whitman Lecture at the Institute of International Economics, April 5, Washington, DC.

Wolf, M. (2005b), *Why Globalization Works*, New Haven, CT: Yale University Press.

Wood, L.J. (2004), "Breaking the bank and taking to the streets: how protestors target neoliberalism", *Journal of World-Systems Research*, **10** (1), 68–90.

World Bank (2008a), "East Asia Update", April, Washington, DC.

World Bank (2008b), *Global Development Finance*, Washington, DC: The World Bank.

World Bank (2008c), *World Development Indicator 2008,* July, Washington, DC: The World Bank.

World Bank (2008d), *Quick Reference Tables, 2008*, Washington, DC: The World Bank.

World Bank (2008e), *China Quarterly Update*, January, Beijing: The World Bank.

World Bank (2007), *Global Economic Prospects*, Washington, DC: The World Bank.

World Bank (2002), *Globalization, Growth and Poverty*, Washington, DC: The World Bank.

World Economic Forum (WEF) (2008), *Global Competitiveness Report, 2008,* Geneva: WEF.

World Trade Organization (WTO) (2008), "World trade 2007, prospects for 2008", press release P/520/Rev.1, April 17, Geneva.

Index